Conflict Assessment and Peacebuilding Planning

Conflict Assessment and Peacebuilding Planning

TOWARD A PARTICIPATORY APPROACH TO HUMAN SECURITY

Lisa Schirch

Kumarian Press

A Division of Lynne Rienner Publishers, Inc. • Boulder & London

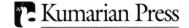

Published in the United States of America in 2013 by
Kumarian Press
A division of Lynne Rienner Publishers, Inc.
1800 30th Street, Boulder, Colorado 80301
www.rienner.com

and in the United Kingdom by
Kumarian Press
A division of Lynne Rienner Publishers, Inc.
3 Henrietta Street, Covent Garden, London WC2E 8LU

Library of Congress Cataloging-in-Publication Data
Schirch, Lisa.
Conflict assessment and peacebuilding planning: toward a participatory approach to human security / Lisa Schirch.
Includes bibliographical references and index.
ISBN 978-1-56549-578-4 (cloth : alk. paper)
ISBN 978-1-56549-579-1 (pbk. : alk. paper)
1. Human security. 2. Security, International. 3. Peace-building. 4. Peacekeeping forces. 5. Conflict management. I. Title.
JZ5595.S34 2013
303.6'9—dc23

British Cataloguing in Publication Data
A Cataloguing in Publication record for this book
is available from the British Library.

Printed and bound in the United States of America

∞ The paper used in this publication meets the requirements
of the American National Standard for Permanence of
Paper for Printed Library Materials Z39.48-1992.

5 4 3 2 1

Inquiry and change are not sequential,
but simultaneous processes.

—David Cooperider

Contents

Glossary

Asset-based approaches — peacebuilding efforts that identify cultural and institutional resources that already exist to support peace and resilience in a conflict-affected context.

Conflict-affected context — an institution, community, state, or region impacted negatively by conflict or violence or both. In a conflict-affected context, people lack human security. They may feel fearful, unable to meet their basic needs, or a sense of humiliation. They need safety and development to meet their basic needs or a sense of dignity and human rights.

Conflict assessment — an interactive research process to conceptually organize factors driving conflict and supporting peace. While "conflict assessment" is a widely accepted term, local sensitivities and even denial that there is a "conflict" may make it difficult to use this term in the midst of conflict. The term "context assessment" can be used instead. But a true conflict assessment is different from a context assessment, which focuses only on the political, economic, social, and historical factors.

Conflict drivers — key people, institutions, or forces that play a central role in mobilizing people to respond violently to the root causes of conflict and shared perceptions of grievances relating to human security. A conflict driver can be something like a famine, unemployment, easy access to weapons, or religious extremism that motivates individuals or groups to engage in conflict.

Conflict mitigators — people, institutions, or forces that support political, economic, security, justice, and social factors related to human security. These are also referred to as *local capacities for peace* or are associated with the concept of *resilience.* Resilience and the concepts of local capacity for peace together refer to the capacity of a system to survive, adapt, absorb, or respond to a crisis or severe change. Individuals, communities, and institutions are resilient in as much as they can adapt, be agile, learn quickly, and improvise new survival methods in a changed environment.

Conflict prevention — an approach to peacebuilding that aims to prevent violence from starting or restarting by addressing factors driving conflict toward violence. *Operational prevention* focuses on short-term crisis response, including preventive diplomacy. *Structural prevention* focuses on long-term efforts to address root causes such as the economic, social, and political exclusion of some groups.

Conflict sensitivity — an approach to programming and policymaking that recognizes the potential influence between conflict-affected context and a policy, program, or project in that region. Conflict-sensitive policies, programs, and projects aim to minimize unintentional negative impacts that may drive conflict and cause further social divisions while maximizing positive impacts on the context that mitigate conflict and bridge social divides. Conflict assessment research and self-assessment research are central to conflict-sensitive policies, programs, and projects in human rights, humanitarian assistance, development, and related efforts.

Conflict transformation — the personal, social, cultural, and structural change that takes place in the process of addressing conflict through forums such as dialogue and mediation that help address the root causes and factors driving violence.

Direct violence — physical harm committed by one person or group against another.

Human security — freedom from fear, freedom from want, and freedom from humiliation for individuals, communities, and their global environment. The term can apply to physical security as well as economic, political, social, and justice systems that protect and support human rights and a freedom from want. Local perceptions of security, peace, justice, and stability are central to defining human security. Peacebuilding's ultimate goal is human security. Strategies to achieve human security are successful in as much as they protect the quantity and quality of life and recognize interdependence between people and their environment.

Insiders and outsiders — classifications that refer to whether the people carrying out conflict assessment and peacebuilding are primarily from within or outside the conflict-affected context. In general, *insiders* live in the area and directly suffer from the conflict; *outsiders* are those who choose to become involved in the conflict, and can choose to also leave the context. People fall on a spectrum and are seen as partially insiders and partially outsiders if they live in the same region but are not directly affected by the conflict.

Outputs, outcomes, and impacts — results of projects, programs, and policies. *Outputs* are the immediate results. For example, the output of a mediation between rival political groups is the meeting itself. *Outcomes* are the results of the output. For example, the outcome of a mediation may be improved communication and trust between rival political groups. *Impacts* are the wider results of the outcomes. For example, the impact of a mediation might be a power-sharing agreement between rival political groups.

Peacebuilding — a wide range of efforts by diverse actors in government and civil society to address the root causes of violence before, during, and after violent conflict. The term "peacebuilding" can have two broad meanings. Peacebuilding can refer to the direct work that intentionally focuses on addressing the factors driving and mitigating conflict. Peacebuilding can also refer to efforts to coordinate a comprehensive, multileveled, multisectoral strategy, including development, humanitarian assistance, governance, security, justice, and other sectors that may not use the term "peacebuilding" to describe themselves.

Projects, programs, and policies — describing different levels of planning and implementation. A *project* is a set of specific activities. For example, a peacebuilding project is a training for journalists in conflict-sensitive journalism that result in outputs such as trained journalists. A *program* is a group of projects that result in a wider set of outcomes. For example, a program in media in peacebuilding includes a variety of projects that aim to train journalists, set up an independent news service, and improve media laws related to protection of journalists. A *policy* is a strategy that guides all related projects, resulting in wider impacts in a conflict-affected region. For example, a policy on media lays out an overall strategy for how to work with and support media-related stakeholders to impact a conflict-affected region.

Self-assessment — a process of identifying one's own cultural biases, perspectives, interests, and assumptions about a conflict, and then identifying one's own resources, capacities, and networks to prioritize planning on what is possible and what will not do harm to others.

Social capital — the quality and quantity of relationships between people. The concept affirms that social networks have value. High levels of social capital between interdependent identity groups correlate with peace.

Structural violence — the disabilities, disparities, and even deaths that result from systems, institutions, or policies that foster economic, social, political, educational, and other disparities between groups.

System-based approaches — peacebuilding efforts that identify the interdependent relationships between people, institutions, and forces in a conflict-affected context.

Theories of change — the "program rationale" or logic of how a program hopes to foster change to produce intended outcomes and impacts. The first part of a theory of change is a belief about what factors are driving or mitigating conflict and need to change. The second part of a theory of change is either implicit or explicit assumptions about how some project, program, or policy will impact a conflict-affected context.

Whole of society — an approach to peacebuilding that includes people from all levels and sectors of society who help to define what peace, security, and justice will look like in their context and develop a shared assessment and plan for peacebuilding. Governments sometimes refer to this as the "comprehensive approach."

The *Conflict Assessment and Peacebuilding Planning* Website

A website, www.conflict-assessment-and-peacebuilding-planning.org, supplements the exercises in this book.

The website contains the following:

Templates: Short, downloadable templates are available for many of the tables and figures in the book. Researchers, students, and planners can use these to fill in their own information for use in their own case studies or work.

Shared exercises and learning tools: Case studies and videos, as well as pedagogical training notes, are presented, and trainers share their ideas for how to teach conflict assessment and peacebuilding planning.

Shared case studies: Researchers and planners can share their completed conflict assessments here for others to see. The website is not intended to be a clearinghouse of conflict assessments, but to provide examples and case studies that can help others learn how to use the methods described in the book.

Acknowledgments

This book grows out of 20 years of practice and teaching on conflict assessment and peacebuilding planning at the Center for Justice and Peacebuilding at Eastern Mennonite University (EMU) and our partner organizations around the world. Thank you to these organizations and their staff and students who tested the material in the book: Kabul University National Center for Policy Research, Afghanistan; Lebanese American University, Beirut, Lebanon; REACH, Erbil, Iraq; Duta Wacana University, Jogjakarta, Indonesia; Pacific Peacebuilding Institute, Suva, Fiji; Daystar University, Nairobi, Kenya; West African Peacebuilding Institute, Accra, Ghana; European Peace University, Stadtschlaining, Austria; and Sri Lanka Peacebuilding Institute, Colombo, Sri Lanka. Hundreds of community-level practitioners from the World Bank, United Nations, and government staff in the fields of development, human rights, governance, community organizing, and peacebuilding also helped to test the material in this book.

The book is also a project of 3P Human Security: Partners for Peacebuilding Policy. 3P is a project of the Alliance for Peacebuilding working in partnership with the Global Partnership for the Prevention of Armed Conflict, EMU's Center for Justice and Peacebuilding, and the University of Notre Dame's Kroc Institute for International Peace Studies. Growing out of partnerships with local civil society groups in conflict-affected regions, 3P Human Security aims to bring local people's perspectives on conflict and peacebuilding to the attention of policymakers.

A special thank-you to the US Institute of Peace for offering a small grant funding the writing of the book.

I extend gratitude to dozens of individuals offering substantial reviews and support during the long development of the book. In particular, gratitude goes to all the students and participants in conflict assessment courses who helped to refine the method described here. A personal thank-you to the following people who read and commented on the book: my husband, Bill Goldberg, and my colleagues Lawrence Woocher, Matthew Levinger, Gloria Rhodes, Jayne Docherty, Catherine Barnes, Karim Merchant, Sigal Shoham, Alys Wilman, Melanie Greenberg, and John Filson.

1

The Purpose of This Handbook

This handbook aims to improve the effectiveness of peacebuilding by better linking conflict assessment to self-assessment, theories of change, and the design, monitoring, and evaluation of peacebuilding efforts at all levels, from community-based projects to international policies. These building blocks of effective peacebuilding elements form the architecture of this handbook illustrated in Figure 1.1.

Conflicts are complex, and assessment can be time-consuming, expensive, and even dangerous. This acronym-free approach aims to provide familiar and easy-to-use conceptual frameworks for seeing and learning about the complex, dynamic conflict system. Recognizing that many groups skimp on assessment, fearing analysis paralysis, this approach provides basic as well as advanced tools for each element of the process. The handbook tackles the problem of untested assumptions and lack of assessment leading to ineffective programs, as well as the problem of too much data and no easy, simple-to-use conceptual framework to turn data into knowledge that is useful for planning peacebuilding. Too often, critical steps in this sequence are missing, as different groups of people conduct the steps without coordination. This handbook addresses these problems.

Audiences

This handbook assists peacebuilding at all levels—from community-based projects to longer-term institutional programs to national and international policies. The level of analysis can be global, national, or local. Researchers can use the exercises in this handbook with groups at different educational

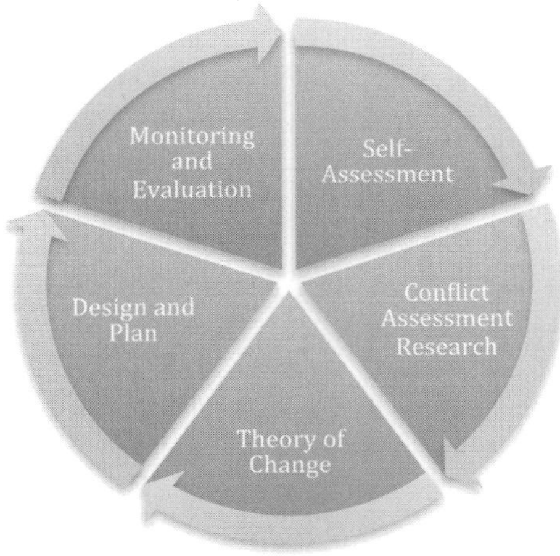

Figure 1.1 Components of Conflict Assessment and Peacebuilding Planning

levels, such as remote tribal groups, urban communities, and high-level policymakers. The handbook's intended audiences include all those individuals and groups from inside and outside of a conflict that are considering how to change the dynamics of conflict to foster peace:

- Local civil society organizations like religious groups, universities, or local community-based organizations
- International nongovernmental organizations (INGOs) and their donors
- Government agencies working on stabilization, statebuilding, or development
- Regional and international organizations like the United Nations, World Bank, or African Union

Many of these different groups already have some sort of assessment process that feeds into their planning processes. But their terminology, approach to planning, organizational cultures, and missions are diverse. Their assumptions about what works and how change happens are also different. This handbook draws on current language and concepts from many of these groups at the same time as they are intended audiences. The handbook aims to help foster more coherent terminology and foundational concepts linking academic sources and practitioner tools in order to enable more effective communication and coordination.

While many insiders and outsiders consider how to best intervene in conflict, the methods in this handbook may lead a group to decide it should not intervene at all. Sometimes the best approach is *not* to get involved. The methods in this handbook offer groups a method for making informed decisions about what they do or opt not to do.

Building Blocks of Effective Peacebuilding

The handbook offers conceptual frameworks for synchronizing self-assessment, conflict assessment, theories of change, design, monitoring, and evaluation to achieve better policy coherence and a comprehensive approach to conflict prevention and peacebuilding. Table 1.1 provides a summary of the conflict assessment and peacebuilding planning conceptual framework used through this handbook.

Self-assessment exercises help narrow priorities and assess abilities of those planning peacebuilding. Conducting a self-assessment identifies your own cultural biases and perspectives on the conflict. From the very start, all individuals or groups should recognize that they are not neutral or objective, but that they bring a certain perspective and their own interests that may or may not overlap with the interests of other people in the conflict-affected context. Self-assessment is an ongoing process, required before beginning conflict assessment and again before designing peacebuilding efforts. It includes a set of questions to examine the potential strengths and challenges of the group planning peacebuilding, taking into account a group's identity, social capital, and financial and skill capacities.

A self-assessment should first decide whether your particular group is the best potential actor to conduct a peacebuilding effort. Groups should question their involvement, recognizing that interventions, especially those by outsiders, carry a risk of making conflicts escalate rather than de-escalate. Questions to ask yourself in a self-assessment include

Where will you work?
Who will you work with?
Why will you do what you do?
What will you do?
How will you shift power sources in support of peace?
When is the best timing for your peacebuilding efforts?

Conflict assessment is a research process involving basic or advanced interactive exercises to map the factors driving conflict and the factors supporting peace. *Factors driving conflict* include a range of lenses to map

Table 1.1 Summary Chart of Conflict Assessment and Peacebuilding Planning

	Self-Assessment	Conflict Assessment Lenses	Theory of Change	Peacebuilding Planning
WHERE	How well do you understand the local context, languages, cultures, religions, etc.? Where will you work?	Where is the conflict taking place: in what cultural, social, economic, justice, and political context or system?	If x parts of the context are at the root of conflict and division or provide a foundation of resilience and connection between people, what will influence these factors?	**How will the context interact with your efforts?** Given your self-assessment, identify your capacity to impact the elements of the context that drive conflict and support peace.
WHO	Where are you in the stakeholder map? Where do you have social capital? To which key actors do you relate?	Who are the stakeholders—the people who have a stake or interest in the conflict?	If x individual or group is driving or mitigating conflict, then what action will incentivize them to change?	**Who will you work with?** Given your self-assessment, decide who to work with to improve relationships between key stakeholders or support key actors who could play a peacebuilding role between key stakeholders.
WHY	How do stakeholders perceive your motivations?	Why are the stakeholders acting the way they do? What are their motivations?	If x group is motivated to drive or mitigate conflict, what will change or support their motivations?	**Why will you work?** Given your self-assessment of your motivations and how stakeholders perceive your motivations, identify how these align with the motivations of the key actors.

(continues)

Table 1.1 Cont.

	Self-Assessment	Conflict Assessment Lenses	Theory of Change	Peacebuilding Planning
WHAT	What are you capable of doing to address the key drivers and mitigators of conflict?	What factors are driving or mitigating conflict?	If x power sources are driving and mitigating conflict, what actions will influence these factors?	**What will you do?** Given your self-assessment, identify which driving and mitigating factors you will address.
HOW	What are your resources, means, or sources of power? How will these shape your efforts?	How is conflict manifested? What are the stakeholders' means and sources of power?	If x power sources are driving conflict, what will influence these sources of power?	**How will you shift power sources in support of peace?** Given your self-assessment, identify and prioritize your capacities to reduce dividers and to increase local capacities for peace.
WHEN	Do you have an ability to respond quickly to windows of vulnerability or opportunity?	Are historical patterns or cycles of the conflict evident?	If x times are conducive to violence or peace, what will influence these times?	**When is the best timing for your peacebuilding efforts?** Given historical patterns, identify possible windows of opportunity or vulnerability and potential triggers and trends of future scenarios.

stakeholders and their means, motivations, and core grievances; to map issues and driving factors; and to identify issues arising from the local context and windows of vulnerability given the historic legacy of the conflict. *Factors mitigating conflict* include a range of lenses to map stakeholders supporting peace; to identify local traditions, values, and institutions supporting peace, resiliency, and social capital; and to assess possible windows of opportunity.

Each section of the conflict assessment using the Where, Who, Why, What, How, and When frameworks progresses from basic to more advanced expertise and exercises. Each section starts with basic conflict assessment methods useful for interpersonal, family, community, regional, and international conflicts to give a broad overview of the dynamics. A basic assessment is definitely better than nothing and may be enough to plan simple programs at the community level, particularly those integrating goals supporting reconciliation between divided groups into support for humanitarian and development projects. Advanced conflict assessment allows for more strategic high-level planning on how to address structural dynamics or how to design a national peace process. An assessment might start with the basic framework and then go deeper into the advanced analysis over time.

Where is the conflict taking place, in what context?
Who is driving the conflict, and who is supporting peace?
Why are the key actors motivated to drive and mitigate conflict?
What are the driving and mitigating factors, and what can be done to impact them?
How are key actors using power to drive or mitigate conflict?
When is the conflict most likely to be open to change for better or worse?

This handbook includes guidance on the research process, including how to

- Gather data sources that are accurate, reliable, and triangulated. Data sources include books, reports, blogs, news articles, Twitter feeds, polling, interviews, focus groups, observations, and the interactive methods described in this handbook.
- Evaluate the quality of each data source. Identify gaps in data or places where there is uncertain or contradictory data. Identify hypotheses for why data may be conflicting. Make a plan to gather further information.
- Examine theories of change or the "program rationale," which articulates the perceived logic between the key factors driving conflict or

supporting peace and what type of peacebuilding efforts can address these drivers. How do local people think change will come about? What are their stories, parables, metaphors, and ideas? What existing research supports or questions these theories of change to help evaluate the likelihood of their impact?

- Design peacebuilding efforts by identifying SMART goals that are Specific, Measurable, Attainable, Realistic, and Timely on who you will work with, what you will do, and where and when you will do it. Planning requires developing strategies to move from micro to macro impacts by scaling up peacebuilding efforts in a variety of ways. Finally, develop a logical framework (also known as a "log frame") that lays out the goals, key audiences, activities, time frames, outputs, outcomes, and impacts of the peacebuilding effort.
- Conduct monitoring and evaluation (M&E), which includes measuring short-term outputs and outcomes as well as long-term interrelated impacts of multiple actors, multiple programs, and multisectors. Research develops indicators and benchmarks for monitoring and evaluating the effects of the peacebuilding effort and the validity of the theory of change. Ultimately, a variety of peacebuilding efforts should synchronize and harmonize with each other to impact broader human security indicators.

Defining Peacebuilding

Peacebuilding includes a wide range of efforts by diverse actors in government and civil society at the community, national, and international levels to address the immediate impacts and root causes of conflict before, during, and after violent conflict occurs. Peacebuilding supports human security—where people have freedom from fear, freedom from want, and freedom from humiliation.

The term "peacebuilding" can have two broad meanings. Peacebuilding can refer to the *direct work* that intentionally focuses on addressing the factors driving and mitigating conflict. Peacebuilding can also refer to *efforts to coordinate* or set up channels for communication to develop a comprehensive, multileveled, multisectoral strategy, including development, humanitarian assistance, governance, security, justice, and other sectors that may not use the term "peacebuilding" to describe themselves.

Before conflict becomes violent, preventive peacebuilding efforts—such as diplomatic, economic development, social, educational, health, legal, and security sector reform programs—address potential sources of instability and violence. This is also termed *conflict prevention.* Peacebuilding efforts aim to manage, mitigate, resolve, and transform central aspects of the conflict through official diplomacy as well as through civil society peace processes and informal dialogue, negotiation, and mediation. Peacebuilding addresses economic, social, and political root causes of violence and fosters reconciliation to prevent the return of instability and violence. Peacebuilding efforts aim to change beliefs, attitudes, and behaviors to transform the short- and long-term dynamics between individuals and groups toward a more stable, peaceful coexistence. Related terms and processes include conflict management, resolution, or transformation; stabilization; reconstruction; and statebuilding.

Peacebuilding is an approach to an entire set of interrelated efforts that support peace. People's efforts to foster economic development, security sector reform, and trauma healing support peacebuilding. But people working in these sectors may not want to call their work "peacebuilding." The concept is not one to impose on specific sectors. Rather, peacebuilding is an overarching concept useful for describing a range of interrelated efforts. But not all development or security programs automatically contribute to peacebuilding. Peacebuilding is distinct from traditional development and security efforts in a variety of ways. Peacebuilding's distinct characteristics include the following:

- Informed by a robust, participatory, ongoing conflict assessment
- Informed by conflict sensitivity that reduces the possibility of unintentional harms that could increase the risk of or actual violence or social divisions
- Designed to address drivers and mitigators of conflict
- Built on local capacities to manage and resolve conflict peacefully
- Driven by local ownership
- Informed by social dialogue to build consensus and trust
- Inclusive of all relevant stakeholders throughout programming and implementation

Note on Terminology

While the terms "conflict assessment" and "peacebuilding" are accepted widely, local sensitivities and even denial that a conflict exists may make it difficult to use these terms in some places. It may be necessary to carry out an implicit conflict assessment and implicit peacebuilding planning process that avoids the explicit use of words like "conflict" and "peacebuilding." Instead, groups can use related terms, such as "context assessment" and "development," even though these more general terms have their own different meanings.

Peacebuilding as a Process

Peacebuilding seeks to change individuals, relationships, cultural patterns, and structures away from harm and toward human security, as illustrated in Figure 1.2.[1]

At the *personal level*, peacebuilding is about changing one's own beliefs, attitudes, and behaviors to monitor and manage one's own physical and emotional reactions to conflict. Peacebuilding requires learning the skills of being nonanxious in the face of conflict and being confident of one's own ability to improvise, facilitate, listen, and transform tense situations.

At the *relational level*, peacebuilding is about changing interpersonal relationships to increase understanding of the differences and commonalities that exist; changing attitudes to depolarize tensions and increase tolerance and acceptance, addressing trauma, grievances, crimes, and perceived injustices between people; and changing the patterns of interpersonal relationships.

At the *cultural level*, peacebuilding is about increasing knowledge of nonviolent ways of addressing conflict, depolarizing tensions and increasing tolerance and acceptance between groups, and changing the pattern of community relationships. This is sometimes referred to as creating a *culture of peace*.

At the *structural level*, peacebuilding is about increasing the knowledge of how and addressing the ways that structures, institutions, and systems impact levels of peace and conflict, changing attitudes about what structural change is possible, and fostering institutions focused on meeting human needs.

Figure 1.2 Dimensions of Conflict Transformation

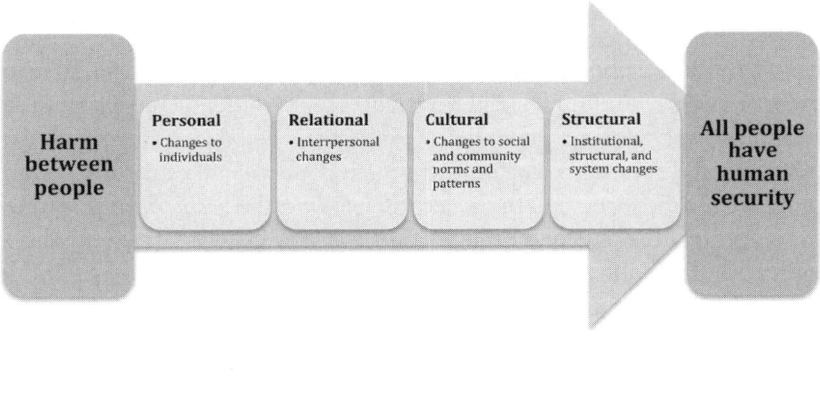

Strategic Design of Peacebuilding

Peacebuilding is strategic when it involves the following:

- Planning is deliberate and coordinated, based on conflict assessments.
- Planning includes a "whole of society" approach involving stakeholders from all levels of an institution, community, or society.
- Planning links short- and long-term efforts.
- Planning links different kinds and sectors of peacebuilding to foster personal, relational, cultural, and structural changes, and support human security.

Peacebuilding is *not* strategic when it is guided by funding availability alone, or when unsubstantiated guesswork and convenience guide planning. Aligning funding, organizational capacity, and access in order to carry out strategic peacebuilding may sometimes be impossible. However, the process outlined in this handbook at least helps move toward asking the right questions and making informed choices.

Peacebuilding and Human Security

Improving human security is the central task of peacebuilding. Human security can both complement and contrast with national security, as illustrated in Table 1.2. Human security requires freedom from fear, freedom from want, and freedom to live in dignity. Human security requires reducing interdependent global and local threats, insecurities, and vulnerabilities related to people's safety, development, and human rights. Peacebuilding strategies aim for sustainable solutions to address immediate and structural factors causing fear, want, and humiliation.

Human security requires a citizen-oriented state, an active civil society, and a robust private business sector, as illustrated in Figure 1.3 on page 12. An elite-oriented state working in support of private business sector without an active civil society results in corruption, instability, and a lack of human rights.

Human security is *people-centered*, focusing on the safety and protection of individuals, communities, and their global environment. When people are suffering direct violence, *protection of civilians* includes all efforts aimed at obtaining full respect for the rights of the individual and of the obligations of the authorities/arms bearers in accordance with the letter and the spirit of the relevant bodies of law. Humanitarian organizations work to prevent and mitigate human suffering to ensure people's access to impartial assistance—in proportion to need and without discrimination; protect people from physical and psychological harm arising from violence and coercion; and assist

Table 1.2 Comparing National Security and Human Security

	National Security Paradigm	Human Security Paradigm
Goal	Securing territorial, economic, and political interests of the nation, such as access to oil or other resources or promoting ideologies such as free-market capitalism	Protecting the well-being of individuals and communities so that they can live free from fear, free from want, and free to live in dignity
Actors	Primarily military	Multitrack efforts at top, mid-, and community levels, including government, civil society, business, academic, religious, media, and other actors
Analysis	Threat assessments primarily focus on terrorism, rogue states, and weapons of mass destruction	Threat assessments include weapons of mass destruction, terrorism from state and nonstate actors, poverty, economic disparity, discrimination between groups, deadly diseases, nuclear and biological materials, and environmental destruction and climate change
Budget	Security budget geared toward offensive military capacity	Security budget requires robust investments in preventive efforts involving economic development, good governance, and multitrack diplomacy
Global Ties	National security seen as relatively isolated from global security	Human security seen as interdependent across state lines

people to claim their rights, access available remedies and recover from the effects of abuse in ways that avoid exposing people to further harm.[2]

A human security approach empowers local people to assess vulnerabilities and threats and then identify and take part in strategies to build security rather than imposing outside definitions and strategies. Human security approaches ask, "Stabilization for whom and for what purpose?" Strategies to achieve human security are successful in as much as local people perceive these strategies as protecting their quantity and quality of life. Human security requires stability. But when governments serve elite interests at the exclusion of their citizens or when governments repress their own citizens, change may be necessary. Many states still use political repression and torture against their own citizens, restrict information via the media, and limit civil freedoms.

Most violence happens within states, not between states. A traditional emphasis on state sovereignty limited international action when a government used repression on its own people or was unable to protect its citizens during civil violence. The Responsibility to Protect (R2P) doctrine

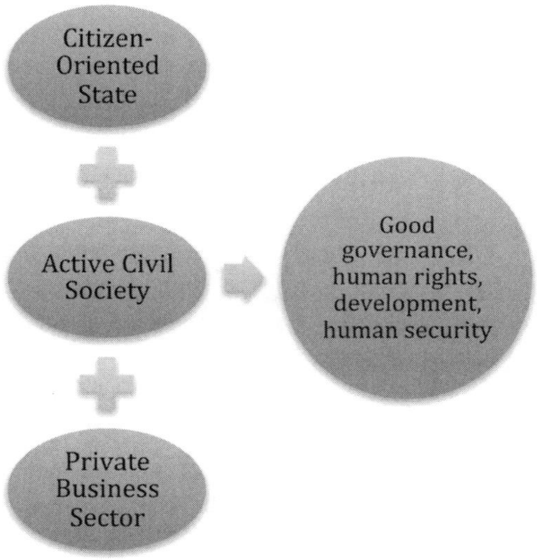

Figure 1.3 Three Elements of a State With Human Security

details each state's responsibility to protect its population from genocide, war crimes, crimes against humanity, and ethnic cleansing (mass atrocities). If the state is unable to protect its population, the international community has a responsibility to help build state capacity for early-warning, mediating conflicts, security sector reform, and many other actions. If a state fails to protect its citizens from mass atrocities or commits these acts against its own citizens, the international community has the responsibility to intervene at first diplomatically using a wide array of peaceful measures, then more coercively through various forms of sanctions, and using force as a last resort.

Peacebuilding Activities

Peacebuilding processes help to build the conditions necessary for five key areas or end states of human security. Table 1.3 illustrates the key concepts of human security and offers examples of the kinds of peacebuilding programs supporting each area and desired end states.[3]

Problems and Principles of Conflict Assessment and Peacebuilding Planning

Too often, conflict assessment does not adequately inform peacebuilding planning. And if conflict assessment is undertaken, it relies on donor-driver outsiders using inadequate research methods that fail to appreciate

Table 1.3 Five Categories of Peacebuilding and Human Security

Levels of Change	Politically Stable Democracy	Sustainable Economy	Safe and Secure Environment	Justice and Rule of Law	Social and Cultural Well-Being
	Predictable and participatory decision making and governance	*Access to basic resources and conducive to socially responsible business*	*Personal safety and freedom of movement*	*Perceived equity in social relations and justice systems*	*Respect and dignity between people of different cultures and identities*
	Peacebuilding efforts include these activities in each category:				
Structural	Build formal and informal **governance** institutions Develop independent **media** Foster **civil society organizations** that advocate for public issues	Build **infrastructure** Promote just, sustainable economic policies within the **regulatory and legal environment** Address institutional obstacles to **economic equity**	Conduct **security sector reform** Create institutions to **restrain perpetrators** of violence Use **security forces** to enforce cease-fires, peace zones **Disarm and demobilize** armed groups **Prevent and mitigate natural disasters**	Foster legitimate and just **legal frameworks** Monitor **human rights** Build **independent courts** **Community policing** Create systems for **restorative and transitional justice**	Create **interreligious or interethnic task forces** on preventing violence Support cultural, religious, and media institutions that provide information on **intergroup relations**
Cultural	Use media programs, and religious and cultural venues to discuss **values of citizenship, political equality,** and **democracy**	Address culture of corruption **Sanction war profiteering** and illicit trade	**Foster respect** for human rights and humanitarian law **Promote understanding** of environmental sustainability	Use media programs, and religious and cultural venues to **promote respect for rule of law and human rights**	Use **media programs, rituals, the arts, and religious and cultural venues** to foster group relations, trauma healing, and peace
Relational	Create **multistakeholder governance processes** Use **mediation and negotiation** to reach political solutions Build state-society relations with **policy advocacy**	Develop processes for **community-based economic development**	Improve relations between security forces and communities **Reintegrate armed groups**	**Mobilize citizens** to advocate for fair and just laws and policies	Use media and the arts for **prejudice reduction** **Intergroup dialogues** Support **women's empowerment and gender sensitivity**
Personal	Train government and institutional leaders in **peacebuilding skills and processes**	Train citizens in starting and supporting **socially responsible businesses**	Train citizens to provide **security sector oversight** and participate in **community watch**		Use rituals, memorials for individual and group **trauma healing**

the complex, culturally unique, local conflict-affected system. Many existing conflict assessment methods and frameworks do not include explicit advice or processes for how to link assessment with planning. Research on whether conflict assessment led to better peacebuilding found no link, suggesting that even when groups conducted conflict assessment, they did not link it to their planning process.[4] This handbook seeks to make a more explicit connection between robust quality conflict assessment research and peacebuilding planning, monitoring, and evaluation.

A conflict assessment process ideally generates ideas that can aid in planning for what to do about a conflict. A conflict assessment can help identify who and what are important factors driving or mitigating conflict. Each of these drivers might lead to a different type of peacebuilding effort. For example,

- If unequal distribution of wealth is driving conflict, development efforts supporting marginalized populations or advocating for policies that provide equal economic opportunities may be an appropriate peacebuilding effort.
- If religious leaders are mitigating conflict, expanding interreligious education, reconciliation workshops, and dialogues may be an appropriate peacebuilding strategy.
- If military raids and house searches are driving conflict, security sector reform efforts and advocacy related to changing military strategies may be important peacebuilding efforts.
- If political power struggles by a repressive elite class are driving conflict between economic classes, a civil society movement supporting participatory democracy may be an important effort.
- If markets run by women in developing countries are mitigating conflict between ethnic groups, peacebuilding efforts that focus on increasing economic interdependence of groups and strengthening the voices of women may be important.

Without rigorous research into who and what are driving and mitigating conflict, planning reflects the biases and limited perceptions of the group doing the planning. Strategic peacebuilding requires a careful assessment of key driving and mitigating factors and then coordinating a range of efforts to address these factors. Peacebuilding also requires careful strategic decision making so that it leads to sustainable change. As detailed earlier, peacebuilding is strategic when it coordinates multiple actors, works at multiple levels in multiple sectors, and works at both short- and long-term change. This approach asks a series of questions about the Where, Who, What, Why, How, and When of conflict so as to design more effective peacebuilding efforts.

Linking Insiders and Outsiders in Participatory, Asset-Based Processes

Conflict assessment and peacebuilding work best when they are locally owned and led or involve partnerships between insiders and outsiders. Outsiders, those people who do not live in the conflict-affected region and who choose to intervene in it, bring resources and expertise, but often only have hypotheses or guesses about insider perceptions on what is driving or mitigating conflict.[5] Peacebuilding driven by outsiders' perceptions, interests, and plans is unlikely to be effective. Conflict assessment and peacebuilding planning require opportunities for local people or "insiders" to provide leadership to their own strategies and to provide feedback to outsiders to ensure local accountability at every phase. Donors' priorities and perceptions of what to do about conflict too often trump or ignore local people's perceptions, resulting in local people seeing donor-driven programs as illegitimate, wasteful, and even neocolonial—reflecting a we-know-what's-best-for-you approach. Too often, planners sitting in foreign capitals conduct a conflict assessment based on their own cultural biases and untested assumptions that significantly depart from realities on the ground for local people experiencing conflict. Too often, foreign planners also impose unrealistic time frames and timelines for peacebuilding efforts. This handbook's focus on self-assessment, insider and outsider partnerships, and participatory processes helps address these problems.

Assets-Based Focus

Most conflict assessments focus only on local problems. This handbook includes a focus on existing local insider assets or resources for peace. It maps existing capacities and solutions as well as problems. When conflict becomes the main focus, people begin to believe their reality is unchangeable and fixed. This perception takes away their agency, power, and will to effect change. Some insiders view their plight as immutable and unchangeable. But in every context, there are local people—including key religious, ethnic, educational, media, and government leaders—who are already making the case against violence and supporting reconciliation through traditional rituals, use of the media, or facilitating social dialogue. A positive approach to peacebuilding assumes that there is a local capacity for peacebuilding.[6] This assessment includes factors, institutions, relationships, traditions, key people, and other "assets" supporting peace.

Outsiders' Interests and Donor-Driven Box Checking

Outsiders' existing capacities, mandates, or self-interests and priorities often shape peacebuilding programs. Some conflict assessments are just a self-fulfilling prophecy for groups that come in looking for evidence that their branded peacebuilding method could work.[7] Outsider-driven solutions are rarely sustainable over the long term. Groups may simply hear what they want to hear in an assessment, or conduct an assessment merely to check a box rather than to truly design more effective peacebuilding. Too many conflict assessment processes rely on external teams that fly into conflict-affected contexts without knowing the language or culture, or the religious, political, economic, and social history. These "expert teams" may interview a handful of locals, but local civil society organizations criticize this research methodology, complaining that donors and outside groups "came to do an assessment already knowing what they wanted to do." Civil society organizations in many regions of the world report that governments see them as "implementers" of projects rather than as having insights into the roots of conflict or ideas for programming. The current approach results in duplication by different donors often asking the same local people to participate in their conflict assessments. This handbook puts local leadership and perspectives at the front end of all conflict assessment and peacebuilding planning, monitoring, and evaluation.

Local Ownership

This handbook highlights the *essential ownership and inclusion of local people*, a majority of whom should at least view peacebuilding as supporting their vision of peace, security, stability, and justice. Insiders are not just victims or implementers of someone else's peacebuilding plans. They are key actors contributing to conflict assessment and peacebuilding. Conflict assessment and peacebuilding planning that do not involve local people, or that only involve token local representatives, will significantly hamper the accuracy of the assessment and the effectiveness of peacebuilding. This handbook draws on diverse approaches to assessment and peacebuilding from around the world that researchers can adapt for local use.

Self-Assessment as Part of Planning

Many conflict assessment processes assume that outside conflict experts are coming in to assess and solve someone else's conflict as neutral outsiders.

This handbook emphasizes the importance of self-assessment for both insider and outsider groups planning peacebuilding. What social capital do they hold with key stakeholders in the conflict? And how does a planning group's skill sets and financial capacity shape their peacebuilding planning? How do diverse local stakeholders perceive the group or groups planning peacebuilding? What are the limits of what they can do based on local perceptions of their interests and intentions? What are the political, economic, and sociocultural interests of those conducting some form of peacebuilding effort? Do these interests overlap with or contradict local people's interests in human security?

A self-assessment helps a group planning peacebuilding focus on what it can and cannot do. Just because there is a need for a certain type of peacebuilding effort does not mean that any group can carry it out. The identity of the group planning peacebuilding impacts how local people view and support the group's efforts. In some places it is very difficult for local people to trust their government's peacebuilding efforts. Some governments may distrust NGO efforts. Some local people typically assume that a foreign government agency working in a conflict-affected context is working on behalf of elite political and economic interests. This presumption may make it difficult if not impossible for local people to trust that a foreign government has the best interest and human security of them in mind.

Required Capacities for Conducting a Conflict Assessment

Any group conducting a conflict assessment should have a variety of skills in their own organization or in the partnerships they form with other organizations. A few groups indeed have all of the skills. But most groups need more capacity in one or more areas. Insiders and outsiders tend to be stronger in different key capacities, which makes use of partnerships a frequent methodology for carrying out conflict assessments. Key skills for conflict assessment include

- Ability to build local networks and relationships to people who can help organize and participate in interviews, focus groups, and so on
- Knowledge of local languages and cultures
- Ability to travel to areas where research will take place
- Ability to design and carry out rigorous research methodologies
- Ability to synthesize data into knowledge and prioritize information
- Knowledge of grammar and writing sufficient to compose a formal paper summarizing assessment and peacebuilding plans
- Access to donors who can fund conflict assessment and peacebuilding efforts

- Access to policymakers to ensure they receive policy recommendations resulting from conflict assessments and peacebuilding processes

Insiders and outsiders should find ways of acknowledging the capacity of each organization. Outsiders may bring comparative experiences and capacities in project management as well as vertical social capital that allows them to conduct policy advocacy related to the conflict. In some cases, some outsiders may be seen as more impartial than insiders. Insiders are more likely to have long-term commitment to and trusting relationships with other local people, flexibility to travel throughout the region, language skills, and a better understanding of local cultures and religions as well as the region's political, social, and economic history.

Insiders Conducting a Self-Assessment

Every insider is also an outsider to others living in the region but belonging to a different identity group. People who live in a conflict-affected region or are part of the local context see and know many things about their context that foreign outsiders do not. But they also may be tied to only one part of the local context through their group identity, so they may need strategies for ensuring that truly diverse local perspectives are part of all elements of conflict assessment and peacebuilding planning, monitoring, and evaluation. In many countries, there are key civil society leaders whom outsiders rely on as their insider partners, but these leaders may or may not truly represent the wide diversity of civil society. Insiders can also be biased, and as a result they need to reach out intentionally to other insiders who are part of other identity groups, other regions, other languages, other age groups and so on. "Insiders" is thus a relative term.

Some insiders act as gatekeepers to their own contexts to decide who they let in as their partners to access relationships and knowledge of the local context and who they keep at a distance. Among insiders' interests are wanting to draw in outsiders who will support their side of the conflict; insiders can then gain from outsiders' financial and political power and influence. Insiders may compete with each other to gain influence with outsiders and to gain more power to be the gatekeepers in their context.[8]

Insiders can lead conflict assessments when they can play all or most of the roles in the list of capacities needed to conduct conflict assessments. Capacity building programs can support insiders' capacities in research methodologies, writing skills, and understanding foreign donors and governments enough to do effective communication and advocacy with them on conflict assessment recommendations for policy changes related to peacebuilding.[9]

Outsiders Conducting a Self-Assessment

Outsiders should always consider that there may be no role for them in peacebuilding and that their well-intentioned efforts may have negative impacts on local people. Most outsiders who come into a conflict-affected region lack understanding of the local cultural, political, religious, economic, and social context. They also may not trust insiders. Outsiders often come from countries that once held colonial policies that viewed local people as "subjects" or even as less than fully human. Many insiders grew up in countries under colonial control and hold vivid memories of blatant discrimination and racism. Ideally outsiders support insiders, and peacebuilding is locally led and locally owned. But in reality, research finds that in many recent peacebuilding efforts led by partnerships of outsiders and insiders, insiders feel that outsiders display a range of disrespectful behaviors, including[10]

- Imposing Western values and being insensitive to local cultures and religious values
- Showing arrogance and a we-know-what's-best-for-you attitude
- Showing ignorance of the complexity of the local context
- Humiliating insiders and denigrating their capacity and local traditions
- Not listening to their ideas upfront during assessment and proposal writing, but rather only wanting to consult after the fact to get approval or seek local partners as "implementers" of foreign-designed projects
- Failing to understand how their own countries' policies are driving conflict in the region
- Focusing on quick-fix solutions rather than the historical and systemic roots of conflict
- Lacking accountability to local people and just leaving if a crisis emerges

Insider-Outsider Partnerships

A "whole of society" approach recognizes that peacebuilding often requires insiders and outsiders—including international organizations, governments, international civil society, and local civil society—to work together. Human security emerges from a combination of a citizen-oriented state and civil society leaders who both complement and supplement the work of governments and hold governments accountable for their responsibilities and transparent governance.[11] Civil society organizations (CSOs) are groups of citizens not in government who organize themselves on behalf of some public interest. Both international (outsider) and insider CSOs are independent from government, making their own plans for meeting human needs and improving the quality of life.

National Interests, Self-Interests, and Human Security

Peacebuilding is rarely seen as neutral. People in the midst of conflict are already in a suspicious and vulnerable position. They are likely to ask questions and make judgments quickly about groups from the inside or outside of their conflict that want to carry out peacebuilding in their community or country. Groups conducting peacebuilding may have any or all of the following interests:

- Supporting human rights and human security
- Pursuing narrow political and economic interests for their identity group
- Gaining funding to continue their organizational existence

In Sri Lanka, for example, countries funding and supporting peacebuilding had a wide range of interests, including regional security, with the Liberation Tigers of Tamil Eelam (LTTE) rebel movement seen as a terrorist organization; trade relations, including selling military hardware to the Sri Lankan government; prevention of refugees, which could destabilize regional countries; promoting human rights and respecting international humanitarian law; reducing poverty; and alleviating human suffering.[12]

Peacebuilding efforts should result in increased human security. Human security is people-centered, focusing on the respect for and safety of individuals, communities, and their global environment. A human security approach empowers local people to assess vulnerabilities and threats and then identify and take part in strategies to build security rather than imposing outside definitions and approaches.

In a conflict-affected context, governments design peacebuilding efforts as well as their economic and military policies with their own national interests in mind. Sometimes these efforts overlap with local people's human security; sometimes they do not. Local people are highly sensitive to outsider's self-interests. Throughout the last decades and centuries, many outsiders have come to their regions seeking to conquer territory, extract resources, or force locals to convert to religious and economic belief systems. Local people often ask, "Do they think we're stupid?" in response to outsider's efforts to hide or distract local publics about their national interests.[13] Rumors and conspiracy theories spread quickly if a program or partnership is not transparent about its interests and intent. Outsiders would do well to put their self-interests up front and have an open conversation with locals about how and if these interests overlap with local perceptions of human security.

Democracy and Public Diplomacy

Local people often have little choice about whether outside donors and peacebuilding planners decide to come to their country. When insiders are left out of key assessment processes and policy decision-making, outsiders send a message that can undercut their public diplomacy efforts promoting democracy. Outsiders who design peacebuilding efforts but fail to include and respect diverse insiders send a clear message that the goal is not to support democracy. Democracy requires a diverse and active civil society, participating with governments when possible to assess conflict and carry out peacebuilding efforts.[14] Ultimately local people also have a right to be heard and to provide oversight and feedback to outsiders working in their home countries and communities.[15] Democracy is both a *means* and an *end*. Democratic policymaking recognizes that promoting democratic political systems requires exercising democratic processes and principles in all elements of outsider interventions in conflict-affected regions.

Contradictions Between Insiders' and Outsiders' Conflict Assessments

While many insiders (such as local civil society organizations) and outsiders (such as foreign governments) use similar conflict assessment frameworks and ask similar questions in focus groups and interviews, they seem to gather contradictory data and receive different answers in their research. Frequent contradictions occur in conflict assessments carried out by insiders and outsiders working in the same region. In many countries around the world, outsiders and insiders develop vastly different conclusions about what is driving and mitigating conflict. Local NGOs in many countries around the world complain that INGOs and foreign donors do not understand their local context.

In Afghanistan, donors—insiders and outsiders—all carried out conflict assessments using very similar conceptual frameworks, yet their results were quite different. Outside donors such as USAID found that unemployment was driving conflict, and thus devoted large sums of aid money to job creation projects.[16] Local think tanks found that government corruption and negative experiences with foreign troops in night raids and house searches were driving the insurgency.[17] The think tanks recommended addressing these drivers of conflict.[18]

In a number of east African countries, some donors pushed NGOs to conduct social dialogue programs between conflicting tribes. But local NGO and think-tank reports saw government corruption and the need for land reform as major drivers of conflict.[19] Local NGOs that had deep knowledge of the local context and clear ideas about what needed to be done to foster peace were largely left out of conflict assessment processes or were asked for their approval of the assessment after donors had already decided what they wanted to do. Foreign donor governments that had sent conflict assessment teams into the country to identify and prioritize aid budgets were reluctant to listen to local NGOs since they had already gone through a long process of developing policy goals, getting budget lines approved, and sending out request for proposals. The disparity between local and foreign conflict assessments meant that relationships between donors and implementers suffered, preventing coordinated action.[20]

In response to this widespread gap in understanding between outsiders and insiders, two large peacebuilding NGOs based in the United Kingdom, SaferWorld and Conciliation Resources, published conflict assessment reports called *People's Peacemaking Perspectives.* These reports aim to help governments and policymakers understand how local people see their own conflict and what they recommend international donors can do to support more strategic approaches to peacebuilding.[21]

Using Systems-Based Approaches to Multistakeholder, Multisector Coordination

An interdisciplinary group of theorists in the mid-1900s developed a new theoretical framework variously called systems theory, cybernetics, complexity theory, or synergetics. According to this framework, everything exists in an ecological relationship,[22] like the relationship between different parts of the biological environment, the parts of a computer, or organs in the human body. A systems-based approach is a meta-theory, or overarching framework for analysis. Systems theory is holistic in that it focuses on the whole, rather than on parts. Systems theorists believe that a part of a system can only be understood by examining its relationship to other parts. A systems-based approach to conflict assessment and peacebuilding grew out of the study of complex systems.[23]

This handbook takes a systems-based approach to assessing conflict, seeing the importance of understanding the whole system rather than just discrete elements of a conflict. This approach to conflict assessment and peacebuilding planning recognizes and respects complexity. A systems-based approach to conflict-affected contexts looks at interrelationships between humans, the institutions they create, social patterns of relationships, and their environment.

Ongoing Assessment in Complex, Dynamic System

Conflicts are systems with interrelated, dynamic parts. Systems are processes, always changing and adapting to change. A systems-based approach reminds researchers that conflicts change day to day as events happen. A onetime conflict assessment is not enough to inform effective strategic peacebuilding. A onetime peacebuilding project cannot bring permanent peace. This handbook sees learning and research on the conflict-affected system and peacebuilding planning as ongoing.

No one part of the system is in control of other parts. Each part of the system influences other parts. Mainstream media and political leaders often provide simple "cause-effect" analyses of conflicts that sound like this: "Bad guys cause conflict. Good guys use military force to kill the bad guys." Often the cause of conflict is seen as some group of people, and the analysis doesn't require understanding complex local cultural contexts. A systems-based approach moves away from a blame orientation in conflict that isolates specific leaders (bin Laden, for example) or groups (al-Qaeda).

In reality, most conflicts have multiple causes that interact with each other, driving a cycle of dynamic causes and effects. A systems-based approach recognizes that a simple identification and removal of an "enemy" is unlikely to change the dynamics of a conflict if underlying driving factors still remain. Rather, a systems-based approach to conflict looks at the entire system of causes and effects and the interplay between groups.

Conflict assessment requires "seeing" as much as possible of the complex social system where conflict takes place. Factors such as inequality, easy access to weapons, shortage of water, extremist leaders, and repressive governments influence each other. Terrorist organizations and repressive governments are often only understandable in relationship to their shared context. A systems-based approach can help provide a view of all the critical elements that perpetuate or drive conflict.

Macro-Level System Impacts

Conflicts happen within complex systems. Small peacebuilding efforts rarely add up to systemic change at the national or global level. Too many conflict assessments capture micro-level conflicts between ethnic or religious groups without looking at global forces that fuel local conflicts, such as the weapons trade, globalization, or climate change. System-based conflict assessments are useful in mapping both the micro and macro dynamics of conflict. Conflict assessment processes should map the system of conflict, all of its stakeholders, and its history, as well as how a conflict at the local level is nested within larger conflicts. Visual maps of the system help identify how parts of the system relate to one another. A systems approach appreciates, for example, why a community in Uganda may suffer from global economic patterns in resource extraction and the weapons trade. A systems-based approach to planning peacebuilding requires humility and strategy in order to have an impact on large, complex systems.

Using Assessment Lenses to See, Rather Than Tools to Take Apart

The metaphor of tools and toolboxes often describes elements of conflict assessment. The tool metaphor suggests that assessment requires taking conflict apart, as one uses a screwdriver to unhinge a locked box. This handbook uses the metaphor of a lens instead. A lens on a camera helps to capture an image or view. Photographers use different lenses to see and preserve different impressions of the world. A magnifying glass is a lens that allows an up-close look at certain elements of conflict while blurring others. In the same way, different assessment lenses help to provide different points of view on a conflict-affected system. The different lenses in this handbook highlight different elements of conflict. Conflict assessment processes contain many elements because each lens brings into focus a different part of reality—such as the social, psychological, economic, or political facets. Focusing on only one element can create a skewed or inadequate understanding of the conflict and leads to program silos and unintended second-order effects.

Drivers and Centers of Gravity: Prioritizing Data into Knowledge

Many conflict assessment tools produce long lists of factors or actors involved in a conflict without a way of prioritizing their importance. A systems approach to conflict assessment helps planners identify key drivers and centers of gravity. A *center of gravity* is a part of the system that has more influence over other parts. Influence can range from financial, moral, and physical power to an ability to act relatively freely, without severe sanctions or repercussions from other parts of the system. The center of gravity in many contexts is the information center. Military forces often destroy their opposition's news broadcast system, which they consider a center of gravity that would have significant impact on how local people respond to foreign forces.

Conflict assessment seeks to identify significant centers of gravity or key drivers or mitigators of conflict in a system that seem to have more influence over the system experiencing conflict. A center of gravity in a conflict system can be a part of the system that is vulnerable to collapse or crisis or has the potential for significant positive or negative influences, such as a mediation effort or an election.

A systems approach to conflict assessment helps filter and prioritize information by helping planners see the relationships and dynamics among key factors driving and mitigating conflict within a conflict-affected system. A good conflict assessment process filters and synthesizes a lot of data to prioritize key driving and mitigating factors in a conflict without sacrificing too much complexity and losing important insights. Planners can thus work with a manageable amount of information. Too much data or long lists of factors and root causes can simply create confusion and make planning more difficult. Information is most helpful when it can be categorized, synthesized, connected with other information, and sorted out by priorities for its relevance. This handbook on conflict assessment should help create knowledge and information out of long lists of unprioritized data.

Viewing the relationships and dynamics among factors allows planners to design integrated programming that reduces program costs and increases program effectiveness by building a broader set of objectives into each policy, program, or project. For example, a microcredit financing program in Iraq included a precondition that loans would go to business plans made by multiethnic entrepreneurs, thus incentivizing people to work together across the lines of conflict while also achieving an economic development goal. This approach is different than creating programs from long lists of factors that are not mapped to show how they relate to each other.

An important caveat is that one's own behavior, choices, or policies can be and often are key drivers and centers of gravity in a conflict. Another key lesson from studying how systems work is that each part of a system has the most influence over its own behavior. The easiest way to shift a system is to focus on those parts of the system closest to us. Too often, peacebuilding plans overlook self-assessment that identifies how one's own group is contributing to conflict and instead focuses on changing other groups.

Program Silos and Unintended Impacts; Second-Order Effects

If planners do not understand complex system dynamics, well-intentioned programs may have unintended impacts or second-order effects that fuel violence and divisions among groups. Consider two examples. First, an economic development program can bring in foreign investment to address unemployment that is driving conflict. But this approach may have a second-order effect of increasing government corruption that rewards some groups and punishes others without understanding and monitoring institutional capacities for keeping track of these investments. Second, a program intending to foster reconciliation between tribes can bring together male tribal elders to identify development programs that they can work on across tribal lines. But a program that reinforces traditional patterns of authority and decision making may have the unintended second-order effect of undermining efforts to foster democratic decision making in situations in which women and younger people also have a voice in decisions that impact their lives.

These types of program silos offer solutions to problems driving conflict without understanding the broader context or thinking outside of their own sector. Some planners focus only on structural factors driving conflict. Others focus only on softer psychological, social, and cultural issues. This handbook emphasizes the need for coordination and complementary planning for strategic peacebuilding that addresses the wider system, including political, economic, social, justice, and security issues.

Multisectoral Integrated Program Planning

Peacebuilding requires coordinating programming by multiple actors in multiple sectors and multiple levels of society to address conflict drivers and support local capacities for peace. Integrated or multisectoral planning builds in an awareness of the systemic context. For example, a health education program integrates conflict transformation and women's empowerment goals by including women from divided ethnic groups in a program to build their capacity to provide health care in their communities. Integrative programs take into consideration a variety of other key factors, such as gender, trauma, justice, culture, and the environment.

- *Gender-sensitive peacebuilding* disaggregates data for men and women in conflict assessment processes, recognizes the relationship between violence against women and broader social divisions, looks at the impact of gender roles on the types of violence that women experience, includes women's empowerment strategies in peacebuilding, and identifies the types of peacebuilding efforts men and women can perform.
- *Trauma-sensitive peacebuilding* looks at the impact of psycho-social trauma on the worldviews and cognitive processes of people driving and mitigating conflict.

- *Justice-sensitive peacebuilding* looks at whether groups perceive institutions and social patterns as fair, reflect universal human rights laws and standards, and include victims, offenders, and their communities in justice processes aimed to foster accountability, restoration, and healing.
- *Environmentally-sensitive peacebuilding* looks at the impact of human activity that negatively impacts the environment and how these environmental changes then play key roles in driving or potentially mitigating conflict.
- *Culturally-sensitive peacebuilding* considers local cultural, communal, and religious values, beliefs, and social rituals as well as natural patterns of change already under way locally.

"Whole of Society" Shared Understanding Required for Coordination

Large conflicts require participation of the whole of society. Neither governments nor civil society can build peace alone. A multistakeholder approach is necessary. Ideally, diverse stakeholders listen to and learn from each other's perceptions in a conflict assessment process. A systems approach to peacebuilding requires coordination of efforts and the design of intentional spaces for diverse groups to share their insights. Lack of coordination or even communication among groups working in conflict-affected regions is a primary reason for duplicative, wasteful, and ineffective peacebuilding efforts. In many conflict-affected regions, government missions and civil society goals are different, making it impossible, or at least challenging, for coordinated action or a comprehensive approach. Goals are different because governments and civil society have different understandings of the problem, and they develop different if not contradictory goals. What governments refer to as a "unity of effort," or a "comprehensive approach" to a shared mission of peacebuilding, is not possible without unity of understanding in conflict assessment. Unity of understanding comes from sharing and discussing conflict assessment data and conclusions. Through this process, depicted in Figure 1.4, key stakeholders can build a shared understanding of the conflict or at least begin to understand where they disagree.

Several decades of successful and failed efforts to prevent violent conflict offer some important lessons for future planning. Every context is different, but countries including South Africa, Indonesia, and El Salvador are moving away from outright war, though they still face considerable challenges from human rights violations and economic inequities. In each of these countries, peacebuilding took place at multiple levels of society in some sort of

Figure 1.4 Components of a Comprehensive Approach

coherent approach that synchronized and harmonized some of the civil society, government, military, and international influences. Local Indigenous stakeholders sustained these peacebuilding efforts over many years and enjoyed solid support from international donors and advisors. This handbook offers a methodology that ideally could synchronize and coordinate or harmonize conflict assessment, design, monitoring, and evaluation processes.

Linking civil society and government approaches to peacebuilding brings challenges, however. First, often there is a lack of shared understanding or conflict assessment between governments and civil society, resulting in divergent approaches to peacebuilding and security. As a result, governments and civil society frequently oppose each other's efforts. Second, civil society organizations (CSOs) often feel that a comprehensive approach that requires integration with governments that call them "force multipliers" makes them soft targets for insurgent groups and hampers their ability to make independent program decisions based on long-term development needs rather than short-term political objectives. A comprehensive approach that respects "civil society space" or the independent roles of civil society is most likely to enable contributions to stability and security. Furthermore, in many regions of the world, global war-on-terror legislation restricts civil society freedoms and intimidates civil society peacebuilding, undermining civil society's ability to hold governments accountable to democratic standards, as some fragile governments label any dissent from civil society as aiding extremism or terrorism.[24]

Finally, many CSOs recognize the benefits of policy dialogue and "communication" with government and military personnel. Yet few consultation structures exist to engage with those CSOs willing to provide policy advice, share conflict assessments, or discuss overlapping human security goals.[25]

Need for a Coordinated Conflict Assessment Center

A coordinated conflict assessment center in each conflict-affected context would enable international and regional organizations, bilateral donors,

International NGOs, and local civil society groups conducting conflict assessments to share data and basic information about drivers and mitigators of conflict. It would also allow them to test and revise theories of change and monitor and evaluate peacebuilding efforts. Ideally, different international and local stakeholders that share a basic understanding of the context can better coordinate their goals so that they complement each other rather than contradict or overlap with each other. Humanitarian and military groups, for example, can benefit from a multistakeholder conflict assessment. A conflict assessment center could provide an impartial place with high-quality facilitation for multistakeholder information exchange. A conflict assessment center could also help protect humanitarian organizations' need to distance themselves from political and security stakeholders, since a wide belief exists that collaborating too closely or directly with them would impact the security and access of humanitarians who work with all sides of a conflict. This form of a comprehensive approach should be based on communication and shared understanding between groups rather than trying to integrate all planning and operational activities on the ground.

- **Assessment.** How are different donors or planners communicating and coordinating their assessments in a conflict-affected context?
- **Planning.** How are different donors or planners communicating and coordinating their planning efforts for a conflict-affected context? In particular, how are insiders and outsiders communicating?
- **Evaluation.** How are different donors or planners communicating and coordinating their planning, monitoring, and evaluation of their theories of change and their policies, programs, and projects?

Improving Research Quality to Save Money, Time, and Mistakes

Untested assumptions drive too many efforts aimed at supporting peace and human security, resulting in failed policies and strategies, ineffective programs and projects, and wasted time and money. Donors and planners often do not adequately invest in the research necessary to collect accurate, reliable, triangulated data—that is, data collected from three or more local sources. Conflict assessment is a research process that reveals new information about diverse stakeholders' perceptions. This new information can help people think nontraditionally to discover new options for transforming the conflict and building on local capacities or resilience that supports peace.

Even a perfect conflict assessment framework cannot result in a perfect conflict assessment without sufficient data quality. The quality of the research process for conducting conflict assessments is as important as the quality of the conceptual framework used to process data. If the people conducting a conflict assessment are not deeply knowledgeable about local languages, cultures, and complex political and economic dynamics, the reliability and accuracy of the assessment is highly questionable. Stated simply, if you put garbage data into a perfect index, you still get garbage out of the assessment. This handbook emphasizes the need for data quality to ensure valid, accurate, reliable, and triangulated conclusions about what is driving and mitigating conflict.

Overconfidence and Lack of Humility to "Know What We Don't Know"

Conflict assessments are too often simplistic, forgoing the work of understanding the complex context in which conflict takes place. Too often, groups design strategies, policies, programs, and projects without a rigorous assessment. People outside the context tend to drastically overestimate what they know, while people inside the context suffer from knowing only one side of the conflict.

Outside interveners first and foremost need humility to know what they do not know. Overconfidence in understanding complex dynamics in a conflict-affected context creates a chain of problems. For example, a quick assessment that unemployment is driving insurgent recruitment can lead to designing programs that may in fact have little to do with local people joining or supporting insurgents because of their frustration with government corruption or their anger at foreign troops in their country. It is better to understand how little we know about conflict from the outset, recognizing that a complex context requires ongoing learning and experimentation. This handbook emphasizes that learning must be ongoing since conflict assessments will only ever see part of the complexity and contexts are constantly changing.

Overcoming Inherent Bias Through Research Rigor

Most people hold opinions about what is causing a conflict that is impacting them personally. But these opinions usually reflect only one side of a conflict. A conflict assessment team may ask all the right questions, but if they are answering the questions themselves, their own biases and limited experiences shape what they hear and see. Two separate groups of people with different political, religious, and cultural affiliations asking the same questions will often come up with two contrary conclusions of what is driving or mitigating conflict.

Development specialists are more likely to see unequal development as driving conflict, while political scientists are more likely to see political power plays doing so. Military forces are more likely to see a military solution to the problem that involves the use of force against specific targets. Westerners may be more likely to perceive the local sources of conflict, while locals from the context may see foreigners as driving the conflict.

Can-Do Attitudes and Fear of Analysis Paralysis

A can-do, eager-to-get-to-work attitude leads people to want to spend less time patiently listening to local people and researching conflict dynamics and more time actually doing something to foster change. Many groups are reluctant to spend program time and resources on assessment research instead of investing funds in actual programming. This fear of "analysis paralysis" also impacts other fields. For example, at the beginning of the Iraq War, military experts reflect that there was a rough balance of 10% of time spent on assessment and 90% of time spent on action. As the years went on, that ratio reversed. Military personnel came to value sitting and drinking tea with village elders and listening to local Iraqi perspectives of what was happening.

All conflict assessment processes face time and resource constraints. But skimping on conflict assessment wastes time and resources. Analysis paralysis is less dangerous than action without assessment.

Data: Overloaded and Mired in Complexity

Analysis paralysis is an actual problem. People can spend too much time collecting information and causing confusion and paralysis by the level of complexity in a conflict assessment. Research shows that when people have too much information or too many choices, they tend to psychologically freeze up and be unable to make decisions.[26] Research finds that most business leaders suffer for lack of a way to make sense of the data they have, not necessarily for having too little data.[27] Groups may analyze a situation so much that the complexity becomes overwhelming, paralyzing them from taking any action. This handbook attempts to provide a conceptual framework for filtering, prioritizing, and making sense of data so as to enable more effective peacebuilding planning. This volume also approaches all peacebuilding efforts as research requiring a humility that balances a willingness to take risks and learn from failures.

Quality, Quantity, and Scale of Research: Saving Money, Time, and Mistakes

The quality and success of peacebuilding planning relate to the quality of conflict assessment. This handbook stresses the *process* of conflict assessment and peacebuilding planning. The data collection and research process may be informal or formal, depending on the level of planning. An inadequate research process lacking quality data collection and community-level input is likely to result in inadequate or ineffective programs and policies. Groups hoping to do a quick and inexpensive conflict assessment may find the quality of the listening or research process more important than the quantity of time invested in it.

Given the strong critiques of wasteful and ineffective programs, quality is likely more important than quantity. The scale of the possible program or policy and the scale of the assessment process should be relative. Larger NGOs, governments, and international organizations may do nationwide conflict assessments involving hundreds of people to develop national peacebuilding plans and policies. Smaller organizations may carry out small-scale conflict assessments in specific communities to help in planning specific programs. This handbook allows for picking and choosing between different exercises according to the time frame and context of the assessment.

Conflict Sensitivity in Assessment: Unintended Impacts and Second-Order Effects

Intervening in a conflict creates opportunities to do harm, and to create unintended impacts and negative second-order effects as well as good at every step. Development researchers document wide-ranging examples of where good intentions of humanitarian aid, for example, have instead increased local conflict, provided resources for warlords to buy more guns, and created more local grievances.[28] Programs aimed at improving a community's quality of life too often inadvertently increase local conflict because outside resources end up in the hands of competing local factions instead of benefiting the whole community. Another scenario is security assistance programs offering weapons to an unstable government without first assessing the impact those same security forces have in repressing nonviolent expressions of conflict in the country, resulting in even greater levels of violence and instability. NGOs have inadvertently escalated conflict by bringing resources into a community to build a well, for example, while unaware of political divisions within the community that would benefit one group over another. Government planners have unknowingly fueled insurgencies when they used repressive security strategies like night raids and drone strikes that impacted the safety and dignity of ordinary citizens, who turned against their government and international allies for using these tactics against them.

New rigor and attention devoted to peacebuilding and statebuilding follow from international processes such as the Busan High-Level Forum on Aid Effectiveness, the New Deal for Engagement in Fragile States, and the International Dialogue on Peacebuilding and Statebuilding (IDPS), in addition to significant reports such as the World Bank 2011 "World Development Report on Conflict, Security, and Development"[29] and the U.N. Secretary-General's peacebuilding reports.[30] These are part of a growing consensus that a peacebuilding approach is necessary for sustainable human development and achievement of the Millennium Development Goals in conflict-affected states. This handbook builds on these common lessons learned and best practices.

All staff—including planners, financial officers, field staff, drivers, and security staff—should have a basic understanding of potential harms that can happen during a peacebuilding effort. Staff tasked with ensuring conflict sensitivity within organizations can review plans to catch a potentially harmful decision before its implementation. Organizations can take the Conflict Sensitivity Capacity Assessment (available at conflictsensitivity.org) to look at their institutional commitment, policies and strategies, human resources, learning and reflective practice, integration into the program cycle, and external relations. All staff should have basic competencies, including in the following areas:

- **Knowledge** of local cultures and the conflict-affected context and of the value of taking a conflict-sensitive approach to all programming.
- **Skills** to talk diplomatically and sensitively about a conflict so as to understand more of the interaction between the conflict and the peacebuilding effort.
- **Attitudes** that are self-aware of one's own biases, cultural differences, and local perceptions, and the **humility** to know that even though one's intentions are good, programs may have a negative impact on others.

Related Research and Assessments

Conflict assessment is related to, but not the same as, other forms of assessment. Conflict assessment is a distinct discipline and produces different types of information that enable peacebuilding efforts. Unlike needs assessments that focus on humanitarian criteria alone, conflict assessments ask a broader range of questions about what is driving and mitigating conflict. Unlike military assessments of "the enemy" that identify targets for violent action, conflict assessment processes aim to inform nonviolent, nonkinetic peacebuilding efforts. Like environmental assessments or gender audits, conflict assessment provides a set of lenses to look at a problem. But unlike any of these other processes, conflict assessment asks a unique set of questions based on interdisciplinary conceptual frameworks from the fields of sociology, political science, economics, psychology, and other disciplines. Information from other assessment processes can be useful in providing data to triangulate with data gathered through group exercises or interviews in conflict assessments. Governments around the world are developing conflict assessment frameworks to complement their other needs-assessment and intelligence-gathering processes.

Research as a Peacebuilding Process

Research processes are not neutral. They are an intervention that changes conflict dynamics. While the final outcome of any conflict assessment will never be perfect, the discussion and learning that happen in the research process constitute a form of peacebuilding. It can produce better intergroup understanding and knowledge, which in turn can mean better group buy-in for peacebuilding planning and therefore more successful outcomes. Bringing diverse groups of people together to jointly discuss and analyze their context can improve relationships between groups. It can also generate ideas for peacebuilding efforts that groups can conduct themselves. Participants in conflict assessment research can and should become the designers and planners of peacebuilding in their own context.[31]

Conflict assessment is essentially the first stage of negotiation or mediation, when stakeholders meet together to share their points of view and discuss their conflicts to clarify issues and identify underlying interests. Peacebuilding groups can use research processes as part of any dialogue, negotiation, or mediation process. The conflict assessment process itself is often used as a form of peacebuilding between adversaries. Known as the Problem-Solving Workshop in peacebuilding literature and theory, academics invite key stakeholders representing opposing sides of a conflict to engage in conflict assessment exercises and dialogue.[32] Through analyzing their conflict together, adversaries can come to understand more about their opponents, identify key differences and common ground, and develop mutually satisfying solutions to key issues.

Notes

1. John Paul Lederach, *The Little Book of Conflict Transformation* (Intercourse, PA: Good Books, 2003).

2. Sphere Project, *Sphere Handbook: Humanitarian Charter and Minimum Standards in Disaster Response, 2011*, http://www.unhcr.org.

3. The chart is adapted from Daniel Serwer and Patricia Thomson, "A Framework for Success: International Intervention in Societies Emerging from Conflict," in *Leashing the Dogs of War*, ed. Chester Crocker, Fen Osler Hampson, and Pamela Aall (Washington, DC: US Institute of Peace, 2007), 369–87. It also draws on Luc Reychler and Thania Paffenholz, *Peacebuilding: A Field Guide* (Boulder, CO: Lynne Rienner Publishers, 2001); Dan Smith, "Towards a Strategic Framework for Peacebuilding: The Synthesis Report of the Joint Utstein Study on Peacebuilding" (Oslo: PRIO, 2003); Thania Paffenholz, *Civil Society and Peacebuilding* (Boulder, CO: Lynne Rienner Publishers, 2009); Lisa Schirch, *Strategic Peacebuilding* (Intercourse, PA: Good Books, 2004); and Cooperation for Peace and Unity, *Human Security Indicators* (Kabul, 2010).

4. Anderson, Mary B., and Lara Olson. *Confronting War: Critical Lessons for Peace Practitioners* (Cambridge, MAMA: Collaborative for Development Action, 2003).

5. Koenraad Van Brabant, "Peacebuilding How? 'Insiders'-'Outsiders' and Peacebuilding Partnerships," Interpeace, Geneva, 2010.

6. Claudia Liebler and Cynthia Sampson, "Appreciative Inquiry in Peacebuilding: Imagining the Possible," in *Positive Approaches to Peacebuilding* (Washington, DC: Pact Publications, 2003), 55–79.

7. Mary B. Anderson and Lara Olson, *Confronting War: Critical Lessons for Peace Practitioners* (Cambridge, MA: Collaborative for Development Action, 2003).

8. Van Brabant, "Peacebuilding How? 'Insiders'-'Outsiders,'" 5–6.

9. Duncan Hiscock and Teresa Dumasy, "From Conflict Analysis to Peacebuilding Impact: Lessons Learned from People's Peacemaking Perspectives," Conciliation Resources and SaferWorld, London, March 2012, ii.

10. Adapted from Reflecting on Peace Practice and the Peacebuilding Effective Partnerships Forum held by Interpeace and the International Peace Academy, Geneva, Switzerland, 2004.

11. OECD, *Supporting Statebuilding in Situations of Fragility and Conflict*, Organisation for Economic Co-operation and Development, Paris, January 2011.

12. Jonathan Goodhand, Tony Vaux, and Robert Walker, *Conducting Conflict Assessments: Guidance Notes* (London: Department for International Development, 2002), 20.

13. Mark Bradbury, "Do They Think We're Stupid? Local Perceptions of US 'Hearts and Minds' Activities in Kenya," http://www.odihpn.org.

14. Aaron Chassy, "Civil Society and Development Effectiveness in Africa," in *Problems, Promises and Paradoxes of Aid: Africa's Experience*, ed. Muna Ndulo and Nicolas van de Walle (Athens: Ohio University Press and University of Cape Town Press, forthcoming).

15. Adapted from Communicating with Disaster Affected Communities Initiative, as cited in the Conflict Sensitivity Consortium, "How to Guide to Conflict Sensitivity," Conflict Sensitivity Consortium, London, 2012, 28.

16. See, for example, USAID Afghanistan, Community Development Program (CDP) Fact Sheet, June 2011, http://afghanistan.usaid.gov.

17. In this situation, the two drivers of conflict found repeatedly by researchers outside of government were the two parts of the system over which outside governments had the most control. While foreign troops did aim to decrease the negative impacts of night raids and house searches, the communication strategies around these tactics either were inadequate, or the degree of change in the house searches—from less respectful involving dogs and body searches on women to more respectful of local culture and religion—the degree of perceived change in the behavior of foreign forces worsened over time, increasing antagonism against foreign forces. The presence of forces then became a primary driver of fence-sitters to support the insurgent groups. International policy in Afghanistan became a "wicked problem" in which the solution (military forces) to the identified problem (Taliban and other insurgent groups) actually reinforced the problem.

18. See, for example, Paul Fishstein and Andrew Wilder, "Winning Hearts and Minds? Examining the Relationship Between Aid and Security in Afghanistan," Feinstein International Center at Tufts University, Medford, MA, January 2012.

19. Karuti Kanyinga, "The Legacy of the White Highlands: Land Rights, Ethnicity, and the Post-2007 Election Violence in Kenya," *Journal of Contemporary African Studies* 27, no. 3 (July 2009): 325–44.

20. Interviews by this author with peacebuilding NGOs in Kenya, Uganda, and those working in parts of Somalia between January 2002 and October 2011.

21. See the websites of Conciliation Resources (http://www.c-r.org/PPP) and SaferWorld (http://www.saferworld.org.uk/where/people-s-peacemaking-perspectives) for copies of 18 separate locally driven conflict assessments and policy recommendations. See also Hiscock and Dumasy, "From Conflict Analysis to Peacebuilding Impact."

22. Fritjof Capra, *The Web of Life: A New Scientific Understanding of Living Systems* (New York: Anchor Books, 1996).

23. See Kenneth Boulding, *The World as a Total System* (Newbury Park, CA: Sage, 1985); Louise Diamond and John McDonald, *Multi-Track Diplomacy: A Systems Guide and Analysis* (Grinnell: Iowa Peace Institute, 1991); John Paul Lederach and Scott Appleby, "Strategic Peacebuilding: An Overview," in *Strategies of Peace*, ed. Daniel Philpott and Gerard F. Powers (New York: Oxford University Press, 2010), 19–44; Robert Ricigliano, *Making Peace Last* (Boulder, CO: Paradigm Press, 2011).

24. David Cortright, George A. Lopez, Alistair Millar, and Linda M. Gerber-Stellingwerf, "Friend or Foe: Civil Society and the Struggle Against Violent Extremism," a report to Cordaid from the Fourth Freedom Forum and Kroc Institute for International Peace Studies at the University of Notre Dame, October 27, 2008, http://www.fourthfreedom.org.

25. See Lisa Schirch, "Civil Society-Military Roadmap on Human Security," 3P Human Security, Washington, DC, 2011; Edwina Thompson, "Principled Pragmatism: NGO Engagement with Armed Actors," World Vision International, Monrovia, CA, 2008.

26. Barry Schwartz, *The Paradox of Choice: Why Less Is More* (New York: Harper Perennial, 2005). See also Dan Heath and Chip Heath, "Analysis of Paralysis," FastCompany.com, November 1, 2007.

27. K. Sutcliffe and K. Weber, "The High Cost of Accuracy," *Harvard Business Review* 81 (2003): 74–82.

28. Extensive research identifies the potential negative impacts of programs related to peacebuilding. See, for example, Mary Anderson's *Do No Harm: How Aid Supports Peace—or War* (Boulder, CO: Lynne Rienner Publishers, 1999).

29. World Bank. *2011 World Development Report on Conflict, Security, and Development*, World Bank, Washington, DC, April 2011.

30. Report of the Secretary-General on Peacebuilding in the Immediate Aftermath of Conflict, United Nations, New York, June 11, 2009.

31. Hiscock and Dumasy, "From Conflict Analysis to Peacebuilding Impact," iii.

32. Christopher Mitchell and Michael Banks, *Handbook of Conflict Resolution: The Analytical Problem-Solving Approach* (London: Pinter, 1996).

2

Research Methods and Challenges

This chapter lays out some of the broad challenges and considerations relating to the conflict assessment and monitoring and evaluation research processes. Research processes are never perfect. This chapter examines how imperfect can a conflict assessment research be and still produce information helpful to planning peacebuilding.

The parable of the four blind people and the elephant holds true for conflict assessment. Each blind man describes the elephant differently. The one holding the trunk, the tail, the leg, or the side of the elephant describe it as a water hose, a rope, a tree, or a wall, respectively. In the same way, four different conflict assessment teams could all research the same conflict and easily come up with four different conclusions.

Contradictions are inevitable. People on different sides of a conflict have different perceptions of what is driving the conflict or what is supporting peace. A conflict assessment process aims to capture not the one truth about the conflict, but rather to map and describe all the different perceptions of diverse stakeholders.

Research Principles

All research is in itself an intervention that can bring harms and benefits in the process. Howard Zehr identifies key elements or principles of "transformative inquiry." Research is more than just pursuing knowledge. Research can foster social action to build community, promote dialogue, increase understanding between groups, and empower people to give voice to their experience and work for justice. Some of these principles include the following:[1]

- **Participation:** Invite people to participate in owning and shaping research about their lives.
- **Empowerment:** Recognize the power dynamics between those sharing their perspectives and the researchers who use these stories to make a case for some sort of policy or program that could affect people's lives.
- **Accountability:** Identify researcher's obligations to subjects including transparency of the goals, methods, and motives of the research; the benefits to subjects; the ability of subjects to voice their perspectives themselves; and recognition of potential harms that may come about through the research process.
- **Respect:** Recognize that each subject has a unique experience that may teach the researcher something new or different and is a gift a researcher should honor as the facilitator, collaborator, and learner in the process.
- **Confidentiality:** Honor requests from people to not share sensitive information that could result in harms to subjects or others.
- **Pedagogy:** Include verbal and written as well as nonverbal, nonlinear, or artistic methods of gathering research data and presenting research findings.

Data Quality

Data quality impacts the quality of conflict assessments, which in turn impacts the quality and effectiveness of peacebuilding efforts. *Data* is raw material gathered from primary sources (e.g., interviews, focus groups, and surveys) and secondary sources (e.g., newspapers, blogs, and publications) through qualitative and quantitative methods. (Qualitative methods lead to descriptive data; quantitative methods lead to data that can be counted.) The conflict assessment framework here organizes data into *information* sorted into conceptual categories (where, who, why, what, how, and when). The resulting *knowledge* from this assessment can lead to conclusions or evidence of what is driving or mitigating conflict. This evidence then leads to development of theories of change used for planning and designing peacebuilding efforts. Ongoing research continues to collect data to measure the implementation or outputs of the peacebuilding effort as well as the larger outcomes and impacts required to evaluate it.

The research process for conducting a conflict assessment requires a methodology that is valid, reliable, accurate, and triangulated.[2]

Valid. Data is valid if it applies to the research questions. Data is most valid if a complete data source (dataset) is available for the selected context and scope, across space, time, or level of detail. Data is least valid if it is incomplete or does not fit with assessment framework questions or categories.

Reliable. Data is reliable if it comes from dependable, respected sources. Data is most reliable when it comes from a primary source (directly accessing the source on location) and the researcher identifies all information as coming from primary, secondary, or tertiary sources. Data is least reliable when it relies on secondary or tertiary sources (more than one or two degrees of separation from the source or source material) and researchers fail to identify the source's reliability.

Accurate. Data is accurate if it can be gathered repeatedly with the same results. Data is most accurate if the research methodology clearly identifies the data providers (interviewers, pollsters, and collectors) and they can be reached for queries. Data is least accurate if no information is available about the data providers. Accuracy also relates to the sampling frame. At best, researchers are transparent, clear, and logical about whom they choose to interview in the sampling frame. At worst, researchers interview only a small sample and are not explicit about reasons for choosing that group. The quality of a conflict assessment relates to the diversity and accuracy of the sources of the information. Do the researchers or participants completing a conflict assessment speak the local languages? Do they read local daily newspapers? Do they spend time with diverse stakeholders from within the context to learn more about their perspectives?

Triangulated. Researchers triangulate data by comparing data from three or more reliable sources. Researchers fact-check data by comparing it to other data sources and then having it peer reviewed by internal and external reviewers. Ideally, data from quantitative sources can provide a numerical scale on how large numbers of people think about some aspect of the conflict. Qualitative sources can examine how smaller numbers of people provide their own, more personal perspectives about conflict.

Triangulation of data sources increases the quality of the conflict assessment. Conflict assessment can easily become an exercise in futility if relatively uninformed participants with a limited range of opinions and experiences use these exercises to make decisions about programming. Too often, conflict assessments include a single person's opinion as evidence that ultimately guides policy or programs. Table 2.1 illustrates how to compare different sources of information or evidence for each theory of what is driving conflict.[3] For example, each stakeholder or local focus group interviewed is a source of evidence. Diverse sources may give contradictory evidence

Table 2.1 Example of Comparing Data Sources

	Landowners' interest in cheap labor drives their treatment of Indigenous people	Landowners' ideology and prejudice drive their treatment of Indigenous people	Landowners' desire for political control drives their treatment of Indigenous people
Evidence 1	Yes	No	No
Evidence 2	No	Yes	No
Evidence 3	Yes	No	No
Evidence 4	Yes	Yes	No
Evidence 5	No	No	Yes

Source: Lawrence Woocher, "Conflict Assessment and Intelligence Analysis Commonality, Convergence, and Complementarity," US Institute of Peace, Washington, DC, June 2011.

on different factors related to conflict. A research team then would have to temper the conclusions of a conflict assessment, noting that there is no conclusive agreement on the conflict's driving factors.

Data quality is not necessarily equal to agreement of data across qualitative and quantitative sources. In conflict-affected contexts, people differ in their perceptions of what is driving a conflict. There is not one truth but rather many different truths for different stakeholders. No one is without bias, although some perspectives are more biased than others. Identifying key issues where disagreement persists can be an important part of conflict assessment. These issues may be important for learning more about the experiences, values, and beliefs that lead groups to hold to different perspectives. Identifying common ground and points of difference is also an important step in developing the curriculum for a dialogue or setting out the issues for a formal negotiation. In this case, triangulated data should support the different perceptions to determine each one's validity or coherency.

Data Validity and Distortion Problems in Current Assessment

Current conflict assessment, monitoring, and evaluation processes face a range of challenges related to data quality. First, the identity of the group collecting the data impacts the quality of the data. In many cultures, people tell data collectors what they think the researchers want to hear. Respondents may do this to be polite, to ensure that aid money continues coming to their community regardless of whether it is resulting in effective programs or not, or because they fear for their safety or position if they explain their true feelings about what is driving the local conflict. Many donors still use a model of outsider teams of experts who go into a community to interview local people. This model does not fully consider the possibility that locals will not provide accurate and complete information to outsiders. Given that local people perceive that many donor countries and outsiders have their own political and economic interests in a conflict, the probability that local people will not give accurate information is high. Outside assessment teams regularly collect distorted data that in turn leads to programs and policies that are ineffective in preventing, managing, reducing, or transforming violent conflict.

Second, data distortion also comes through translation. Conflict assessment questions themselves may be politically charged or offensive to interviewees. A translator may misinterpret the question, or may not be able to fully translate a response to a question. The translator may even come from a particular ethnic or ideological group and intentionally misinterpret a response so as to shape the data.

Third, outside teams of experts often assume they hold a neutral, unbiased approach to the conflict. Many donors still collect the bulk of their data from people outside the conflict. They assume that "nationals"—insiders and local people—are more biased than "internationals" or outsiders. These expert outsider teams often fail to conduct a self-assessment of their own biases shaped by what they have read in media reports about the conflict and their own political assumptions and perceptions of their interests in the conflict. Without a clear self-assessment, researchers are often blind to their own biases and are more likely to hear what they want to hear. Assessment teams on tight budgets and with tight timelines may look for shortcuts to quickly articulate a concise statement of what they see as key drivers of a local conflict. In the search for cognitive consistency, outside assessment teams may start to dismiss or ignore data that contradicts their beliefs or conclusions about the conflict. Without a process to check whether psychological processes of selective perception and groupthink (described more fully later in this chapter) are occurring, researchers may not detect data warping.

Psychological Processes That Hamper Research

Everyone participating in a conflict assessment is subjective—including researchers and research subjects. No one person or group can conduct an accurate conflict assessment. By necessity, conflict assessment is a process involving a wide variety of diverse voices and perspectives. At every step of conflict assessment and peacebuilding planning, an important question to keep in mind is "Whose perspectives are shaping the discussion?"

Psychological processes greatly influence conflict assessment. People tend to hear and see what they want to hear and see. People's worldviews shape and filter the world that they see. Research on conflict is particularly challenging, as people with an interest in a conflict tend to filter data to fit into their current worldview.

The process of perception is the way a person makes sense of a complicated world of information. Understanding basic facts about the human brain and psychological processes is essential to understanding the problems of bias and data distortion during research for conflict assessment, monitoring, and evaluation.

There are two simple principles of perception. First, people desire *cognitive consistency* or a steady, predictable understanding of the world. Second, when people perceive something that is inconsistent with their past experiences or beliefs, they seek to hide or deny it from existence. Contradictions or new information that goes against one's current worldview is stressful. If individuals perceive the world in a way that is incongruent with their worldview, they experience *cognitive dissonance*; they have anxiety and discomfort about a new experience or idea that does not fit with their current understanding.

Humans perceive only a small part of any system or context. The process of perception shapes and limits what people see in a conflict. People maintain cognitive consistency and avoid cognitive dissonance in two ways:

1. People *filter their experiences* with the world in a way that only retains the information consistent with their current way of viewing the world. People reinforce preexisting views of what the conflict is about based on personal experience or professional expertise.
2. People *actively create the world* they expect and want to experience. People jump to conclusions about what is best to do in a conflict based on the programs or resources already available or what one's own organization would like to do.

A pair of glasses in Figure 2.1 represents how the process of perception filters and creates what people perceive as reality. A few definitions and examples demonstrate the relevance of perception and psychological processes for conflict assessment research. These psychological processes are

Figure 2.1 Psychological Processes

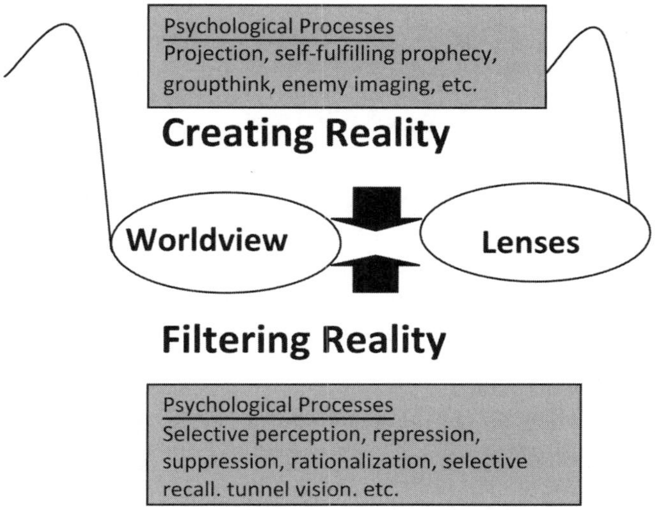

also important for analyzing key stakeholders' worldviews, as discussed in Chapter 7.

Selective perception Humans selectively perceive information by either discarding dissonant information or distorting it to fit into current understandings. For example, conflict assessment teams may discard information suggesting that their own identity group is driving conflict. A person from the conflict may discard or distort information that appears to show an adversary's positive qualities.

Repression Repression and suppression are processes of avoiding dissonant memories. For example, a researcher may avoid memories that formed her own worldview about the conflict. A person from the conflict may repress memories of growing up peacefully beside his adversary.

Tunnel vision Tunnel vision is a process in which humans perceive only a small part of the world consistent with previous experiences. Researchers can have tunnel vision in regard to how they understand others' actions. Depending on their biases, researchers may see only the bad things others do and disregard the good.

Rationalization Rationalization is the process of explaining to oneself why discarding dissonant information is acceptable. Researchers may rationalize any positive actions by another group, such as an organization labeled as "terrorists," by believing that the other group's good actions are only exceptions to the rule.

Projection People create their own sense of reality by *projecting* their current beliefs and values onto the world. People may project their biases and stereotypes of other groups onto others. For example, researchers may project untrustworthiness on corporate executives or on illiterate people, depending on their biases. People in conflict may project untrustworthiness onto their adversaries. The more distrustful people are of others, the less likely an adversary is to actually attempt building trust. In conflict, the psychological process of projection may become a self-fulfilling prophecy as groups labeled as "terrorists" become more committed to using violent strategies if others exclude them from political processes.

Groupthink Another factor to consider is *groupthink*, which happens as people within a group start to reinforce each others' points of view. Researchers may start to think alike, reinforce false assumptions, and fail to see alternatives. Group members may minimize conflict with each other by not asking critical questions about a dominant point of view, by permitting "mind guards" to censor anyone who veers from unanimity, or by promoting self-censoring of views that deviate from the group consensus. In groupthink, people become overly optimistic with a sense of invulnerability and an inherent belief in their morality. Foreign policy analysts detail how groupthink is responsible for failure to predict major international crises because policymakers were too likeminded and failed to ask critical questions of each others' assumptions.[4]

Each of these psychological processes is at work in all members on a research team, in the organizations they work for, and in every research subject. Skilled researchers recognize psychological tendencies and seek out dissonant information that can challenge their own perceptions.

Identifying Missing Information and Overconfident Assertions

A misinformed conflict assessment leads to ineffective, wasteful, and even harmful peacebuilding programs. People often do not know what information they are missing. On the one hand, the process of cognition itself hides alternative perspectives that challenge our own worldviews. On the other hand, the human ego leads many people to assume that they know more than they do. Particularly in well-educated or elite policymaker settings, participants tend to be overconfident about what they know about a conflict. If conflict assessment happens in a group process, people may compete with each other to look knowledgeable and assert strong, albeit inaccurate, opinions.

Conflict assessment researchers should understand these dynamics in order to minimize collective blindness due to these perceptual processes, especially groupthink. A facilitator or research team should seek to create a group dynamic in which people can challenge each other respectfully. One way of challenging the quality of information offered is to ask a group doing a conflict assessment to fill in a chart such as presented in Table 2.2. Participants can list what information is missing and ideas about how to develop a process for discovering the information.

Another option for testing the accuracy of information in a conflict assessment is to develop a review process. Sharing a final report of the assessment with diverse stakeholders can help test its accuracy. This review process can then identify areas where inaccurate or overconfident assumptions exist about the conflict.

Government agencies sometimes use "red-teaming"—also known as a "skeptics core"—to address the problem of groupthink and tunnel vision. When gathered to discuss an issue, a designated group identifies and challenges the dominant themes and assumptions. The red team provides different points of view.[5] However, red-teaming cannot replace how someone from another culture or another side of a conflict actually thinks. Without having people of diverse backgrounds involved, red teams are an inadequate

Table 2.2 Identifying Research Gaps

What information are we missing?	Whose perspectives do we need to seek out?	What research process could we use to discover this information?

substitute for people with different life experiences and different perceptions of the conflict.

Constructing Conflict Assessment Teams and Processes

The output from each conflict assessment process will be different depending on who participates in the process. Ideally, conflict assessment processes include joint teams of people along a spectrum of those more or less inside or outside of the conflict. This mixed team would ideally participate in the design and implementation of conflict assessment and then help to choose theories of change, design policies and programs, and influence research to monitor and evaluate the peacebuilding effort. If the people conducting a conflict assessment are not deeply knowledgeable about local languages, cultures, and complex political and economic dynamics, the output of the assessment may not enable effective planning. Diverse groups of local people, including women and youth—as well as different ethnic, religious, regional, class, linguistic, and other identity groups—should be involved in planning every aspect of conflict assessment, monitoring, and evaluation.

Implicit Messages in Research

Implicit power relationships are in place within any conflict assessment process. The assessment process can send an implicit message about whose goals and voices are most important and whose analysis is most trusted. When a conflict assessment process hears radically different perspectives from the national government, a foreign ambassador, and a local farmer who lives and works in an area with public violence, whose opinions about the root causes of the conflict are most valid, and whose perspectives most shape the planning process?

Identifying the sources of power of potential participants in a conflict assessment—such as whether they have local authority, donor funds, or government access—is an important step in ensuring an accurate assessment. These power sources may influence how people think about conflict. If they are in a position of responsibility or authority, they may want to underplay their role or the impact of conflict. If they are seeking donor funds for a project, they may overemphasize the conflict's impact.

Outsiders and Insiders—Researchers and Research Participants

Inclusive, respectful processes where diverse stakeholders discuss, decide, and implement conflict assessment and peacebuilding planning together demonstrate democratic decision making about what peacebuilding goals are legitimate. People with different backgrounds naturally view a conflict in different ways. A diverse range of people from within a community or region complemented by outsiders who bring interdisciplinary and comparative insights from outside the region is likely to produce the best conflict assessment.

Assessment processes that rely only on outsiders with limited or token participation by elite local representatives are likely to miss a wide array of cultural and contextual insights. Outsiders, for example, are often unable to adequately understand the divisions and social ranking systems within a country. Insiders of different socioeconomic, ethnic, religious, or linguistic groups may defer to other groups in public settings, or say what they think outsiders want to hear. Outside donors and programmers should be aware that insiders may not be able or willing to communicate directly about complex dynamics of conflict. The identity and presence of outsiders and translators who have their own biases skew data about local conflict dynamics. For example, in some countries, people from some of the country's minority ethnic groups may not speak publicly on the dynamics of conflict when outsiders or other ethnic groups are present.

Diverse teams of insiders and outsiders representing a country's spectrum of socioeconomic, ethnic, religious, lingual, age, educational, and regional backgrounds are more likely to provide a conflict assessment that is adequate for peacebuilding planning. Ideally government and civil society leaders could participate in an ongoing conflict assessment forum. Civil society includes religious leaders, NGOs such as charities, community-based development organizations (CBOs), women's groups, media, business associations, faith-based organizations, professional associations, trade unions, self-help groups, coalitions, and advocacy groups. Often the same local elites from government and civil society are repeatedly chosen to participate in donor assessments. Yet the strength of civil society is its diversity. Conflict assessment processes should ensure that local voices truly represent this.

Data Collection Challenges

Regardless of whether they are insiders, outsiders, or a mix, researchers have a difficult time finding reliable and accurate data in conflict-affected regions. Rumors, misinformation, and outright deception are commonplace. In the midst of conflict, people feeling fearful and threatened and those who stand to gain or lose in the conflict communicate with researchers based on self-interests. It may be difficult to reach people with different points of view because of safety concerns or political forces that block access.[6] People unfamiliar with political and structural discussions might have a hard time participating in complex discussions of conflict drivers and mitigators or root causes. And there may be a lack of funding or local capacity to conduct long-term assessments that illustrate changes over time.[7] Still, it is absolutely essential to do community-level research with a diverse set of local people from all sides of a conflict.

Conflict Sensitivity in Assessment, Monitoring, and Evaluation Research

Research processes are not neutral. They are an intervention that can change conflict dynamics. Asking questions can create conflict. A conflict-sensitive approach to research follows a number of basic practices, guided by certain principles.[8]

Choose who designs the research process. Every conflict has people who bridge different communities. These insiders are often best placed to help design the research process so that it accurately gathers information from all sides of the conflict. Outsiders may inadvertently bias the design of the research process itself and entirely miss the diversity of perspectives necessary for understanding the context. Where a research team travels and whom they interview create perceptions about the fairness of the process as well as the political interests behind those carrying out the research.

Choose who conducts the research. The identities of the people carrying out the research make first impressions and shape perceptions about the purpose of the research. If the team is made up of outsiders only, or with only one or two insiders who belong to a certain social group, local people will interpret the political and economic interests of the team based on their supposed allegiance to their larger social group. Given the sensitivities about research on conflict and violence, researchers for conflict assessment and peacebuilding monitoring and evaluation need a special set of skills. Trained facilitators and researchers are essential to help groups use exercises and effectively dialogue with each other in the conflict assessment research process. Trained facilitators are skilled in how to involve all group members, create a safe space where people can surface underlying perceptions, and ask probing questions that seek clarification and synthesis. Collecting information about people's perceptions of conflict requires asking "open" questions that allow individuals to use their own language, terms, and symbols to describe the world as they see it. Asking open-ended questions—

rather than closed-ended questions that can be answered yes or no—is a skill.

Facilitation skills are also necessary when stakeholders participating in an assessment express opposing views. A facilitator can model nonanxious behavior and encourage participants in a focus group, for example, to acknowledge or recognize that different people view the conflict in different ways.

A trained research team can facilitate the use of these assessment exercises with key individuals, focus groups, organizations, government offices, and other sections of a community, city, or region facing conflict. The research team can then compile and compare the results of the different exercises to produce a conflict assessment that is more valid and accurate.

Make the process transparent. People interviewed want to know who is carrying out a conflict assessment and what interests lie behind the process. As with all research projects involving human subjects, an ethic of transparency is essential.[9] Conflict assessments carried out by local groups with longstanding relationships with communities still need to be transparent about why they are conducting the assessment at a particular time. Outside assessment teams need to develop a strategy for explaining their research to local leadership, possibly asking these leaders for an introduction to the broader community. But asking leaders for an introduction can also shape local perceptions of what these outsiders want to hear. Local media may want to cover the research process if a community consultation is taking place. The assessment team should have a strategy for clearly communicating the purpose of the assessment and deciding if, when, and how media cover the process.

Pilot-test trauma-sensitive research questions. Asking questions of people experiencing trauma or having lived through traumatic experiences is delicate, if not dangerous. Victims can feel revictimized if researchers attempt to evoke an emotional response by asking questions about how they feel about a tragic experience. Research questions can raise sensitivities and even increase local conflict. If outsiders come into a community asking about ethnic divisions, inequality, or gender relations, they may change the way local people view their own problems and issues. Assessment can change the relationships between groups of people. If planned and managed as an intervention itself, conflict assessment can be a valuable part of a larger peacebuilding effort. But if assessment teams are not aware of the sensitivity of their questions, they can do harm to local people without ever understanding or knowing what they have done.

The Organisation for Economic Co-operation and Development (OECD) Development Assistance Committee (DAC) Guidance on Evaluating Humanitarian Aid in Complex Emergencies summarizes these concerns:

> Psycho-social trauma may affect much larger numbers of people than is often evident to an outsider, particularly one unfamiliar with the local language and untrained in the diagnosis of post-traumatic stress disorders [PTSD]. People being interviewed during or after a major violent conflict may have experienced violence first-hand; they may have been forcibly displaced, had relatives and friends killed, or perhaps seen their personal, social or cultural identities shattered. Chronic insecurity and widespread gender-based violence, including the systematic use of rape and other forms of torture compound trauma. Widespread trauma will no doubt impact interactions between local people and [assessment and evaluation] teams and should be handled with great care. The value and use of information collected from locals will have to be weighed against the potentially harmful effects of explaining traumatic experiences to [assessment and evaluation teams].[10]

Pilot testing research questions with trusted insiders from across known social divides can help sensitize researchers to possible effects certain questions will elicit. Researchers can adapt and change the terminology to ask more open-ended questions.

Conflict assessment researchers can learn from the Dart Center for Journalism and Trauma. The Dart Center advises journalists to ask questions like "What did you see?" and "Who was there?" rather than "How do you feel?" Questions asking for facts are less likely to cause harm and more likely to elicit an accurate story about what happened.

The Dart Center suggests that journalists always ask a series of self-assessment questions before interviewing victims: Is it necessary to immediately interview those who have suffered a traumatic event? Is there a value of intruding on people when they are grieving, disoriented, shocked, and frightened that makes the interview worthwhile to prevent future violence? If I were chronicling events directly affecting my family, would I alter the wording of my question in any way? Is it necessary to include graphic descriptions or images in the research? Could any of the research prove harmful to any of the people involved?[11] Their recommendations also include:

- Be sensitive to the emotions and trauma of people providing information.
- Be aware of any dynamic of coercion or power that may apply pressure on someone to provide data.
- Plan security measures to ensure the safety and anonymity of people talking to researchers, which can mean traveling at certain times of the day and meeting in places where there is either complete transparency or protection for those meeting to talk.

- Ensure confidentiality of data. Let people know that their names will not be included in the report, and efforts to protect their anonymity and safety are of top priority.

Manage expectations and follow-up. Researchers should be aware of elements of power and coercion in collecting data. Who will benefit from the research? What are possible political and economic interests in the outcome of the research? People participating in an assessment want to know what happens with the information they provide. Those who participate in an assessment process may do so because of their hope that it will bring financial or political rewards to their community. Assessment teams should provide an explanation of what happens with the information. Will the community see a public version of the assessment? Will the assessment team decide on which communities receive funds for programs? Will the assessment team give information to the military or armed forces that may decide to use the information to target individuals in the community? How are researchers and their organizations accountable to local people in sharing their assessment?

Data Collection Research Methodologies

Many data collection strategies can use the tools, lenses, and exercises described in this handbook, many of which grew out of the development field's use of Participatory Rural Assessment (PRA) models, which help villages identify development goals. This handbook offers interactive exercises and guides for group dialogue that are especially helpful for gathering qualitative data from community consultations, workshops, and focus groups. These exercises can be carried out in boardrooms, strategic planning retreats, or community centers; around the kitchen table; or in the middle of the jungle or desert. These group exercises use a variety of conflict lenses outlined in the following chapters. Computer-based mapping software, graphics features in word processing programs, and PowerPoint drawing tools can re-create all of the diagrams in this handbook. In more rural areas, groups can use portable sticky walls and markers on sheets of paper,[12] chalkboards, or even using a stick to draw in the dusty ground.

Other data collection strategies rely on using the Internet, mobile phones, surveys and polls, or desk research on publications. These do not require participatory methodologies. However, this form of research can triangulate and support—or call into question—the degree of consensus on information that emerges from interviews, focus groups, and these participatory methodologies.

Local research teams made up of amateur insiders who want to help collect data can play important roles in collecting data from diverse groups. Some NGOs, for example, support youth research teams. They offer young people basic training in interviewing and give them cameras or video cameras to go into the streets to interview their peers and strangers.

Figure 2.2 illustrates these various data collection methods, which are then described more fully.

Interviews ask key research questions of a wide range of diverse local stakeholders from different identity groups, including religious, ethnic, class, education, region, sex, language, age, and other identity groups.

Community consultations and workshops ask diverse groups to participate in both generating and sorting data into categories for the conflict assessment, monitoring, and evaluation frameworks. These community workshops can take various cultural models. For example, in Central Asia, community shuras and jirgas are a familiar way of organizing discussions at the local level. Some groups use these traditional forums as their community consultations or focus groups.[13] In the United States, a methodology called Listening Projects uses trained facilitators to ask open-ended questions that help people in communities express their fears, hopes, needs, and solutions.[14] As citizens begin to understand their own and others' points of view, they may open to new ideas and possibilities and find common ground with opponents.

Figure 2.2 Data Collection Methods

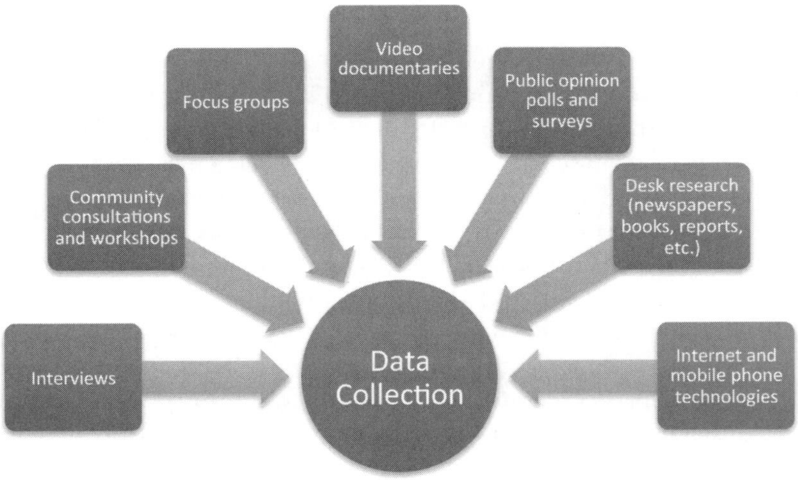

Focus groups can include people from the same region or cultural group (women, youth) to help generate, sort, and prioritize data into categories. Data from focus groups can help shape questions for larger surveys and polls. After collecting survey and polling data, focus groups can help interpret this data as well.

Focus groups differ in the level of diversity they allow members. Some people feel safe to share different points of view in a focus group. Other groups develop a culture in which people show evidence of pressures to conform and silence dissent within the group. In places with active violence, people may be silent and too traumatized to talk. In some regions where identity conflicts play an important role, having an identity caucus focus group may be helpful, including only members of an identity group who would not speak freely when mixed with other identity groups. For example, a women's caucus may help women share more freely their insights into conflict. In another region, a minority identity group may share completely different information in a minority caucus focus group. Insiders could help organize and facilitate conflict assessment caucuses to provide safe spaces for specific minorities or identity groups to discuss together and develop an assessment that reflects their own unique perspectives. If comfortable, they can then share a public report of their analysis while maintaining some degree of individual anonymity that can protect them from reprisals from other identity groups. Insider teams can help to pull together the information developing out of caucus assessments to feed into donor decision making.

Rapidly changing events impact how focus groups respond. On the day before a marketplace bombing, a group of elders may feel hopeful and positive about the future. On the day after a bombing, another similar group of elders may share different perspectives.

Video documentaries capture focus groups, exercises, and key findings in their conflict assessment process. They can create a mirror or self-portrait of a conflict-affected region, helping researchers, local people, and donors listen to diverse points of view. The NGO Interpeace uses video documentaries to help researchers remember and analyze more deeply what people have said. Videos can be shown later to the same focus group to reflect on changes over time, or to invite them to build on their analytical discussion. Or the video can be taken to new focus groups to invite them to respond or to feel empowered and comfortable about taking part in a difficult conversation.

Researchers can show a video to large audiences to invite them to reflect on the conflict-affected context. A facilitator can ask large groups of people to reflect on whether the video is an accurate mirror or portrait of their context, or whether something is missing in the analysis. Videos then serve as a way of checking on the accuracy and reliability of the data.

Researchers can also show a video to elite groups to help them understand broader public opinions. A video can foster understanding of how diverse groups understand conflict; videos can illustrate how people in other regions, identity groups, or social classes think about the local context—capturing, for example, perspectives of women and youth that these discussions often omit or neglect.

Video documentaries help give a voice to local people, allowing people to hear directly from those impacted by conflict, rather than from the researchers themselves. This approach might make people more trusting that the assessment is not biased or did not manipulate the data of what people said in interviews or focus groups. Videos can serve as a form of evidence of how people think and act before and after a peacebuilding effort to provide insight on and proof of the transformation.[15]

Public opinion polls and surveys ask a limited number of exact questions to large numbers of people to develop quantitative data. Pilot testing carefully formulated questions with focus groups can help ensure that bias is not inherent in the question itself.

Desk research can find conflict assessments carried out by other organizations in a conflict-affected region. Because there is no center for coordinating conflict assessments, many different groups carry out assessments without ever knowing about other researcher's efforts. International and local universities, NGOs, and think tanks publish conflict assessment reports or research that contains data that support conflict assessments. Desk research can also find newspaper and media reports related to conflict that contain useful data. Online desk research, covered in the next section, also can reveal useful data through search engine queries and Internet sites that collect conflict assessment research conducted on different topics and in different regions.

Internet and mobile phone technologies allow individuals to write SMS text messages, tweets, and blogs that provide eyewitness accounts and analysis of conflicts. New technologies allow data sources to come from satellites, computer-generated information collection, or crowdsourcing when people use their mobile phones or the Internet to share their perspectives on conflict. Mobile phone technologies allow researchers to conduct surveys more easily and cheaply with populations that may otherwise be difficult to reach. Mobile phones allow individuals to share their photos and videos that illustrate their account of conflict dynamics. These technologies also allow people to make visual geographic maps of where crowds are gathering, where attacks have happened or where violence is happening, and where humanitarian crises are unfolding. For example, FrontlineSMS collects and shares reports on incidents of conflict collected from people who text message information. Kenyans used a crowdsourcing technology called Ushahidi during the 2008 electoral violence to gather data from citizens who texted from their mobile phones to a central location information on where violence was occurring. Ushahidi now works in many other places using geospatial mapping to inform early warning and conflict assessment. This type of data can help to indicate if violence is spreading.

Notes

1. Adapted from Howard Zehr, "Us and Them: A Photographer Looks at Police Pictures: The Photograph as Evidence," *Contemporary Justice Review* 1 (1998): 377–85.

2. This section benefited from the work of Brian Efird and the DataCards webportal on Socio-Cultural Data Evaluation Criteria following a one-day seminar, Socio-Cultural Data Evaluation Summit, held at the US National Defense University, January 18, 2012.

3. Lawrence Woocher, "Conflict Assessment and Intelligence Analysis Commonality, Convergence, and Complementarity," US Institute of Peace, Washington, DC, June 2011.

4. Irving L. Janis, *Groupthink: Psychological Studies of Policy Decisions and Fiascoes* (Boston: Houghton Mifflin, 1983).

5. University of Foreign Military and Cultural Studies, "Red Team Handbook," vol. 5, no. 15, U.S. Army, April 2011.

6. Organisation for Economic Co-operation and Development, "Guidance on Evaluating Conflict Prevention and Peacebuilding Activities," Working Draft for Application Period, 2008, 37.

7. Ibid., 65.

8. Some of these principles are adapted from the Conflict Sensitivity Consortium, "How to Guide to Conflict Sensitivity," February 2012, and Cheyanne Church and Mark Rogers, *Designing for Results: Integrating Monitoring and Evaluation in Conflict Transformation Programs* (Washington, DC: Search for Common Ground, 2006).

9. See, for example, the National Institutes of Health, "The Belmont Report: Ethical Principles and Guidelines," National Commission for the Protection of Human Subjects of Biomedical and Behavioral Research, 1979, for the protection of human subjects of research, http://ethics.iit.edu.

10. OEDC, "Guidance on Evaluating Conflict Prevention."

11. Dart Center for Journalism and Trauma, "Self-Study Unit 2: Covering Terrorism," http://www.dartcenter.org.

12. See Technology of Participation Sticky Walls, http://www.mntop.us/sticky wall.html.

13. Duncan Hiscock and Teresa Dumasy, "From Conflict Analysis to Peacebuilding Impact: Lessons Learned from People's Peacemaking Perspectives," Conciliation Resources and SaferWorld, London, March 2012, 17.

14. See Rural Southern Voice for Peace, Burnsville, NC, http://www.listening project.info.

15. This entire section draws on Koenraad Van Brabant, "The Uses of Video in a Participatory-Action-Research Process for Peacebuilding," Interpeace, Geneva, 2005.

3

Self-Assessment

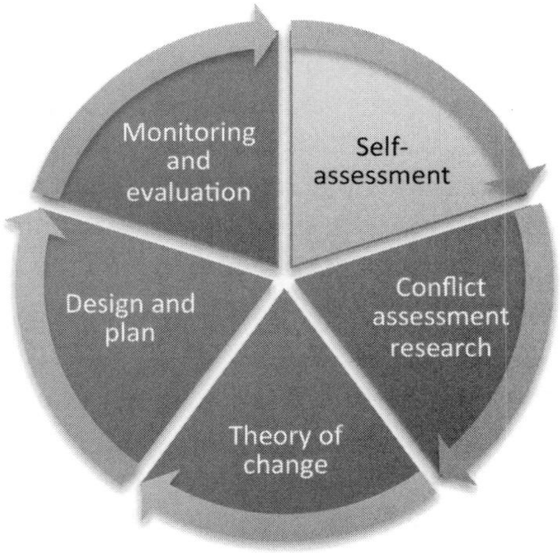

Graphic 3.1

Reflective peacebuilding researchers and practitioners recognize that the gap between intent and impact is often large. Even when people set out to do good, they inadvertently harm others. All too often, groups carrying out conflict assessment processes examine the problems and capacities of others in the conflict without looking inward at their own issues and resources. The easiest way to shift a system is to focus on those parts of the system closest to us. Each of us has the most control over our own behavior in a system. Rather than focusing on how to change the other parts of a system, reflective peacebuilding should identify the ways we can change a conflict-affected system by altering our own behavior in the system. A reflective peacebuilding approach spends less time examining the question of

"What can we do to change them" and more time asking the question of "What can we do differently that might influence our own role in the conflict?" Sometimes, groups conducting a self-assessment and a conflict assessment come to the conclusion that their involvement in peacebuilding has a greater risk of escalating conflict or having no impact. This conclusion can lead to a reasonable and strategic decision to not continue to plan a peacebuilding effort.

Self-assessment is an ongoing process. It should start at the very beginning, before any research on the conflict itself. Researchers need to reflect first on their motives and resources. They need to understand how people within the conflict perceive those conducting the research. Researchers need to reflect on each of their decisions about the research process to ensure that they are conflict-sensitive, recognizing potential harms that could come through the research process.

A second round of self-assessment takes place after conflict assessment. This step helps to narrow the scope of planning from possible strategic peacebuilding options resulting from the assessment to filtering and prioritizing the pragmatic list of what is possible and strategic for a particular organization or group to do, given its identity and capacities. Some of the self-assessment questions in this chapter make reference to frameworks and concepts introduced in later chapters describing conflict assessment lenses. Readers should come back to this chapter to revisit self-assessment questions before they begin peacebuilding planning.

Methods

Self-assessment research can use questionnaires, staff discussions, limited focus groups, and interviews with people in a conflict-affected context, and a desk review of any relevant written reports or evaluations.

Where, Who, Why, What, How, and When Questions

First and foremost, a group conducting a conflict assessment should assess its overall purpose. Groups should shape the conflict assessment to meet their purposes. This handbook includes many different lenses, and not all lenses fit the needs of different groups. Likewise, the responses to the following questions and prompts relate to the overall purpose.

Where

1. Where will the assessment take place? In what geographic area? Do you have access and transportation? Is safety an issue?

2. How well do you understand the local context, language, cultures, religions, and so on? Do you know and recognize the limits of your knowledge of the local cultures, languages, and systems? Do you know what you don't know? What range of insiders or local people could you consult with who could critically review and raise questions on your peacebuilding plan? *Identify the limits of your understanding of the local context. List types of information about the local context to which you do not have access and describe how you will continue to gather information about the context throughout the conflict assessment effort.*

3. Where—which region, community, or city—will be the focus of your peacebuilding efforts? Why choose this place over other places? Where will you rent an office or hold conferences or events? Where will you buy your supplies? How will others perceive the location of these choices? *Identify the rationale, costs, and benefits of the locations of your peacebuilding effort, the location of any office or site used in your efforts, and the sources of your supplies.*

Who

1. Who will you interview? What individuals and groups? Do you already have relationships with them?

2. Who will conduct the interviews? What are the researcher's identities and life experiences, and how do these shape what the researcher will be likely to perceive or miss in doing research?

3. How do other stakeholders perceive your group's identity? How might this limit your ability to conduct conflict assessment? Will you have local staff or foreigners to conduct conflict assessment research? How will others perceive your staff's identities? How will your group make decisions about who to hire and what qualifications are necessary? Do potential interviewees see researchers as impartial or as stakeholders in the conflict with self-interests that may conflict with local people's interests? What are the identities of your organization's staff? How do key stakeholders view your organization? Do other groups perceive your behaviors as driving the conflict? You may need to carry out research to determine how stakeholders view your group. *Fill out an identity group diagram (see Chapter 6) for your organization along with a description of how the key stakeholders may view your organization based on their perceptions and experiences. You may need to carry out research to determine how stakeholders will view your group.*

4. Where are you or your organization on the stakeholder map and peacebuilding pyramid (see Chapter 6)? Which stakeholders are your adversaries or allies? Where do you have social capital? *Circle or highlight where your organization fits in the stakeholder map and peacebuilding pyramid.*

5. To which key actors or relationships do you have access? Who will you choose to work with in your peacebuilding effort? Who will be left out of your effort? *Choose who you will work with based on your conflict assessment. Circle or highlight these stakeholders in both the stakeholder map and peacebuilding pyramid diagrams for the potential placement and focus of your peacebuilding. Be ready to give the rationale for who is included and excluded from the program.*

6. Who else might inadvertently benefit from your peacebuilding and thus have an interest in shaping your conflict assessment research? Who may feel threatened by your peacebuilding? *List people or groups that may benefit from your efforts (such as hotel staff, drivers, food providers, etc.) and those who may feel threatened by your peacebuilding.*

Why

1. What are your motives? What values drive your work? How explicit have you made these motivations to other stakeholders?

2. What do stakeholders perceive about your motivations? Have public figures or media outlets commented on your motivations? *Describe how you will explain your motivations and address others' criticisms or suspicions of your motives.*

What

1. What are your narratives or assumptions about what is driving and mitigating the conflict? Where and how did you develop these beliefs? What experiences shape your point of view?

2. What are your ultimate goals? What type of change are you seeking: individual, relational, cultural, or structural? What beliefs, attitudes, or behaviors do you intend to change? *Describe how the types of peacebuilding goals and activities you plan will relate to the conflict assessment. Explain how your conflict assessment and peacebuilding effort connects with stakeholders' needs and interests.*

3. What are the worst-case scenarios for unintended impacts of your conflict assessment process and your peacebuilding efforts? *List worst-case scenarios, potential unintended impacts, and negative consequences that could happen as a result of your conflict assessment research and your peacebuilding effort.*

How

1. What are the resources, means, or sources of power available for your conflict assessment and peacebuilding efforts? How will these shape or limit your efforts? *List your organization's human, financial, and other*

resources. Identify specifically how your group is different from other groups and what makes it uniquely positioned to conduct conflict assessment research and peacebuilding.

2. What partnerships does your organization already have with organizations working in this region? How could your organization consult with governmental and nongovernmental groups to better foster coordination of conflict assessment and peacebuilding planning?

When

1. How long do you have to complete a conflict assessment? What time pressures do you face?

2. What is your organization's capacity for crisis response or to adapt your plans quickly in response to windows of vulnerability or opportunity? *Identify how your organization will adapt to changes or crises that may emerge before or during the conflict assessment.*

3. When is the best timing for your peacebuilding given the assessment of the timeline and possible triggers or windows of opportunity or vulnerability as described in Chapter 10? *Identify possible specific times for your peacebuilding efforts that take advantage of windows of opportunity or that address windows of vulnerability.*

4. Does the peacebuilding effort aim to foster change in the immediate future (6 to 12 months) or in 5 to 10 years, or does it take a long-term approach, aiming at 20- to 50-year impacts? How long will the project last? Is your funding limited, or will ongoing peacebuilding efforts continue in this region? When will the project end? *Identify the rationale for the length of time for the peacebuilding effort and the likely length of time that may be necessary for the effort to make an impact or bring about change. List indicators that will be used to monitor the progress of the peacebuilding effort and signal the end of the project.*

SWOT Analysis

Businesses often conduct a "SWOT" analysis before designing a new product or project. In the same way, peacebuilding actors should conduct this analysis before planning and designing peacebuilding.[1]

Strengths

Given the conflict assessment, what are the strengths that your organization brings to peacebuilding in the conflict-affected context?

Weaknesses
Given the conflict assessment, what are the weaknesses your organization brings to peacebuilding in the conflict-affected context?

Opportunities
Given the conflict assessment, what are the opportunities that might develop to your ability to contribute to peacebuilding in the conflict-affected context?

Threats
Given the conflict assessment, what are the threats that might develop to your ability to contribute to peacebuilding in the conflict-affected context?

Peacebuilding Partnerships

Peacebuilding requires partnerships between groups from inside and outside of the conflict-affected context and those working at different levels (from government down to community) as well as those working in different sectors. Partnerships are opportunities for developing better conflict assessment processes and creating macro-level changes. But partnerships also require energy and pose challenges.[2]

Capacity mapping. Some common principles and steps apply when identifying potential partners.[3]

- Map existing conflict assessment research and peacebuilding efforts related to the conflict-affected region and identify existing partnerships or coordination mechanisms.
- Identify potential partners by considering those groups that share basic values, would complement your own groups' capacities or your identity as an insider or outsider and the level and sector of your work.
- Identify the organizational culture and protocols of potential partners for assessment and planning to assess if and how to align or harmonize these processes.

Set up communication and grievance resolution forums. Partnerships require regular communication to check in on each group's perceptions of the peacebuilding effort at each stage. Partnerships should also include a regular review of how the relationship is functioning and include grievance resolution processes.

Conduct joint assessment, planning, monitoring, and evaluation. Partnerships work best when built on a principle of mutual learning and planning. All research on the local context should bring all partners together in thinking through decisions on what research questions and indicators to use and how to carry out the research for conflict assessment, monitoring, and evaluation.

Understand perceptions of partnership. If nongovernmental groups partner with governments, militaries, or donors with obvious ties to political interests, the partnership can change the way local people view the NGO. It may be denied access to local communities that oppose the government, or it may suffer from security attacks by insurgents opposing the government. Likewise, governments that partner with certain civil society organizations may also receive criticisms for bias or favoritism of one group over others. An assessment should map how local people view different donors or interveners in their community so that potential partners can assess the risks and opportunities of such a partnership.[4]

Make partnerships known. Use the logos and names of all partners together on public statements and reports.

Include a joint statement defining the partnership. Partnerships work best when they have explicit principles. For example, Save the Children and its local partners in Sri Lanka wrote that they were "partners by choice working together interdependently towards a common goal with a clear understanding of roles, responsibilities and mutually agreed norms, and commitment to accountable and sustainable development practice."[5]

Maintain principles of transparency and security. Be transparent and discuss difficult issues of financial remuneration and security protocols with local and international staff.

Visit the website accompanying this book at www.conflict-assessment-and-peace building-planning.org to learn more or share your own ideas on self-assessment.

Notes

1. The technique is credited to Albert Humphrey, who led a convention of business leaders at Stanford University in the 1960s and 1970s.

2. Koenraad Van Brabant, "Peacebuilding How? 'Insiders'-'Outsiders' and Peacebuilding Partnerships," Interpeace, Geneva, 2010.

3. International Alert, *Codes of Conduct for Conflict Transformation Work*, International Alert, London, 1998.

4. Conflict Sensitivity Consortium, "How to Guide to Conflict Sensitivity," Conflict Sensitivity Consortium, London, February 2012, 20.

5. Ibid.

4

Conflict Assessment

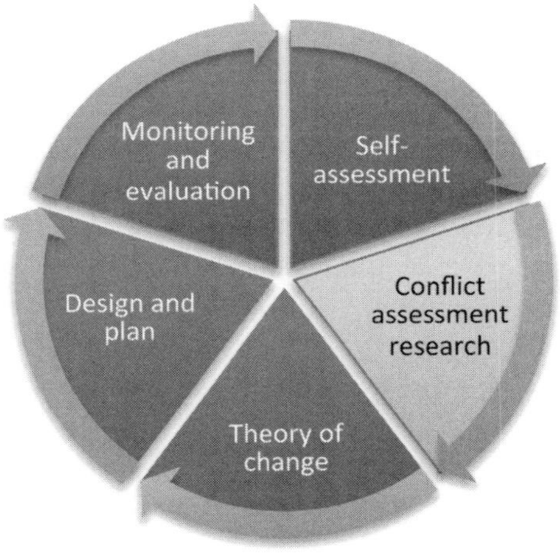

Graphic 4.1

Conflict Assessment Framework

There are a variety of ways to structure conflict assessment frameworks. Some frameworks emphasize political economy.[1] Others include elements relevant specifically to trying to do development in conflict-affected regions.[2] Others emphasize state fragility and stability,[3] or social capital.[4] Effective conflict assessment frameworks include several tools or lenses that offer insight into different elements or dimensions of conflict. But most other conflict assessment frameworks either include long lists of questions to capture the complexity of conflict or they create simplistic frameworks that leave out important elements. Complex frameworks make it difficult for people to easily learn and remember the key questions in a conflict assessment. In addition, most existing conflict assessment frameworks use categories that do not relate directly to planning, making it more difficult for planners to see the link between conflict assessment and peacebuilding design. Only a few of the existing conflict assessment frameworks attempt to link conflict assessment and peacebuilding planning explicitly.[5]

The framework in this handbook uses the familiar categorization schema of Where, Who, Why, What, How, and When. This framework is a basic journalistic inquiry approach, familiar to many people, and it provides an easy-to-remember set of questions for all elements of assessment and planning. This handbook links every aspect of conflict assessment to the planning process. The summary chart of conflict assessment and peacebuilding planning in Table 4.1 (also Table 1.1) summarizes the key Where, Who, Why, What, How, and When of self-assessment, conflict assessment, theories of change, and peacebuilding planning.

Lenses for Conflict Assessment

Each of the following conflict assessment chapters offers lenses, conceptual frameworks, exercises, and dialogue questions to bring insight into these six categories of conflict: Where, Who, Why, What, How, and When. Each lens helps to answer one of the questions in each category of this framework.

Where

What is the **context** of this conflict? What is working well? What **connects** and **divides** people? What **institutions** drive or mitigate conflict? What are **micro and macro** manifestations of conflict?

Who

Who are the **key stakeholders** driving and mitigating the conflict? Which **identity groups** are most important in this community or society? Who are the people or groups that could play **peacebuilding roles**?

Why

What are the **motivations** and **grievances** that drive conflict? How do people articulate their public positions and what are the underlying **interests** and **needs** that drive a group's desire for change?

What

What are the driving and mitigating factors related to conflict? How are these factors interrelating with each other? What types of peacebuilding efforts and incentives could address conflict drivers or support mitigating factors?

Table 4.1 Summary Chart of Conflict Assessment and Peacebuilding Planning

	Self-Assessment	Conflict Assessment Lenses	Theory of Change	Peacebuilding Planning
WHERE	How well do you understand the local context, languages, cultures, religions, etc.? Where will you work?	Where is the conflict taking place—in what cultural, social, economic, justice, and political context or system?	If x parts of the context are at the root of conflict and division or provide a foundation of resilience and connection between people, what will influence these factors?	**How will the context interact with your efforts?** Given your self-assessment, identify your capacity to impact the elements of the context that drive and mitigate conflict.
WHO	Where are you in the stakeholder map? Where do you have social capital? To which key actors do you relate?	Who are the stakeholders—the people who have a stake or interest in the conflict?	If x individual or group is driving or mitigating conflict, then what action will incentivize them to change?	**Who will you work with?** Given your self-assessment, decide whom to work with to improve relationships between key stakeholders or support key actors who could play a peacebuilding role between key stakeholders.
WHY	How do stakeholders perceive your motivations?	Why are the stakeholders acting the way they do? What are their motivations?	If x group is motivated to drive or mitigate conflict, what will change or support their motivations?	**Why will you work?** Given your self-assessment of your motivations and how stakeholders perceive your motivations, identify how these align with the motivations of the key actors.

(continues)

Table 4.1 Cont.

	Self-Assessment	Conflict Assessment Lenses	Theory of Change	Peacebuilding Planning
WHAT	What are you capable of doing to address the key drivers and mitigators of conflict?	What factors are driving or mitigating conflict?	If x power sources are driving and mitigating conflict, what actions will influence these factors?	**What will you do?** Given your self-assessment, identify which driving and mitigating factors you will address.
HOW	What are your resources, means, or sources of power? How will these shape your efforts?	How is conflict manifested? What are the stakeholders' means and sources of power?	If x power sources are driving conflict, what will influence these sources of power?	**How will you shift power sources in support of peace?** Given your self-assessment, identify and prioritize your capacities to reduce dividers and to increase local capacities for peace.
WHEN	Do you have an ability to respond quickly to windows of vulnerability or opportunity?	Are historical patterns or cycles of the conflict evident?	If x times are conducive to violence or peace, what will influence these times?	**When is the best timing for your peacebuilding efforts?** Given historical patterns, identify possible windows of opportunity or vulnerability and potential triggers and trends of future scenarios.

How

How do the key stakeholders exert **power**? What forms of social capital exist? How do stakeholders use power? What are their **means** to drive or mitigate conflict? What are the local resources for peace?

When

What is the **timeline** of events from each side's perspective? What are the trends and **triggers** that push conflict into violence? What are potential future scenarios? Are there windows or certain holidays, seasons, or events that make people more likely to be violent against others or to enable peace?

Each section of this framework begins with basic concepts and exercises and then proceeds to more advanced lenses. Each lens can draw on a range of data sources. Researchers may use the exercises with focus groups or community consultations, or may use the conceptual frameworks and questions to consider information from polling, surveys, interviews, blogs, or collected SMS texts. The exercises are a way of collecting new data, but also processing existing data and sorting it into the conflict assessment categories. Each lens ends with an "Output" summary that synthesizes the data into information useful for peacebuilding planning.

Groups conducting a conflict assessment can pick and choose which lenses are most appropriate for their purposes. An organization assessing a relatively small, internal conflict might just choose to use the basic lenses that begin each section. Government donors looking to design countrywide peacebuilding policies and programs might choose to focus mostly on the advanced lenses.

Each lens contains the following:

- The purpose of the lens, and what it helps to see
- How the lens can contribute to peacebuilding
- Concepts explaining the lens
- Methodology or the suggested ways of collecting data for the lens
- Exercises and questions for discussions or interviews
- Summary Output statements prioritizing the data

Each lens also provides a conceptual framework for organizing information in a way that directly enables peacebuilding planning. (Figure 4.1 depicts this process.) Each lens suggests data collection methods that can be sorted into the different conceptual frameworks. Drawing on the research principles in Chapter 2, researchers should check the validity, accuracy, reliability, and triangulation of the data. Unlike other research, the goal of some

Figure 4.1

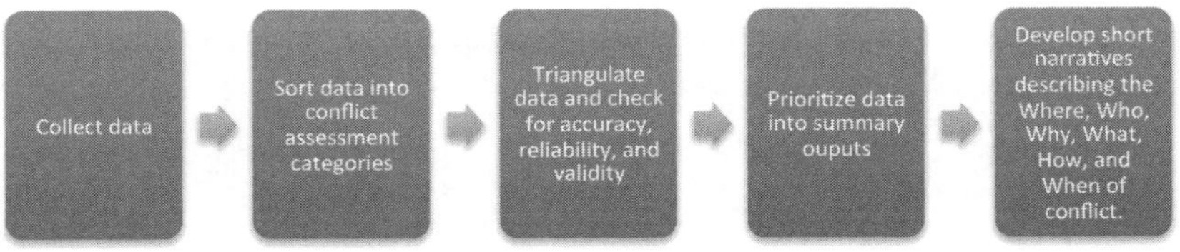

Example of Final Narrative Summary of a Conflict Assessment Process

Where

This region has an abundance of resources and a long cultural tradition of civil society struggling peacefully against extractive corporations. The history of colonialism followed by abusive political leadership and continued foreign exploitation of resources contributes to a traumatized population, ethnic divisions, and dysfunctional political, economic, judicial, and security institutions. The immediate electoral crisis takes place within a broader struggle for ethnic self-determination. [**Note to Researchers: Add Output Summary of each Where lens here.**]

Who

Military and nonstate armed groups are the major forces driving conflict. Foreign corporations and governments are backing the repressive government. A variety of religious leaders are working together to establish a peacebuilding network and are mitigating conflict. Media professionals are opening up channels of communication between supporters of armed groups on all sides by inviting them to call into radio dialogue programs. [**Note to Researchers: Add Output Summary of each Who lens here.**]

Why

Ethnic divisions exist in the region. But these divisions are only meaningful in districts where political leaders and armed groups feed on ethnic tensions to increase their own support. Corporate interests in the regions and economic interests focused on controlling natural resources seem to be the primary motivating factors. [**Note to Researchers: Add Output Summary of each Why lens here.**]

What

A struggle for control over resources and territory and foreign support for the government are key conflict drivers. Open fighting is taking place in most of the country. Conflict mitigators include broad public weariness from war, a desire for a political solution, and strong religious beliefs. There are five major peacebuilding initiatives in the region, but none of these work in partnership or coordinate with the others. [**Note to Researchers: Add Output Summary of each WHAT lens here.**]

(continues)

> **Example of Final Narrative Summary of a Conflict Assessment Process (cont.)**
>
> ***How***
> The importation of arms by three opposition groups and the government is creating a climate in which military power is more important than political power. In some districts, religious leaders seem to be able to draw on their authority, networks, and moral power to influence other stakeholders. Women's groups in some districts are working across the lines of ethnic divide. [**Note to Researchers: Add Output Summary of each How lens here.**]
>
> ***When***
> Elections, natural disasters, and media stories breaking news on corruption scandals have been significant triggers historically related to escalation of violence. In the near future, before the next election, there appear to be a variety of openings for preventive action. But forecasters note impending crises related to climate change–induced changes in flooding and drought patterns—and ongoing land-grab scandals. [**Note to Researchers: Add Output Summary of each When lens here.**]
>
> *Visit the website accompanying this book at www.conflict-assessment-and-peacebuilding-planning.org to learn more or share your own ideas on conflict assessment.*

conflict assessment lenses is to find the areas of disagreement. Researchers should make note of where different groups provide different information or perspectives, such as when different key drivers of conflict are identified. These insights could help planners identify issues for discussion in peacebuilding efforts such as multistakeholder negotiation or dialogue.

Ultimately, each lens asks researchers to prioritize information so that it becomes useful for peacebuilding planning. Each lens asks researchers to develop an Output Summary that will provide a direct link to a peacebuilding planning recommendation. At the end of a conflict assessment process, an ideal output could be a one- to two-page document that summarizes the key factors in the Where, Who, Why, What, How, and When into short statements or narratives that contain the condensed information from the entire process.

These statements could accompany a longer report that goes into more detail and provides more examples and citations of how the data backs up this summary. The summary document and the longer document are then both useful for designing and planning peacebuilding.

The quality of these summary statements depends on the quality of the process, how many people participated, whether they were from diverse backgrounds from a variety of different stakeholders, and whether the data they use is accurate, valid, reliable, and triangulated.

Visit the website accompanying this book at www.conflict-assessment-and-peacebuilding-planning.org to learn more or share your own ideas on conflict assessment.

Notes

1. See, for example, "Political Economy Assessments at Sector and Project Levels: How-To Note," World Bank, Washington, DC, May 2011, http://politicaleconomy.org.

2. See, for example, Conflict Management and Mitigation Office, "Conflict Assessment Framework (CAF) 2.0," United States Agency for International Development, Washington, DC, June 2012; *InterAgency Conflict Assessment Framework (ICAF)*, US Department of State, Washington, DC, 2008; Jonathan Goodhand, Tony Vaux, and Robert Walker, *Conducting Conflict Assessments: Guidance Notes* (London: Department for International Development, 2002); SIDA, *Manual for Conflict Analysis*, Division for Peace and Security through Development Cooperation, Methods Document (Stockholm: Swedish International Development Cooperation Agency, 2006).

3. See, for example, Suzanne Verstegen, Luc van de Goor, and Jeroen de Zeeuw, "The Stability Assessment Framework: Designing Integrated Responses for Security, Governance and Development," Clingendael Occasional Paper, prepared for the Netherlands Ministry of Foreign Affairs, the Hague, 2005; Michael Dziedzic, Barbara Sotirin, and John Agoglia, eds., *Measuring Progress in Conflict Environments (MPICE): A Metrics Framework* (Washington, DC: US Institute of Peace, 2010); Pauline Baker, *Conflict Assessment System Tool (CAST)* (Washington, DC: The Fund for Peace, 2006); Monty G. Marshall and Benjamin R. Cole, *Global Report 2011: Conflict, Governance, and State Fragility* (Vienna, VA: Center for Systemic Peace, 2011).

4. Anirudh Krishna and Elizabeth Shrader, *Social Capital Assessment Tool* (Washington, DC: World Bank, 1999).

5. See Simon Fisher, Dekha Ibrahim Abdi, Jawed Ludin, Richard Smith, Steve Williams, and Sue Williams, *Working with Conflict: Skills and Strategies for Action* (London: Zed Books, 2005); Manuela Leonhardt, *Conflict Analysis for Project Planning and Implementation* (Bonn: GTZ, 2002); Irma Specht, "Conflict Analysis: Practical Tool to Analyse Conflict in Order to Prioritise and Strategise Conflict Transformation Programmes," ICCO, Kirk in Action, and Transitional International, Utrecht, the Netherlands, 2008.

5

WHERE

Understanding the Conflict Context

This chapter examines the system or broader context in which conflict is taking place. A basic approach will answer the questions in Table 4.1. An intermediate approach will answer the summary questions outlined here from each of the five lenses in this chapter. A more advanced approach will use the suggested methodologies in each lens exercise to answer a longer set of related questions.

Basic conflict assessment questions	Where is the conflict taking place—in what cultural, social, economic, justice, and political context?
Lenses for conflict assessment	**1. Nested model of micro and macro context:** How does the immediate crisis relate to the broader regional or international context? What is the relationship between micro and macro views on the conflict? **2. Cycle of violence map:** What forms of direct and structural violence are occurring? **3. Appreciative inquiry:** What is already working to reduce violence and foster resiliency? What specific institutions and relationships are resilient, and able to be flexible and adapt in times of crisis? **4. Connectors and dividers:** What are the most significant connectors and dividers between people in the local context? **5. Institutional capacity mapping and human security baseline:** What are the dividers, early warning indicators, and connectors or local capacities for peace in this context?

Basic Self-Assessment	How well do you understand the local context, language, cultures, religions, and so on? Where will you work?
Theory of Change	If x parts of the context are at the root of conflict and division or provide a foundation of resilience and connection between people, what will influence these factors?
Peacebuilding Planning	How will your peacebuilding effort interact with the conflict context and system? How will the context interact with your efforts? Given your self-assessment, identify your capacity to impact the elements of the context that are at the root of conflict and divisions between people and your ability to foster institutional and cultural resiliencies that support connections between people.

Where 1: Nested Model of Micro and Macro Context

What Does This Lens Help Us See?

People undertake a conflict assessment because of some presenting issue—in other words, some problem or conflict that has become so painful that someone decides something needs to be done to bring about change. Often these are smaller, *micro* problems that relate to larger, *macro* problems. This *nested model*[1] lens begins a conversation about how that presenting issue at the micro level relates to or is nested within a larger, macro system.

How Does This Lens Contribute to Planning Peacebuilding?

This lens illustrates how a strategic, coordinated peacebuilding effort can address systemic, macro-level issues as well as the immediate, presenting micro issue. There may be ways of addressing each level of the nested model through unique peacebuilding efforts. A program, for example, aimed at the immediate issue may look quite different from a program aimed at addressing the regional or systemic level of the conflict. Peacebuilding planners can use this model to map out different efforts at different levels of the system.

Key Concepts

In Figure 5.1, the innermost oval is the immediate issue; the next oval is the relationship, followed by the subsystem, and finally the entire conflict system on the outside.

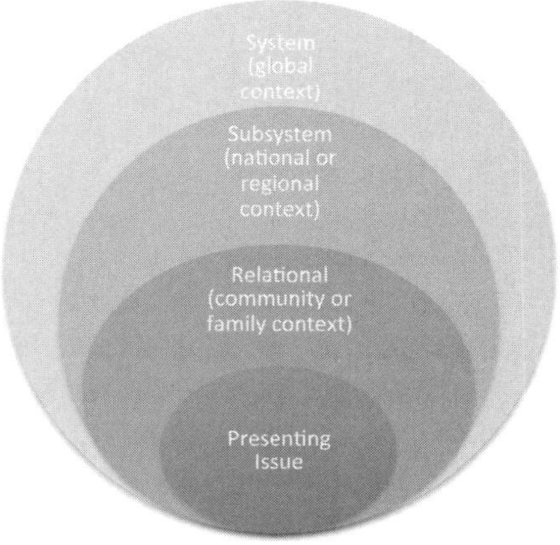

Figure 5.1 Nested Model

For example, imagine that the presenting issue is two youths of different backgrounds who have a playground fight. Perhaps these two youths have a history of problems with each other, and their respective ethnic groups also have a pattern of tensions with each other. At the subsystem level is the school and educational system that also has a history and patterns of challenging conflict between these ethnic groups. The system level includes the national and international social forces and history of racial discrimination that impact the conflict between these two ethnic groups.

For groups that have a limited mission devoted to presenting issues such as humanitarian crises, a macro conflict assessment identifies trends that impact their work. Some of these groups, recognizing the impact of macro forces, will sign onto advocacy campaigns to address global forces such as the arms trade led by other organizations. For example, many development NGOs have taken an advocacy position on the Kimberly Process, aiming to address the global economic forces in the diamond markets that have driven civil wars in West Africa. World Vision's macro conflict assessment tool helps equip NGO staff to analyze and articulate the macro trends and triggers of ongoing and sometimes chronic political and economic instability.[2]

How Does This Lens Work?

Methodology

Interviews or focus groups and desk research.

Exercise

1. Opening discussion: What is the presenting issue that prompted someone to call for a conflict assessment? How is the conflict seen as a

limited issue? How is the presenting issue or conflict seen as part of a relationship? How is it seen as part of the subsystem or regional level? How is it a conflict of the entire system? How is that presenting issue nested within a larger set of relationships and systems?

2. Draw a diagram like the one in Figure 5.1 about a presenting issue or conflict which you are familiar. Identify a description of the conflict at each level. What types of peacebuilding efforts are needed to address each level?

Output Summary

Given your self-assessment, are you best situated to work at micro or macro levels of this conflict? How might you design your peacebuilding efforts so that they address all levels or coordinate with peacebuilding efforts working at other levels of the system?

Where 2: Cycle of Violence Map

What Does This Lens Help Us See?

This lens identifies different types of violence, illustrating the relationship between structural violence and forms of secondary violence, such as intergroup, interpersonal, and self-destructive violence.

How Does This Lens Contribute to Planning Peacebuilding?

Peacebuilding requires addressing each part of the cycle of violence. Peacebuilding includes keeping people safe in the midst of a crisis, and addressing the structural root causes driving conflict while also reducing harms from self-destruction and interpersonal forms of violence stemming from this cycle.

Key Concepts

Direct violence refers to physical harm committed by one person or group against another. **Structural violence** refers to the disabilities, disparities, and even deaths that result from systems, institutions, or policies that foster economic, social, political, educational, and other disparities between groups.[3]

Secondary violence refers to the intergroup violence, interpersonal violence, and self-destructive violence that stem from structural violence. The cycle of violence diagram[4] (see Figure 5.2)[5] illustrates how structures that perpetuate social, political, and economic exclusion and discrimination that

Figure 5.2 Cycle of Violence Diagram

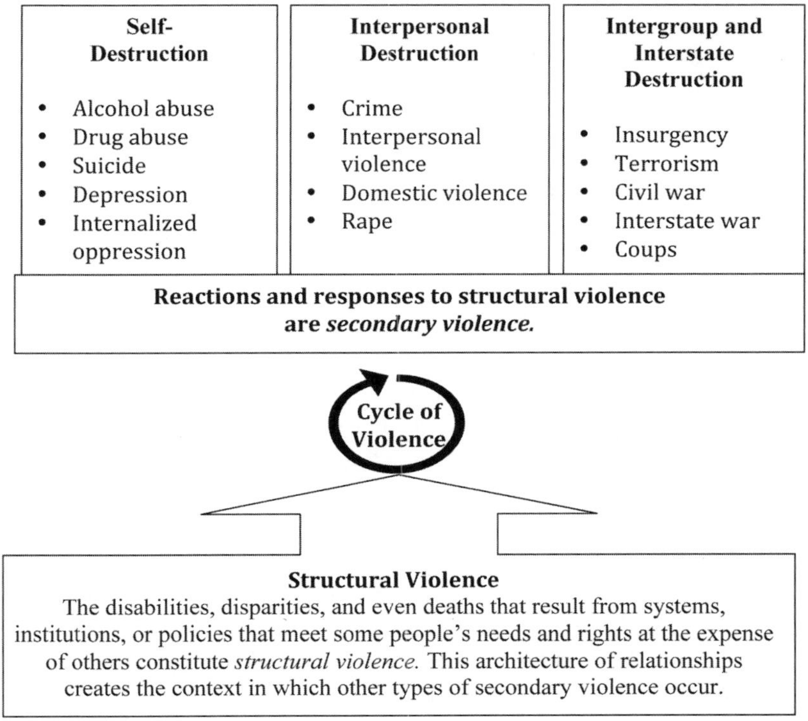

benefit small, elite groups at the expense of other people can lead to "secondary violence," including self-destructive, interpersonal, and intergroup violence.

Self-Destruction
• Alcohol abuse
• Drug abuse
• Suicide
• Depression
• Internalized oppression
Interpersonal Destruction
• Crime
• Interpersonal violence
• Domestic violence
• Rape
Intergroup and Interstate Destruction
• Insurgency
• Terrorism
• Civil war
• Interstate war
• Coups
Reactions and responses to structural violence are secondary violence.
Cycle of Violence
Structural Violence
The disabilities, disparities, and even deaths that result from systems, institutions, or policies that meet some people's needs and rights at the expense of others constitute structural violence. This architecture of relationships creates the context in which other types of secondary violence occur.

Intergroup and intrastate violence. At the state and international levels, violent insurgent movements seek to change, overthrow, or replace the existing state structure. Increasingly, repressive governments and insurgents target civilians to induce terror and fear, or to control their allegiance and loyalty. Mass atrocities are attacks on large numbers of civilians. *Systematic violence* refers to ongoing direct violence against certain groups over a prolonged period of time.[6] Social movements advocating for human rights and democracy can be violent or nonviolent. A goal of peacebuilding is to find nonviolent expressions of advocacy to respond to structural violence. For example, African Americans used nonviolence primarily in the civil rights movement to respond to the structural violence of segregation and institutionalized racism.

Interpersonal and community violence. At the interpersonal and community levels, some people respond to the sense of injustice brought about by structural violence and seek to regain a sense of power by releasing their anger on people in their families and communities. Family violence, sexual abuse and rape, gang violence, youth violence, and all forms of interpersonal crime are examples of secondary forms of violence.

Conflict assessments often overlook statistics on violence against women, particularly if this violence is primarily interpersonal, in the privacy of the home. If large numbers of any other identity group were experiencing violence, conflict assessments would no doubt identify the social pattern. But the privacy of the violence, and cultural acceptance of violence against women, means that too often violence against women does not gain the attention of peacebuilding efforts.

Self-destruction. Depression, alcoholism, drug abuse, and suicide are all ways that some people cope with structural violence. Self-destruction is an effort to regain power and control. Rather than suffer destruction at the hands of others, people self-destruct as a form of self-determination.

The cycle of violence diagram illustrates how ineffective, corrupt, and dictatorial state structures that benefit small, elite groups at the expense of the majority of citizens can lead to secondary violence or the types of violence that grow out of citizen frustration and grievances.

Different forms of violence are interrelated. For example, apartheid in South Africa was a form of structural violence that excluded black South Africans from political power. But after political apartheid, economic structures continued to separate the black and white communities. While the armed insurgency ended along with the end of political apartheid, self-destructive and community-level violence increased. Overall, the end of the war did not lead to fewer deaths.

How Does This Lens Work?

Methodology

Interviews, focus groups, or community consultations or workshops using group discussion. Researchers may also use secondary sources in desk research and polling data.

Exercise

1. Identify and list types of violence in Figure 5.2.
    a. What forms of structural violence exist that discriminate against certain individuals or groups?

b. What forms of direct violence exist? Do armed groups target civilians? Do security forces aim to protect civilians? Do vulnerable populations such as women, children, minorities, and refugees experience direct violence in private or public? Is there systematic violence between groups or against certain groups of people? Are there mass atrocities or large numbers of civilians suffering direct violence?

c. What forms of interpersonal violence exist? How are these related to structural violence?

d. What forms of self-destructive violence exist? How are these related to structural violence?

2. Discuss the relationships between different forms of violence. Are secondary forms of violence related to structural violence? Are there symptoms of structural violence such as self-destructive patterns, community or interpersonal destruction, or intra- or interstate destruction?

3. What types of peacebuilding efforts could address each type of violence in the system? What could interrupt the cycle of violence?

Output Summary

Given your self-assessment, what forms of violence are you most able to address? How might you build in an awareness of other forms of violence into your peacebuilding effort?

Where 3: Appreciative Inquiry

What Does This Lens Help Us See?

An appreciative inquiry process identifies the capacities of local individuals and institutions to respond to conflict and crisis and bring resilience to a social system experiencing conflict.[7] Rather than looking at what is wrong or missing from a local context, examining what is working can inspire, provide energy, and offer hope for strengthening peacebuilding. What is working well in the context? This lens identifies the capacities of local individuals and institutions to respond to conflict and crisis and bring resilience to a social system experiencing conflict.

How Does This Lens Contribute to Planning Peacebuilding?

A formal appreciative inquiry process can be an entire assessment and peacebuilding planning approach. The focus is on improving and strengthening what is already working well in the local context. A peacebuilding effort that helps or supports a system's existing components may more naturally help to moderate conflict and violence within the system rather than importing a new peacebuilding effort. Beginning a conflict assessment with storytelling about what is working provides a foundation for building on these existing narratives and examples. It fosters an appreciation that there are local solutions to local problems.

Key Concepts

Appreciative inquiry and assets-based assessment is a research process widely used among business leaders, sports teams, education systems, and other groups to focus on and learn from what they do well.[8] In appreciating their assets, successes, and talents, groups can expand these good elements. This is a counterintuitive approach to a focus on problem identification and problem solving. Albert Einstein noted, "We can't solve problems by using the same kind of thinking we used when we created them." Rather than focusing on problems, positive approaches to peacebuilding seek to discover the successes and strengths that can be built on and supported through peacebuilding interventions. Any new peacebuilding effort will best harness and expand the local resiliencies and capacities for peace.[9]

Local capacities for peace include individuals and institutions that work to sustain some sort of harmony or intergroup peace in social systems. The Do No Harm project of CDA Collaborative Learning Projects documented the existence of local capacities for peace in their research. They identify local capacities for peace such as justice and policing systems that protect all people fairly (many do not), elders and women's groups, schoolteachers, business professionals, or religious leaders and other respected and trusted figures. CDA found in its research that these local capacities for peace were often not sufficient to prevent violence. However, they did function to help depolarize and rebuild tense relationships.

Resilience refers to the capacity of a system to survive, adapt, absorb, or respond to a crisis or severe change. Resilience requires an ability to learn quickly and improvise new survival methods in a changed environment.[10]

Ecosystem resilience, for example, is measured by a system's ability to survive through droughts, floods, and other shocks and to rebuild itself after the crisis. Human or social resilience is the capacity to anticipate and prepare for crises and the ability to survive and respond to a crisis, and then adapt to a destroyed environment.

Individuals, families, and communities are resilient when they prepare for crises and have plans for coping and adapting to a postcrisis environment. Institutions are resilient when they prepare themselves to continue playing their social functions in the midst of and after a crisis. Social systems are most resilient when they combine strong, interdependent elements that help communities provide care for each other with some weaker or more flexible elements that help individual people and institutions continue functioning even if others are no longer functioning.

How Does This Lens Work?

Methodology

Interviews, focus groups, or community consultations or workshops using group discussion. Researchers may also use secondary sources in desk research and polling data. An appreciative inquiry process or quest creates a forum for people to discuss their future. Local people interview each other or talk in small groups in workshops, seminars, or community consultations about what is working well in their local context.

Exercise

Participants may ask each other the following questions:

1. What are three examples of who or what works well in your local context?
2. What are the strengths, passions, unique initiatives, or projects that are positive examples?
3. What resilience or capacity do individuals, communities, and institutions have in each of these areas?

- Ability to manage differences and tensions between groups through local cultural mechanisms.
- Ability to improvise solutions to complex problems such as providing health care, food, and shelter, and organizing search-and-rescue teams and efforts to promote law and order.
- Ability to restore institutions such as schools and hospitals and infrastructure such as electricity, roadways, and gas stations.
- Ability to organize community members to work together in the midst of the chaos or crisis.
- Ability to find, communicate with, and organize support from external groups.

Output Summary

What key assets in the local culture stand out as holding potential for supporting or expanding in a peacebuilding effort?

Where 4: Connectors and Dividers

What Does This Lens Help Us See?

This lens examines a wide range of factors in the broader context that can contribute to divisions between groups (dividers) or help to foster better relationships between groups in order to bridge their differences (connectors).

How Does This Lens Contribute to Planning Peacebuilding?

The lens helps organizations maximize the impact they are having by harnessing the power of local capacities for peace. This lens helps organizations identify creative ways that they can support connections between groups. It also allows organizations to redesign and correct their programs to avoid negative or harmful unintended impacts.

Key Concepts

Created by CDA Collaborative Learning Projects,[11] this lens identifies two sets of forces: "dividers" and "connectors." **Dividers** are tensions or fault lines that refer to those forces that divide people or interrupt their human needs. Dividers include sources of conflict, or the issues in conflict. **Connectors** refer to everything that links people across conflict lines, particularly those forces that meet human needs. Each of the following connectors can supply natural linkages.

Systems and institutions. In all societies in which violence erupts, systems and institutions—like markets and communications systems—can cause further division between people or can continue to link people across conflict lines. For example, local markets or the continued need to trade goods may bring together merchants from opposing factions in a conflict. Media sources (foreign or local news broadcasts on the radio or television) also provide linkages between people regardless of their affiliation. Irrigation systems, bridges, roads, and electrical grids are additional examples of institutional and systemic connectors and dividers.

Attitudes and actions. As people on all sides of violence experience harms, they may develop hateful attitudes and actions that cause further divisions. Even in the midst of war and violence, it is possible to find individuals and groups that continue to express attitudes of tolerance, acceptance, or even love or appreciation for people on the "other side." Some individuals act in ways that are contrary to what we expect to find during war—adopting abandoned children from the opposing side in the conflict, continuing a professional association or journal, or setting up new associations of people opposed to the war.

Shared values and interests. People use violece against each other to pursue their religious values or interests. But a common religion can bring people together, as can common values such as the need to protect a child's health. UNICEF, for example, has negotiated days of tranquility based on the shared value of inoculating children against disease.

Common experiences. The experience and effects of war on individuals can increase divisions or provide linkages across conflict lines. Citing the experience of war and suffering as "common to all sides," people sometimes create new peacebuilding alliances across conflict lines. Sometimes the experience of war unites individuals who are traumatized by violence, regardless of their different affiliations.

Symbols and occasions. Art, music, historical anniversaries, national holidays, monuments, and sporting events (e.g., the Olympics) can divide people by prompting memories of past traumatic events, bring people together or link them across conflict lines, or some combination of the two.

How Does This Lens Work?

Methodology

Interviews, focus groups, or community consultations or workshops. Researchers may also use secondary sources in desk research.

Exercise

Make a list of connectors and dividers. If some of the same forces are on both lists, try to qualify them. For example, if "water" is listed as both a connector and a divider, ask the group why and wait for the answers. It could be that wells are connectors, as communities share these public spaces. But lack of water for farmers may be a divider as community members involved in agriculture don't have enough water to irrigate their crops.

Output Summary

Identify two to four of the most significant connectors and dividers from the discussion and research. Are you best situated to increase connectors or decrease dividers in your peacebuilding effort? How might you do both? How will you ensure that your peacebuilding effort does not inadvertently increase dividers?

Where 5: Institutional Capacity and Human Security Baseline

What Does This Lens Help Us See?

This lens identifies how well existing formal and informal governance structures are performing to meet human needs and protect human security. The lens identifies both the strength and resilience of governance structures as well as gaps. Assessing the resilience of governance institutions means listening to how local people think institutions support human security.

How Does This Lens Contribute to Planning Peacebuilding?

This lens gives a sense of how well existing formal and informal governance structures are meeting human needs and protecting human security. It can guide planners on how to strengthen and support functioning governance structures and help fill gaps.

Key Concepts

Violence is not distributed equally across all individuals, families, communities, and nations. Some people suffer much more from violence and conflict than others. Violence correlates with the level at which people perceive that structures or institutions are fair and just.[12] The five categories of governance institutions related to peacebuilding and human security include

- *Politically stable democracy:* Need for predictable and participatory decision making
- *Sustainable economy:* Need for basic resources and freedom from want
- *Safe and secure environment:* Need for security and freedom from fear
- *Justice and rule of law:* Need for predictable social relations and justice
- *Cultural and social well-being:* Need for respect and dignity with others and need for meaning, identity, and belonging

Governance for peace. The concept of governance refers to traditions and institutions that exercise political authority and resources to manage society's problems and affairs. State structures help to manage environmental, economic, political, and social systems. But prior to the Westphalian state system, humans had a long history of organized societies and communities governed via religious groups and tribal, patronage, business, and other institutions. In most societies today, informal, nonstate governance structures complement or exist outside of formal state governance. Government, businesses, and civil society organizations such as tribal groups, professional associations, NGOs, and academic and media organizations all perform governance functions by helping to manage resources to address social problems and meet human needs.

In places like Afghanistan, Pakistan, Somalia, and elsewhere, traditional governance institutions continue to play major roles in the absence of a central state that extends to the subdistrict level. Calling these places "ungoverned spaces" is misleading. More accurately, areas like Somalia experience nonstate or informal governance in a variety of shapes and forms, such as tribal and religious leadership. These nonstate forms of governance can function very well in some contexts to provide for local human security. Even countries with strong central governments have robust forms of nonstate governance. In some sectors, such as the environment, civil society, businesses, and the state all play important roles in governance to manage and build sustainable environmental systems. Watershed management boards are an example of public-private partnerships enabling better governance.

A hybrid approach to governance includes a citizen-oriented state or other governing institutions and an active civil society. Ideally, a responsive state practices inclusive politics, whereby all citizens have regular opportunities beyond elections to participate in democratic decisions that impact their lives. Inclusive politics allows individuals and groups peaceful and legitimate channels to express their interest in, support of, or opposition to a public issue.[13]

A citizen-oriented state is responsive to citizen needs and orients its governance toward the public good, which includes an active private sector. An elite-captured government orients its governance toward the elite private sector or a specific identity group at the expense of the public good.

An active local civil society is an indicator of a functioning and democratic state. Civil society both works in partnership with the state to complement and supplement its capacity and to hold the state to account for its responsibilities and transparent governance.[14]

Assessing the legitimacy of governance is then a combination of a variety of factors, including the degree to which people participate in decisions that affect their lives and the degree to which governance institutions serve all people with equal opportunity.

Judging the degree of functional and legitimate governance includes looking at three areas, illustrated in Figure 5.3. These include the institutional capacity or bureaucratic structure and revenue; the institutional performance in different sectors, such as providing for transportation,

Figure 5.3 Components of Legitimate Governance

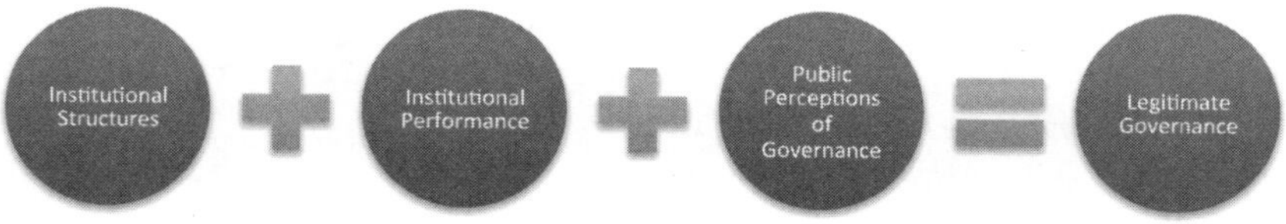

education, health care, economic stability, security, and other human needs; and the public perception of how well their economic, social, political, and other needs are met through these governance structures. For each sector researchers can examine how the public would answer these critical questions: Governance for what purpose? For whom? By what process? Resourced how?[15]

Institutional resilience and performance. A human security baseline measures the level of institutional performance perceived by different groups. Which institutions mitigate or manage conflict? Are there religious leaders working together across the lines of conflict, or are there multiethnic organizations, artists, political leaders, or independent media that play a role in managing conflict?

People can measure and perceive inequality and injustice in different ways, such as these categories identified by Catholic Relief Services.[16]

Procedural fairness refers to whether people perceive public institutions operating in an impartial and transparent way. For example, people look at media coverage and ask whether it treats all groups fairly and provides information relevant to each of their interests.

Decision-making access refers to whether people perceive that their interests and perspectives are reflected in public policies.

Resource allocation refers to whether people perceive the just sharing or distribution of public resources, funds, and services.

Quality standards refers to whether people perceive that everyone receives the same quality of public goods and services.

In a context in which people perceive power inequities between identity groups, peacebuilding involves improving governance to make it more fair and responsive to all groups. Citizens can start this process by identifying shared values and collective interests to improve their lives and then working together to advocate for change. This can include implementing reforms to foster equal treatment of identity groups, setting minimum levels for participation and access to public institutions, using redistributive or preferential treatment to redress historic grievances, and ensuring that institutions have mechanisms for setting standards of quality assurance for the public.

Human security baseline index on governance and institutional performance. This framework of five categories of peacebuilding and human security, adapted from a number of similar sources, identifies different sectors of governance and institutional performance.[17]

Politically stable democracy. Do people perceive they have political security to protect and promote human rights and processes to foster peaceful discussion and negotiation? What institutions address these needs? How legitimate, transparent, and effective is the government? Political parties? Elections? The legislature?

Sustainable economy. Do people perceive that they have basic economic security to earn and access a basic income? What institutions address these needs? How well do government and nongovernmental service institutions meet citizen needs for water, education, health care, electricity, roads, markets, and so on? How well does the economic system work in terms of rewarding entrepreneurship, managing sustainable use of resources, reducing the gap between rich and poor, and fostering economic stability for all people?

Safe and secure environment. Do people perceive that they have community security, freedom of movement, and freedom from fear? How well do security forces protect all civilians, regardless of their identity? Do institutions protect ethnic, religious, and cultural groups—particularly women, children, and minorities—from violence? What institutions address these needs?

Justice and rule of law. Do people perceive that they have predictable social relations and a justice system that is coherent and legitimate, and that uses just legal frameworks to monitor and protect human rights? What institutions address these needs? How fair and consistent are the police, courts, and corrections institutions to all people, particularly women, children, and minorities?

Social and cultural well-being. Do people perceive that they have a sense of meaning and social order in their lives along with respect, dignity, identity, and a sense of belonging with others? Do people have freedom to practice their religious beliefs and cultural traditions? How independent, fair, and professional are the news media that are providing information to people about their context? What is the quantity and quality of civil society organizations and their ability to monitor human rights, hold government accountable to its functions, and mediate public disputes? What institutions address these needs? Do people have access to programs to aid in psychosocial recovery and trauma healing?

Indicators of institutional performance dividers, early warnings, and connectors. Researchers identify patterns that accompany the escalation or de-escalation of conflict. The indicators in Table 5.1 identify preexisting tensions or dividers, early warning signs, and connectors and local capacities for peace that relate to institutional performance and grievances in the five categories of peacebuilding and human security. A variety of indexes and other assessment frameworks capture information or metadata related to a human security baseline,[18] including those in this box, as well as many others. These can measure the amount of services, such as the number of schools or health clinics, the number of paved roads and bridges, or the amount of financial activity and banking institutions and credit available in a country. People's perceptions of how institutions are performing are also important, though more difficult to measure.

Key Indexes and Research Related to Human Security

Conflict Early Warning and Response Mechanism (CEWARN)
Country Policy and Institutional Assessment (CPIA; World Bank)
Crisis Watch (International Crisis Group)
Failed States Index (Fund for Peace)
Global Peace Index
Human Development Index (HDI)
Human Security Index
Peace and Conflict Instability Ledger (University of Maryland)
Peace Research Institute Oslo (PRIO)
Uppsala Conflict Data Program
World Bank's Institutional and Governance Reviews

Table 5.1 illustrates three columns that identify potential dividers within the context, early warning indicators that these dividers may trigger violence, and connectors or indicators that there are openings for peacebuilding in each of the five categories of peacebuilding and human security.

How Does This Lens Work?

Methodology

Interviews, focus groups, community consultations or workshops, and public opinion polling. Researchers may also use secondary sources in desk research. There are many sources of data already available that are relevant to this lens for many countries.

Exercise

Discuss the following:

1. Identify the dividers, early warning indicators, and connectors in each of the five categories in Table 5.1.

Table 5.1 Connectors, Dividers, and Early Warning Indicators

Politically Stable Democracy		
Dividers	**Early Warning Indicators**	**Connectors or Peace Indicators**
Politicizing along ethnic, economic, religious lines	Adopting violence to advance the political cause of identity groups, such as increased hate crimes	Increasing willingness of dominant political opposition groups to talk peace and do justice in situations of hate crimes
One group dominates government and military	Increasing dominance or absolute control of one group in the military and state structures	Establishing political institutions with increased representation and power sharing
Some groups are systematically excluded from government institutions	Increasing systematic exclusion of groups from government institutions	Encouraging an inclusive government
Restricting the constitutional rights of some groups	Increasing restrictions and denial of constitutional rights of some groups	Granting political power and reserving seats for disadvantaged groups; releasing political prisoners and returning of exiles
Little sense of participatory democracy, winner-take-all political system	Rigged elections, no elections, or violence during elections	Free and fair elections accompanied by robust public-private dialogue in all sectors and with active participation at all levels
Lack of accountability of political leaders and institutions with citizens	Increasing lack of accountability of political leaders and institutions with citizens	Encouraging accountability and serious attempts to build trust in government, involving stakeholder groups in consultations, and considering the views of communities in decision making
Weakening democratic system of elections, parliament, district/local levels	Failing democratic systems	Moving to consociational democracy with power sharing or federalism where regions have a great deal of power
Widespread corruption accepted	Escalating corruption	Addressing issues of corruption
Limited freedom of the press to travel or publish without restrictions	Media increasingly restricted in their ability to travel or publish	Limited freedom of the press to travel or publish without restrictions

(continues)

Table 5.1 Cont.

Dividers	Early Warning Indicators	Connectors or Peace Indicators
	Sustainable Economy	
Unequal economic growth among different territorially situated groups	Increasing geographic divisions of economic growth	Economic growth more equitable across the region
Unequal access to social services and/or relief and development programs	Increasing disparity of access to social services and/or relief and development programs	Conscious efforts to ensure equal access to social services and/or relief and development programs
Scarcity of natural resources, exploitation of resources, deforestation, and population increases	Worsening scarcity of natural resources, increasing exploitation of resources, and rapid population increases	Introducing policies to prevent deforestation and exploitation of resources
Unequal access to natural resources and/or politicization of resource scarcity	Increasing inequality of access to natural resources and/or politicization of resource scarcity	Introducing policies for equitable access to natural resources
Low economic growth rates, inflation, large debt	Slowing economic growth rates, growing inflation, growing debt	Rising economic growth rates, lowering inflation, managing debt
Rich/poor divide is widely accepted	Growing disparity among rich/poor, particularly along identity lines	Lowering rich/poor disparity, particularly along identity lines
Dependence on primary commodities or natural resources such as diamonds, timber, oil, and water	Increasing dependence on primary commodities or natural resources such as diamonds, timber, oil, and water	Decreasing dependence on primary commodities or natural resources such as diamonds, timber, oil, and water, and encouraging production of alternate commodities
Development programs favor one group	Development programs favor one group	Development programs systematically ensure that programs do not alienate any groups
Population movements (forced or due to no opportunities to participate in economic life)	Rising or potential population movements through threats to civilians, expulsion or forced internal displacement disrupt economic activity and limit access to markets	Fostering resettlement and reintegration, and ensuring the resumption of productive activity and increasing incentives for all groups

(continues)

Table 5.1 Cont.

Dividers	Early Warning Indicators	Connectors or Peace Indicators
Increase in child malnutrition	Increase in child malnutrition	Introduction of health-care programs to reduce child malnutrition
Increase in female-headed households	Increase in female-headed households because of men leaving for war, dying; gender exploitation	Increasing number of programs to assist victims of war, especially female-headed households
Safe and Secure Environment		
Large numbers of potential recruits for armed groups due to lack of other options	Active recruiting for armed movements, especially of youth	Increased employment possibilities, particularly for youth
Availability of arms and resources for armed movements	Mobilization of arms and resources for armed movements	Decrease in availability of arms and resources for armed movements
Large and powerful military with little relationship to or control from civilian leadership	Military increasingly controlling political decision making	Increasing accountability of military to civilian leadership, and division of powers between state and military enforced
Large military budgets	Increase in armed forces, military budget, and/or availability of arms	Reducing military budget, arms control agreements, and restrictions to prevent the availability of arms
Justice and Rule of Law		
Inequitable laws that discriminate between groups (or the perception of such discrimination)	Increasing number of or implementation of laws that discriminate between groups (or the perception that they are increasing)	Strengthening the judicial system and efforts to remove or correct the perception of biases
Abuse of human rights, particularly along identity lines with arrests, rapes, disappearances, army/police brutality	Escalating human rights violence with political murders, arrests, brutality, etc., and increasing abuse of civil rights and liberties	Establishing human rights committees and implementing and protecting civil rights

(continues)

Table 5.1 Cont.

Dividers	Early Warning Indicators	Connectors or Peace Indicators
Sporadic acts of violence, such as armed robberies	Increasing cases of violence and armed robberies, and increasing inability to protect civilians	Decreasing levels of violent crime and increased determination to protect civilians
Volatile region, with violence happening close by	Increasing level of violence in the region; military interventions, increased flow of arms, influx of refugees from neighboring countries, demonstration effect of identity groups in neighboring regions fighting for self-determination	Resolution of violent conflicts in the region, return of refugees, maintaining positive relationships
	Social and Cultural Well-Being	
Media controlled by separate identity groups and reinforces negative attitudes toward other groups	Growing politicization and division of the media, which increasingly acts as a propaganda tool to reinforce negative stereotypes of other groups	Encouraging neutral and fair media; media used to support coexistence and tolerance between groups
Preexisting social divisions, such as limited intermixing in schools, businesses, and marriage, and a sense of "us vs. them"	Increasing divisions between groups; growing segregation in schools, businesses, social groups, marriages, and cultural events	Increased respect and cohesion between groups; increased intermixing in schools, business, social groups, and marriages
Divisions between groups are overlapping along lines of ethnicity, religion, economic advantage, or territory	Increasing political consciousness among groups and sanctioning of cross-group associations	Growing incentives to cooperate and increasing number of cross-group associations, such as women's groups across ethnic lines

(continues)

Table 5.1 Cont.

Dividers	Early Warning Indicators	Connectors or Peace Indicators
Negative stereotypes and inflammatory rhetoric between groups	Worsening negative stereotypes and dehumanizing images and language to describe the "other"	Diminishing negative stereotypes and rehumanizing efforts to make the enemy fully human
Different versions of history taught to children	Increasingly different versions of history taught to children	Correcting historical untruths or myths and creating shared histories to teach children
Tradition of solving problems with violence; using violence seen as a cultural tradition	Leaders highlight, glorify, and praise the cultural traditions of violence and use of arms	Leaders highlight a history of positive relationships between groups and portray the current situation as the exception, and discourage the use of arms or violence to solve problems
Historic trauma continues to play an important symbolic role in narratives of conflict and identity	Active recalling of historic traumas by media and key public figures	Media and public figures use narratives emphasizing shared traumas and collective desire to end war
Support for identity groups from diaspora or kindred identity groups outside the country with the goal of increasing their group's power in the country	Growing material, military, and political support from identity groups	Diaspora and kindred identity groups from outside the context support peace in the region

2. What are examples of institutions that are working well in each of these categories? Where are institutions resilient and capable of addressing human needs?

3. Where are the gaps in human security? What institutions are not performing? Which institutions are mobilizing grievances and driving the conflict?

4. Where are the needs for governance efforts to support peacebuilding?

Output Summary

Given your self-assessment, which of the key problems or resiliencies most relate to your existing capacities? Identify the top two to four dividers, early warning signs, and connectors/resiliencies that you may be able to address.

Notes

1. Maire Dugan, "A Nested Theory of Conflict," *Women in Leadership* 1, no. 1 (Summer 1996): 9–20.

2. World Vision, "Making Sense of Turbulent Contexts," World Vision International, Washington, DC, 2006.

3. Johan Galtung, "Violence, Peace, and Peace Research," *Journal of Peace Research* 6, no. 3 (1969): 167–91.

4. Lisa Schirch, *Strategic Peacebuilding* (Intercourse, PA: Good Books, 2004).

5. Ibid.

6. Max Kelly with Allison Giffen, "Military Planning to Protect Civilians," Henry L. Stimson Center, Washington, DC, 2011, 49.

7. David L. Cooperrider, Diana Whitney, and Jacqueline M. Stavros, *Appreciative Inquiry Handbook* (Bedford Heights, OH: Lakeshore Publishers, 2003).

8. Claudia Liebler and Cynthia Sampson, "Appreciative Inquiry in Peacebuilding: Imagining the Possible," in *Positive Approaches to Peacebuilding* (Washington, DC: Pact Publications, 2003), 55–79.

9. Ibid.

10. Andrew Zolli and Ann Marie Healy, *Resilience: Why Things Bounce Back* (New York: Free Press, 2012).

11. Adapted from Mary B. Anderson, *Do No Harm: How Aid Supports Peace—or War* (Boulder, CO: Lynne Rienner Publishers, 1999). See also CDA Collaborative Learning Projects at www.cdainc.com/.

12. James Gilligan, *Preventing Violence* (New York: Thames and Hudson, 2001).

13. Robert Muggah, Timothy D. Sisk, Eugenia Piza-Lopez, Jago Salmon, Patrick Keuleers, *Governance for Peace: Securing the Social Contract* (New York: United Nations Development Program, 2012).

14. OECD, "Supporting Statebuilding in Situations of Conflict and Fragility: Policy Guidance," DAC Guidelines and Reference Series, OECD Publishing, January 2011.

15. Hamish Nixon, "The Dual Face of Subnational Governance in Afghanistan in DCAF Afghanistan Working Group, Afghanistan's Security Sector Governance Challenges," DCAF Regional Programmes Series 10, Geneva Centre for the Democratic Control of Armed Forces, 2011.

16. Mark Rogers, Aaron Chassy, and Tom Bamat, "Integrating Peacebuilding into Humanitarian and Development Programming: Practical Guidance on Designing Effective, Holistic Peacebuilding Projects," Catholic Relief Services, Baltimore, MD, 2010, 15.

17. The chart is adapted from Daniel Serwer and Patricia Thomson, "A Framework for Success: International Intervention in Societies Emerging from Conflict," in *Leashing the Dogs of War,* ed. Chester Crocker, Fen Osler Hampson, and Pamela Aall (Washington, DC: United States Institute of Peace Press, 2007), 369–87. It also draws on Luc Reychler and Thania Paffenholz, *Peacebuilding: A Field Guide* (Boulder, CO: Lynne Rienner Publishers, 2001); Dan Smith, "Towards a Strategic Framework for Peacebuilding: The Synthesis Report of the Joint Utstein Study on Peacebuilding" (Oslo: PRIO, 2003); Thania Paffenholz, *Civil Society and Peacebuilding* (Boulder, CO: Lynne Rienner Press, 2009); Schirch, *Strategic Peacebuilding;* and Cooperation for Peace and Unity, *Human Security Indicators* (Kabul, 2010).

18. See the following publication for a more complete list: Matthew Levinger, *The Practical Guide to Conflict Analysis: Understanding Causes, Unlocking Solutions* (Washington, DC: US Institute of Peace, 2013).

6

WHO

Identifying Stakeholders and Potential Peacebuilders

This chapter identifies key people or groups that are driving or mitigating conflict. A basic approach will answer the questions in Table 4.1. An intermediate approach will answer the summary questions outlined here from each of the three lenses in this chapter. A more advanced approach will use the suggested methodologies in each lens exercise to answer a longer set of related questions.

Basic conflict assessment questions	Who are the stakeholders—the people who have a stake or interest in the conflict? **1. Stakeholder mapping:** Who are the key stakeholders related to the conflict? **2. Culture and identity group dynamics:** What are the stakeholder's identity and cultural groups? What are the stakeholder's worldviews and perceptions related to the conflict? **3. Peacebuilding actors and mapping capacity:** Who are the key stakeholders supporting peacebuilding?
Basic Self-Assessment Questions	Where are you in the stakeholder map? Where do you have social capital? Which key actors do you relate to?
Theory of Change	If x individual or group is driving or mitigating conflict, then what action will incentivize them to either stop driving the conflict or expand their mitigation?

Basic Peacebuilding Planning Questions

Who will you work with? Given your self-assessment, decide who to work with to improve relationships between key stakeholders or support key actors who could play a peacebuilding role.

Who 1: Stakeholder Mapping Lens

What Does This Lens Help Us See?

A stakeholder map creates a visual image of the main stakeholders and the absence or presence of relationships or social capital between them. Stakeholder maps illustrate alliances and divisions between simplified stakeholders. A stakeholder map can illustrate an entire system of actors, those driving, mitigating, and impacted by conflict. Figure 6.1 provides an example of a stakeholder map of the conflict in Afghanistan from one perspective. But sometimes these maps become too complex. Narrowing down on a subset of the entire system can give new insights. Smaller maps can focus on

- Relationships between key stakeholders mobilizing grievances and driving the conflict

Figure 6.1 Example of a Stakeholder Map on Afghanistan

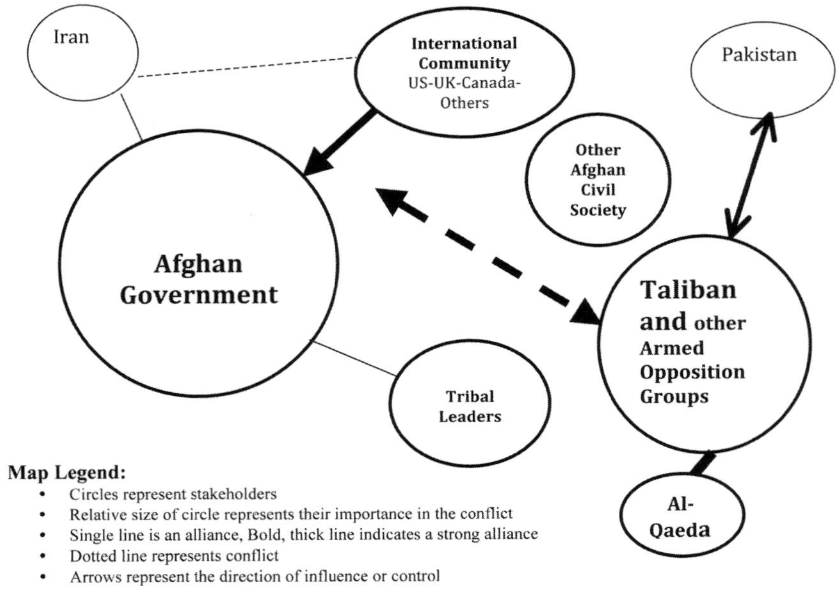

- Relationships between key peacebuilding organizations, groups, or individuals who are mobilizing resiliencies to mitigate conflict and play peacebuilding roles
- Relationships within one group of stakeholders to illustrate intra-group divisions and alliances.

How Does This Lens Contribute to Planning Peacebuilding?

Effective peacebuilding requires knowing those individuals or groups that are driving and mitigating conflict and developing peacebuilding efforts that specifically aim to influence these groups. This lens helps prioritize which relationships to focus on, and what peacebuilding efforts could do to address spoilers and groups driving conflict, such as offering negotiation training to or conducting a mediation between key stakeholders.

Key Concepts

Key people and groups are those that are driving or mitigating conflict. They may mobilize grievances around governance, institutional performance, or social patterns that exclude or discriminate against certain identity groups. Key people may also mobilize others around resiliencies and local capacities for peace.

Spoilers are groups that aim to drive violent conflict and disrupt peacebuilding processes because they perceive themselves to benefit more from ongoing violent conflict.[1] Governments typically restrict spoilers from participating in negotiations or peace processes with the belief that isolating them is the best strategy. They often conclude that "violence is the only language" understandable to their opponents, but engaging with armed groups is not equal to legitimating their cause.[2] Negotiation processes can uncover legitimate grievances buried beneath a group's radical rhetoric. Excluding potential spoilers can increase their commitment to violence by removing viable political alternatives. Managing spoilers means preparing for the reality that certain stakeholders will sabotage peacebuilding efforts and, as much as possible, identifying spoilers' underlying interests and understanding their worldview. Peacebuilding efforts can then help reduce the costs and maximize the benefits of allowing a peace process to move forward.[3]

Many peacebuilding efforts exclude spoilers or stakeholders driving conflict. Peacebuilding efforts often work with groups that are easy to reach and accessible such as youth in schools or victims in internally displaced persons (IDP) camps.[4] While these groups may be able to play a significant role in peacebuilding, other peacebuilding efforts will likely need to focus on those key actors already driving and mitigating conflict. A conflict assessment and theory of change should help shape the decision of which groups to involve in a peacebuilding effort.

For example, in Uganda, peacebuilding efforts included key actors working together to develop a national policy on oil production. The theory of change was stated, "If there is constructive engagement among key stakeholders on political economy issues, then it will improve information flow and lead to a shift in policy and decision making."[5] A stakeholder map can aid in the design of a program like this, which brings together relevant stakeholders from across the lines of conflict.

How Does This Lens Work?

Methodology

This lens can be used alone in an interview setting. However, it is a useful lens for fostering dialogue in a group, as well as gathering information from diverse people with a variety of perspectives on the conflict. People see conflict differently and thus draw stakeholder maps in different ways. If people with different viewpoints map their situation together, they may learn about each other's experiences and perceptions. The process of creating a map is just as important as the outcome. The dialogue and discussion can help a group identify the key stakeholders and relationships that they perceive as most important to address.[6]

Exercise

1. Make a list of all the stakeholders in a conflict. If it is a small conflict, you may want to list individuals. In large conflicts, list groups that share key worldviews, interests, and grievances. In total, have no more than 10 to 12 stakeholders in order to make a map clear enough to understand. Create a separate stakeholder map for each subgroup conflict if needed. For every stakeholder, think about how important they are to the key drivers of the conflict. Which key people or individuals have maximum motivation to drive the conflict? Which key people are also mitigating conflict or playing peacebuilding roles?

2. Create a circle for each stakeholder, with the largest circles for the most influential. Be careful how you place the circles, as you want to plan your space so that all the relevant stakeholders appear. If there is a decision-making hierarchy involved, place those with the most decision-making power at the top of the map and those with the least amount of power at the bottom of the map.

3. Draw lines of relationship between the circles representing stakeholders. If they are close allies, use a thick or double line. If they are in conflict

with each other, use a dotted line or a zigzag line. If one stakeholder is exercising influence or controlling another, use an arrow at the end of the line to illustrate the direction of influence. For stakeholders not directly involved, distance them on the map to illustrate their level of influence. Make sure to include a map legend to interpret whichever types of lines you use.

4. Identify where you, as the analyst and peacebuilding planner, are on the stakeholder map. Almost everyone involved in peacebuilding at the community, national, and global level is, in some way, viewed as related to one or more stakeholders in the conflict. Neutrality is rarely possible outside of interpersonal disputes. How do others view your relationships with key stakeholders? How does this self-assessment affect the other stakeholders with whom you are most able to work?

5. *Optional:* Assign a number from 1 to 10 to the strength of the relationship between stakeholders. This provides a quantitative measure of the social capital between groups, with 10 being the strongest relationship. If you are conducting this lens within a community dialogue, the values can be averaged between groups.

Output Summary

Given your self-assessment and how others view your relationships to key stakeholders, identify the peacebuilding actors whom you think are most significant to driving and mitigating the conflict and whom you can access through your networks.

Who 2: Culture and Identity Group Dynamics

What Does This Lens Help Us See?

This lens lays out a variety of principles of identity as they relate to the dynamics of conflict. Conflicts are "protracted" or "intractable" when people begin perceiving themselves in an identity struggle of "us against them." Understanding cultural and identity group dynamics helps to explain more about the stakeholders and how they see themselves and others in the conflict.

How Does This Lens Contribute to Planning Peacebuilding?

Peacebuilding can help people both understand their identity differences and build on the common ground and shared values across groups. Identity analysis can assist in creating contexts where key stakeholders are able to see the common identities that they share. Key breakthroughs in negotiations sometimes happen between those smoking in the hallway or over dinner as people share photos of their grandchildren.[7] Peacebuilding planners who understand identity group dynamics can help foster programs that uncover common ground between identity groups.

Key Concepts

Everyone belongs to a variety of cultural identify groups relating to their ethnicity, region, religion, education level, age, gender, and other social groups. (See Figure 6.2.) **Cultures** structure how groups of people think and act according to shared beliefs. Cultural groups share a common identity as members of that group. **Identity** is defined in relationship to others. People create a sense of who they are—their identity—through their relationships with others.

Each person's identity is complex. People belong to a variety of identity groups that influence and shape them. Different elements of a person's identity mix together. To describe a person as "white" says very little about that individual's identity.

Identities can be based on *sameness* or *difference.* Identity groups based on sameness use positive comparisons with others: *I know who I am because of my positive relationships with others.* For example, adopted children may belong to an association of other adopted children to find social support. Identity groups based on difference, on the one hand, use negative comparisons with others: *I know who I am by knowing who I am not.* For example, people in some countries display a type of nationalism that conveys feelings of superiority over others. Identities can be *biologically* or *socially constructed.* People distinguish themselves from others through biological differences (such as sex, height, or age) or socially constructed differences (such as religion, ideology, or class).

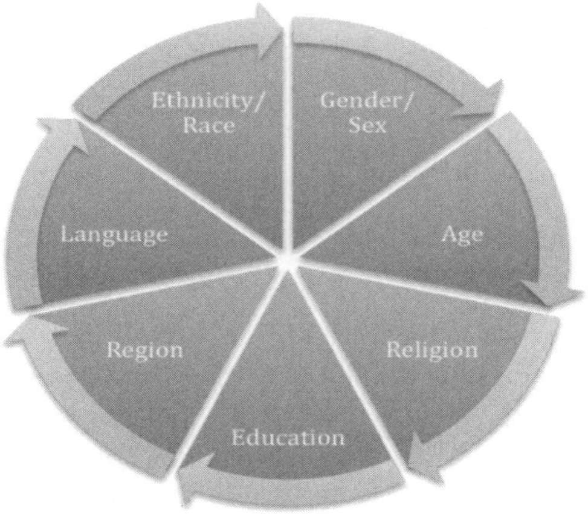

Figure 6.2 Aspects of Identity

Forms of identity based on difference are often a *source of conflict.* The psychology of ethnocentrism leads people to believe that their own identity group is superior to others. People may be willing to both kill and die defending certain group identities. For example, some people were so certain that capitalism was superior to communism that many said they "would rather be dead than red" during the Cold War. In other words, some people were willing to fight and die to preserve one identity group related to the economic ideology of their country.

Forms of identity based on difference may also *result from conflict.* Conflict plays a role in creating in-groups or allies, and out-groups or enemies. Conflict strengthens perceptions of who is good and who is bad, allowing people to create simplified ways of understanding the world. Often people live with each other side by side for decades before a violent conflict. The conflict itself pushes them to see each other as enemies instead of neighbors.

Conflict distorts a person's identity, making one element more important than all others. In nonconflict situations, people seem to define themselves and others broadly according to the multiple cultural groups to which they belong. People may come to see themselves and others through the lens of conflict; for example, those engaged in gender conflicts may perceive being "male" or "female" as their primary or sole identity. In conflicts involving race, people may see themselves as primarily "white" or "black." The psychological process of ascribing an identity to another person or group seems to increase in conflicts. People dehumanize each other by stripping each individual of other sources of their identity and humanity.

Crosscutting relationships between groups on different sides of conflict helps to prevent violence and enable peacebuilding. Identity groups that have crosscutting social, economic, security, or political bonds with other identity groups are more likely to be able to address conflicts through nonviolent channels of communication.[8]

Peacebuilding often requires transforming perceptions of identity. Rehumanizing oneself and the enemy requires transforming the way people identify themselves and others. Identity transformation means increasing the flexibility or relative importance of the ways people identify themselves. As people become aware of common identities and values shared with their enemy, they gain a fuller sense of their own and their enemy's identities. For example, Palestinian and Israeli women share aspects of their lives as mothers, widows, sisters, wives, and victims of a painful conflict even while their ethnic identities are in conflict.

Perceptions of identity change according to physical and relational contexts. A person's sense of identity can shift throughout the day while moving from home to work to place of worship to market. The typical negotiation room encourages people to identify each other as "negotiators" or members of only one identity group related to the conflict. Peacebuilding efforts can intentionally create contexts where adversaries see themselves and others as full human beings with many identities—such as mother, sister, tennis player, teacher, gardener—and not just representatives of one identity group. Rehumanizing people means finding common ground between people.[9] For example, at Camp David, Israeli and Egyptian negotiators shared photos of their grandchildren, enabling them to build greater trust with each other and develop a peace plan.[10]

How Does This Lens Work?

Methodology
Interviews, focus groups, or community consultations or workshops. Researchers may also use secondary sources in desk research such as newspapers and blogs to analyze identity groups.

Exercise

1. Identify identity groups related to the key actors and stakeholders that are driving and mitigating conflict using Figure 6.2.
2. How is identity a driving or mitigating force in the conflict?
3. What overlapping identities do key stakeholders share?
4. How can peacebuilding efforts create a context that emphasizes these shared identities?

Output Summary
Given your self-assessment, what identity groups do you belong to that overlap with the key actors' identity groups? How could your identities shape your peacebuilding effort? Identify how might you construct a context or situation where these shared identity groups would be highlighted.

Who 3: Peacebuilding Actors and Capacity Mapping

What Does This Lens Help Us See?

This assessment lens is helpful in identifying existing and potential peacebuilding actors and peacebuilding roles. This lens uses a pyramid to show or map stakeholders with a capacity for peacebuilding in different sectors of society and at three different levels of leadership—with decision making at the top, middle, and community levels.

How Does This Lens Contribute to Planning Peacebuilding?

The "peacebuilding pyramid"[11] lens (see Figure 6.3), developed by John Paul Lederach, identifies existing and potential peacebuilding leadership and capacity at each level of society. Peacebuilding efforts can offer support and resources for existing peacebuilding actors to expand their leadership potential to play a variety of different peacebuilding roles.

Key Concepts

Mapping existing and potential peacebuilding capacities requires identifying key people in a variety of tracks or sectors and the diverse peacebuilding or third-party roles that they can play.

Key people and opinion shapers for peacebuilding. Key people or opinion shapers have greater influence over larger numbers of people than other people. Key people can mobilize large numbers of people for peace. John Paul Lederach uses two metaphors to describe key people.[12]

Key people are like adding yeast to flour and water in a bread recipe. A small amount of yeast can make the flour and water mixture double or triple in size.

Figure 6.3 Peacebuilding Pyramid

Top-level leaders include political, economic, military, and religious elites with decision-making power to begin high-level negotiations, cease-fires, and so on.
Mid-level leaders include local political leaders, media professionals, religious leaders, academics, and ethnic leaders, and sports, business, labor union, and nongovernmental organizations that foster economic development, promote values supporting peace, and build capacity for responding to conflict.
Community-level leaders include grassroots religious, ethnic, women's, youth, and business groups, and health workers, local unions, community-based organizations, and others who initiate peacebuilding activities from the ground up, including local dialogues, social movements and advocacy, trauma healing, peace education, local economic development, and civilian peacekeeping.

Key people may also be like a siphon by pulling people, like water, into a new way of thinking and acting. Siphons work by using suction to move liquid through a tube. Once a small amount of liquid is pulled, the rest of the liquid follows, moving from one container to another.

Identifying key people for peacebuilding roles requires thinking about who can have the effect of yeast or a siphon on public opinion or groups of people.

Multitrack diplomacy. The concept of multitrack diplomacy,[13] developed by Ambassador John McDonald and Louise Diamond, describes the diverse sectors that play a variety of roles in peacebuilding. Listed here are some of the groups involved in peacebuilding:

- **International institutions** like the United Nations and regional organizations like the Organization for American States can play important roles in creating legal norms, preventive diplomacy, mediation, capacity building, and sanctioning state actors in ways that restrict space for violence and foster peace.
- **Governments** can play essential roles in creating legal frameworks and justice systems, regulating economic activity, and providing an environment in which citizens have fair opportunities to pursue education, obtain jobs, and live healthy and secure lives.
- **NGOs** can play important roles in delivering humanitarian assistance in times of crisis and fostering long-term development and peace.
- **Religious organizations** can offer programs that emphasize values tolerance and coexistence, and religious leaders can play important roles in mediation and de-escalating violence.
- **Businesses and professional associations** can provide needed goods and services to customers in a way that benefits the common good.
- **Universities and schools** can research and teach on the causes of conflict and methods for peacebuilding.
- **Journalists and news producers** provide essential information to the public about the causes of conflict and options for peace.
- **Media professionals, artists, and musicians** can design programs to foster the values of tolerance and coexistence.
- **Citizens and community-based organizations**, including women and youth of all ages and classes, can engage in peacebuilding in their communities.
- **Traditional and tribal organizations**, still thriving in many parts of the world, can play roles in development, mediation, dialogue, and other aspects of peacebuilding.

Peacebuilding roles. Harvard University's Global Negotiation Project runs a project called "The Third Side" that outlines how insiders and outsiders can play a variety of "third-side" roles.[14] A third side is anyone who tries to understand all sides to the conflict from a larger perspective to see the points of views and needs from each side. Someone from a third side encourages a process of cooperative negotiation and supports a wise and fair solution that meets the needs of each side of a conflict. In this definition, someone whose identity belongs to one of the groups in conflict, but who sees the conflict from a larger perspective that includes the needs of opposing groups, can also play a third-side role. Third-side or peacebuilding roles include the following:

- **Researchers** listen to people to learn their perspectives and provide information.
- **Humanitarians** provide emergency assistance to people in the midst of crises.
- **Development and governance planners** help develop functioning political, economic, and social institutions at all levels of society.
- **Educators** provide skills and knowledge to people so that they can better address their own conflicts.
- **Conciliators, envoys,** and **mediators** help people communicate across the lines of conflict by shuttling information and helping groups identify their interests, needs, and alternatives to negotiation.
- **Reality testers** challenge stakeholders to identify their best alternatives to a negotiated agreement and to identify the costs of not reaching an agreement.
- **Catalysts** create new forums, programs, and institutions to foster peacebuilding.
- **Arbitrators** use rules, laws, precedents, or merits of the issues to make decisions to help resolve a conflict.
- **Advocates** can mobilize disempowered stakeholders and help them develop and exercise collective forms of power to increase the chance that mediation or negotiation will become more appealing to all stakeholders.
- **Healers** help people process deep emotional wounds and find appropriate ways of expressing and transcending the wounds.
- **Monitors** and **witnesses** draw attention to human rights violations, grievances, and key issues to mobilize others to act.
- **Rule setters** and **referees** set forth rules for fighting that can limit atrocities and harm, especially to civilians.

- **Peacekeepers** separate people who are fighting and monitor ceasefires to de-escalate the fighting so as to allow for mediators or other third-side roles to try to address the root causes driving the violence.

How Does This Lens Work?

Methodology
Interviews, focus groups, or community consultations or workshops using group discussion. Researchers may also use secondary sources in desk research and polling data.

Exercise

1. Draw a pyramid as in Figure 6.3 to identify leaders and important groups playing peacebuilding roles at each level of society. Circle the names of those leaders who can help draw in both moderates and extremists into peacebuilding processes.
2. Who are the people in different tracks or sectors of society who can initiate a change process? Assess whether there are internal divisions within levels. In societies divided by ethnic and religious lines, the pyramid may have one or more vertical lines dividing it. Many peacebuilding efforts aim primarily to build horizontal social capital across these lines.
3. Who can foster vertical capacity among the grassroots, middle, and top levels of society? Assess whether there is sufficient vertical social capital between peacebuilding actors at the top, middle, and community levels. Are there people at the mid-level who could help build a bridge between the top- and community-level leaders through creating forums and meetings between them? See Chapter 9 for a discussion of social capital.
4. Identify which key actors are already playing third-side roles. Are evaluations of these peacebuilding efforts available? What has worked and not worked? Should they be expanded and supported? Or did they cause unintentional harms?
5. Identify which stakeholders could be trained or coached to play third-side or peacebuilding roles. Who has access to them to offer this support?

Output Conclusion
Given your self-assessment and your social capital, identify the key people you could best support to play peacebuilding roles and which roles you think are most needed in this context.

Notes

1. Stephen Stedman, "Spoiler Problems in Peace Processes," *International Security* 22, no. 2 (Fall 1997): 5–53.

2. Guy Oliver Foure and I. William Zartman, eds., *Negotiating with Terrorists* (New York: Routledge Press, 2010).

3. Desiree Nilsson, "Partial Peace: Rebel Groups Inside and Outside of Civil War Settlements," *Journal of Peace Research* 45, no. 4 (2008): 479–95.

4. Care International UK, *Peacebuilding with Impact: Defining Theories of Change,* Care International UK, London, 2012, 5.

5. Ibid.

6. Simon Fisher, Dekha Ibrahim Abdi, Jawed Ludin, Richard Smith, Steve Williams, and Sue Williams, *Working with Conflict: Skills and Strategies for Action* (London: Zed Books, 2005).

7. Lisa Schirch, *Ritual and Symbol in Peacebuilding* (Bloomfield, MA: Kumarian Press, 2005).

8. Ashutosh Varshney, *Ethnic Conflict and Civil Life: Hindus and Muslims in India* (New Haven, CT: Yale University Press, 2002).

9. See chapter on "Identity Transformation" in Schirch, *Ritual and Symbol in Peacebuilding.*

10. Ibid.

11. John Paul Lederach, *Building Peace: Sustainable Reconciliation in Divided Societies* (Washington, DC: US Institute of Peace, 1997), 39.

12. John Paul Lederach, *The Moral Imagination: The Art and Soul of Building Peace* (New York: Oxford University Press, 2005), 91.

13. Louise Diamond and John McDonald, *Multi-Track Diplomacy: A Systems Approach to Peace* (Grinnell: Iowa Peace Institute, 1991).

14. See The Third Side website at www.thirdside.org/.

7

WHY

Motivations

This chapter explores the motivations that drive people to pursue conflict or peace with others. A basic approach will answer the questions in Table 4.1. An intermediate approach will answer the summary questions outlined here from each of the three lenses in this chapter. A more advanced approach will use the suggested methodologies in each lens exercise to answer a longer set of related questions.

Basic conflict assessment questions	Why are the stakeholders acting the way they do? What are their motivations?
	1. Human needs, human rights, grievances, and perceptions of justice: What are the key stakeholder's underlying interests and needs as well as their best alternative to a negotiated agreement (BATNA) and negotiation skill level? Are there existing forums for communication between stakeholders?
	2. Worldview perceptions, brain patterns, and trauma: How is trauma impacting key stakeholders? Would a trauma-sensitive peacebuilding approach enable them to move to more productive and positive relationships with others?
	3. Incentives for peace: What types of incentives might work best in this context to incentivize groups to support peace?
Basic self-assessment questions	How do stakeholders perceive your motivations?

Theory of change	If x group is motivated to drive or mitigate conflict, what will change or support its motivations?
Basic peacebuilding planning question	Why will you conduct a peacebuilding effort? How does your self-assessment of your own motivations align with stakeholders' perceptions of your motivations and their own motivations in driving or mitigating conflict?

Why 1: Human Needs, Human Rights, Grievances, and Perceptions of Justice

What Does This Lens Help Us See?

This lens helps to identify the perceptions of needs, rights, grievances, and justice that motivate people to engage in conflict. Also called "the onion," this lens helps to distinguish between key stakeholders' public, stated positions and their underlying interests and needs.

How Does This Lens Contribute to Planning Peacebuilding?

A key task of peacebuilding is helping people identify and create processes to satisfy human needs and addressing grievances of all people involved in a conflict or crime. Satisfying basic human needs is the most effective way to foster healing, change behavior, end violence, and transform conflict.

This lens helps planners to prioritize legitimate motivations driving conflict that can be addressed through peacebuilding efforts. This assessment lens is useful for people involved in negotiation, to clarify distinctions between needs, interests, and positions. It becomes easier to find a mutually satisfying "win-win" solution when negotiating at the level of needs rather than negotiating over positions often framed in terms of "win-lose" competitions. This lens also helps groups to develop a narrative to distinguish illegitimate greed that may require a rule-of-law approach to peacebuilding, and legitimate grievances that may require structural changes to address.

Key Concepts

People engage in conflict for various reasons. People often decide to fight and die to protect their basic human needs for dignity, respect, identity, and economic and physical safety. In the "onion" diagram in Figure 7.1, needs and interests are often hidden underneath public positions.

Positions are what people say they want in public. These can be political demands or conditions under which people will stop fighting.

Figure 7.1 The Onion Diagram

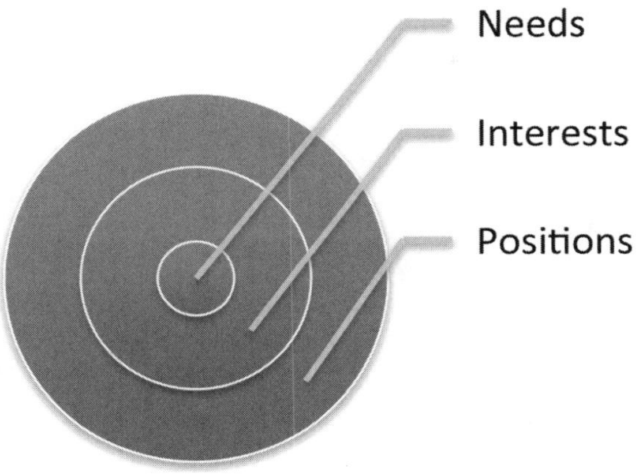

Interests are desires, concerns, and fears that drive people to develop a public position.

Needs are the most basic material, social, and cultural requirements for life that drive people's behavior and their positions and interests. There does not appear to be a hierarchy of needs, unlike Maslow's pyramid.[1] Context seems to shape which needs take precedence over others. In some cases, people do without food or even risk their life to protect their identity and dignity.

The drive to satisfy core human needs shapes human behavior. Conflict occurs when people perceive that others are obstructing or threatening their needs and rights. People are often willing to fight, die, or harm others to satisfy their needs. People fight to preserve their sense of identity just as much if not more than to obtain power or resources. Threats and punishments are ineffective at changing the behavior of people trying to satisfy what they perceive to be their basic human needs.[2]

Human rights and human needs are basically the same. People have a right to these basic needs.[3]

Material needs and rights include basic physical safety, food, shelter, health care, and the necessary resources to survive physically.

Social needs and rights include a sense of dignity, respect, recognition from others, belonging to a group while having a sense of participation, and self-determination in decisions that affect one's life.

Cultural needs and rights include a sense of meaning in one's own identity, cultural groups, and religious beliefs.

Researchers can use Table 7.1 to compare how stakeholders perceive their material, social, and cultural needs.

Table 7.1 Dimensions of the Conflict

	Dimensions of the Conflict
Material	
Social	
Cultural	

Core grievances develop as a deep sense of frustration and injustice that emerges out of persistent social patterns that obstruct human needs. Grievances emerge as people perceive a social pattern of discrimination or exclusion of some groups in favor of an elite group. Core grievances could also develop when social institutions are ineffective, corrupt, or illegitimate, or do not exist at all. Grievances shape people's perceptions of what they see as just and fair. Sometimes these grievances look illegitimate to others. People desire a *sense of justice* in how material resources are distributed, power to control their lives, participation in decision making, and a sense of identity and culture. People experience justice as a satisfaction of these basic human needs.

"**Greed**" is a term that refers to people who meet their own interests at the expense of others. For example, some armed groups use violence to take resources away from other groups so that they can increase their own wealth and finance further armed struggle. Sometimes people act in ways that harm others in an effort to defend or achieve their needs. People may satisfy their own needs at the expense of others. Some people *perceive* that their lives are worth more than others, and therefore it is "just" for them to have more resources and power. This *internalized superiority* develops from cultural values and is shaped by one's sense of identity of self and other. Most people tend to view themselves as good and their own motivations as legitimate. People tend to avoid seeing their own actions as greedy. Instead, they justify the reasons for their actions, describing them as legitimate grievances instead.

Perception plays a key role in assigning motivation. Greed and grievance are a matter of *perception.* People make decisions based on their *perceptions* of reality. A complex understanding of how people perceive justice and develop a sense of deprivation and grievance provides a richer understanding of the causes of conflict and violence. While some people's grievances and perceptions of their deprivation of needs may be more accurate and just than others', in practice the distinction may be less helpful.

A scholarly debate persists about whether people are motivated to engage in conflict because of greed or for legitimate grievances. This literature often poses these two motivations for conflict as opposite; some groups fight for legitimate grievances (unmet needs) and others fight with greedy motivations.[4]

Perception shapes whether others see a motivation as "need" or "greed." What one person views as greed another may see as a legitimate grievance. For example, even within an armed movement such as the one in Chechnya, some will articulate their struggle as a motivation for respect, identity, and self-determination. Others talk in a language of fighting for power and resources. The Chechnyan fighting for power and resources may look greedy to an outsider but likely sees him- or herself as fighting for legitimate grievances.

Justice is a perception of fairness. People perceive there is justice when their own human needs have been met. People perceive an injustice or trauma when others are seen to obstruct their human needs or human rights. People who engage in conflict, crime, or violence almost always have a story or narrative that justifies their actions as helping to meet their human needs, addressing their grievances, or bringing about their perception of justice. People tend to see pursuing their needs and rights as pursuing justice. People who cannot satisfy their needs often feel a sense of injustice or trauma.

Restorative or **transformative justice** efforts are peacebuilding processes that address wrongdoing or injustices by focusing on human needs. Crime and violence harm relationships between people, creating even more human needs.[5] Restorative justice processes focus on acknowledging and repairing the harms done to restore relationships between people. In restorative justice, those responsible for harming others by violating their human needs or human rights are accountable directly to their victims. Injustices and harms against people create obligations. Restorative justice processes include those accountable for the harms, the people impacted, and the broader community. All participate in a process that asks the following questions to heal and put right the harms:

1. Who has been hurt?
2. What are their needs?
3. Who has the obligation to address the needs, put right the harms, and restore relationships?

These questions are different from a normal criminal justice procedure that asks, What rules were broken? Who did it? What do they deserve? Restorative justice processes can serve either as an alternative or as a supplement to state-based criminal justice systems.

In a postwar context, the process of **transitional justice** uses some restorative justice principles that attempt to address victims' needs and rights. Truth and reconciliation processes aim to identify people or groups that harmed others and to give victims a process to identify their needs and to receive symbolic and financial reparations. The challenge of doing justice in a context experiencing war is to look at the multiple harms and perceptions of injustice on all sides of the conflict and to find a process for mutual accountability and responsibility for making things right.

Win-win negotiations on needs and win-lose negotiations on positions. Positions are almost always stated in a way that is mutually exclusive. For example, groups demand territory and threaten to bomb others if they do not get their way. Or a group demands a policy that supports its position and threatens to retaliate if it does not get its way. Most people approach conflict as a win-lose game. They assume that people's goals are actually in conflict, and in order for one group to win, another must lose. In reality, in most conflicts it is possible for all sides to satisfy their underlying needs and achieve an outcome that all groups can view as a win-win solution.

Win-win solutions rely on principled negotiation and problem-solving processes to identify the underlying needs and interests that can be met. Positions are almost always stated in a way that is mutually exclusive. Groups demand territory or reject the presence of foreigners in their country. Peacebuilding processes like principled negotiation can satisfy the underlying interests and needs of these positions, which could include a need for identity, self-determination, and respect. There are multiple ways of satisfying human needs, and while these needs are not negotiable, the ways to satisfy them are negotiable. Everyone needs respect, but people earn and give respect in different ways. Needs are never in conflict. Only strategies to meet those needs are in conflict.

For example, a group of Indigenous people has a need for land, identity, well-being, and justice. Their interest is in international recognition of their right to statehood, access to markets and trade, respect for human rights, and protection of their land rights. But because of the crisis in which they are involved, what they express publicly is their position—the rights of their group to fight back at those taking their land to make way for a shopping mall.

An opposing group in government has a need for security and land. Their interest is in protecting the survival of their state and to thrive politically and economically. Their public position condemns what they see as illegitimate terrorism, which they say justifies denying the rights of these

Indigenous people who are not of their ethnic and religious group. In this situation, the goal of peacebuilding would be to foster recognition of and negotiation at the level of each group's needs.

A long-term goal of peacebuilding is to improve communication and trust to the point where people can reveal their own needs and also understand and try to meet others' needs. This lens also helps groups develop a narrative to distinguish illegitimate greed that may require a rule-of-law approach to peacebuilding, and legitimate grievances that may require structural changes to address.

Reality checking and BATNA. All stakeholders—including armed groups, governments, business leaders, farmers, drug traffickers, military contractors, and ordinary citizens—calculate their interests and speculate on how to achieve them through political, economic, social, or military means. Stakeholders assess their best alternative to a negotiated agreement (BATNA) to determine whether to continue fighting.[6] If stakeholders believe they can achieve more on the battlefield, through other means of coercion, or by the continuation of the status quo, they will likely not negotiate in good faith. Stakeholders calculate their BATNA depending on the calculus of the costs and benefits, incentives and sanctions for participating or not participating. The "ripeness" for negotiation centers on whether the groups in conflict believe they have more to gain from peace or continued fighting.[7]

How Does This Lens Work?

Methodology

Interviews, focus groups, or community consultations or workshops. Researchers may also use secondary sources in desk research.

Exercise

1. Draw an onion as shown in Figure 7.1 for each key stakeholder. Identify the public positions, underlying interests, and deeper needs of each of the key actors in the stakeholder map.

2. Ask people to discuss and identify unmet material, social, and cultural needs that relate to perceptions of grievance and injustice. Create a chart as shown in Table 7.1. In each row, detail and describe each dimension of the conflict. To discover what is underneath their positions, ask key stakeholders the question "Why?"—as in "Why do they hold this position?" What is their deeper interest? Keep asking the "Why?" question until you get to the level of basic human needs such as identity, respect, and belonging.

3. Discuss whether people perceive the stakeholder's motivations as legitimate grievances or driven by greed. How do they think the stakeholders themselves see their motivations?

4. Do key actors tend to focus on their own or other group's public positions, or do they understand the interests and needs that drive these positions?

5. Do key actors have the skills to negotiate on interests and underlying needs instead of battling and bargaining over positions?

6. Do key actors have forums for communicating with each other? Are there trained facilitators and mediators who are creating channels for negotiation?

7. Do key actors have an accurate sense of the best alternatives to a negotiated agreement (BATNA)? Are there trained facilitators and mediators who can help them reality test their own self-assessment of their options?

Output Summary

Identify the underlying interests and needs as well as the BATNA, negotiation skill level, and existing or potential forums for communication of the key stakeholders you are most likely to work with in a peacebuilding effort.

Why 2: Worldview Perceptions, Brain Patterns, and Trauma

What Does This Lens Help Us See?

This lens highlights how key stakeholders' worldview perceptions, brain structure, and experiences of trauma shape their beliefs, attitudes, and behaviors in a conflict.

How Does This Lens Contribute to Planning Peacebuilding?

Peacebuilding is a process of changing worldview perceptions and narratives. It requires people to see the world from others' point of view. Understanding the existing worldviews of stakeholders is essential to planning efforts to shift these perceptions. Planners should be aware of how perceptual defense mechanisms and brain structure can make this challenging. Peacebuilding efforts can create spaces where people will encounter information and other people who will influence their worldview. But this worldview transformation may only be possible if peacebuilding efforts reduce the defense mechanisms that prevent worldview change.

Key Concepts

Each stakeholder in a conflict views the world in a different way. **Worldview** refers to the dynamic perspective from which one sees and interprets the world. Conflict is not just over scarce resources or competition over goods. Conflict is at least partly driven by perceptions and the story or **narrative** that we tell about conflict. Everyone wants to make sense of the world. The worldviews of the key stakeholders shape how they think, feel, and act in conflict, as well as the story they tell about who the conflict involves and why the conflict is happening.[8]

Two simple principles of perception exist. First, people desire **cognitive consistency,** or a steady, predictable understanding of the world. Second, when people perceive something that is inconsistent with their past experiences or beliefs, they seek to hide or deny it from existence. Contradictions or new information that goes against one's current worldview is stressful. If individuals perceive the world in a way that is incongruent with their worldview, they experience **cognitive dissonance**; in other words, they have anxiety and the discomfort of a new experience or idea that does not fit in with their current understanding.

The process of perception shapes and limits what people see of a conflict. People maintain cognitive consistency and avoid cognitive dissonance in two ways:

1. People *filter their experiences* with the world in a way that only retains information that is consistent with their current way of viewing the world. People reinforce preexisting views of what the conflict is about based on personal experience or professional expertise.
2. People *actively create the world* they expect and want to experience. People jump to conclusions about what is best to do in a conflict based on the programs or resources we already have available or what our organization would like to do.

Chapter 2 in this book detailed how the process of perception can hamper research quality. In the midst of conflict, the process of perception can hide the humanity of the other side and the complexity of the issues at hand. No individual is able to be unbiased or to see the whole truth of any reality. People may **dehumanize** each other by creating diabolical or animal *enemy images* of the other so that they may kill freely, without having to experience cognitive dissonance over treating a fellow human cruelly.

The structure of the brain itself impacts the process of perception. Conflict, violence, and trauma greatly impact people's ability to think and perceive accurately. In the midst of conflict, people respond to traumatic or fear-producing situations via their brain stem (see Figure 7.2[9]). The *reptilian brain* or *brain stem* is the unchanging base of the human nervous system that controls basic animal functions such as digestion and perspiration, and automatic reactions such as breathing. It is the place of instinctual responses to conflict, such as the impulse to freeze, to fight, or to flee. The *limbic system* is the emotional core of the brain where people feel fear, anger, hatred, joy, and so on.

The cerebral cortex, in the front and outside layer of the brain, controls rational thinking. This part of the brain observes, anticipates, plans, responds to, and organizes information. It helps people make logical decisions and to reflect and create ideas. Ideally, it controls the other two parts of the brain. Because this part of the brain helps to integrate, regulate, and control emotional impulses, people can learn to control their emotional reactions and even their physiological responses to conflict such as tightened muscles, cold hands, and sweating resulting from fear or trauma. It is the last part of the brain to engage in a situation of crisis. The rush of adrenalin and chemicals through the body can trigger a range of physical reactions.

In the midst of conflict or some sort of traumatic experience, the rational brain is often overwhelmed, and the other two parts take over with emotional or instinctual reactions. The "memory" of the trauma or crisis can stay in the brain for years afterward if the rational brain has not had the ability to identify and process the crisis situation. Each individual develops particular buttons that, when pushed, lead to patterned reactions that

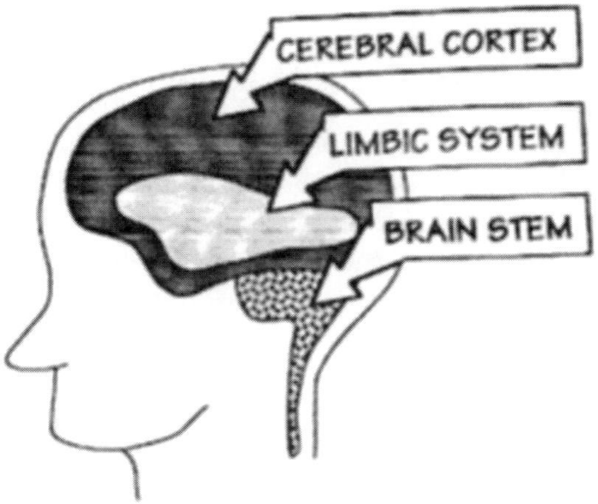

Figure 7.2 Brain structure

often flow along deeply engraved biological grooves in the structure of the brain. For example, when a person sees someone considered an enemy or someone who may attack, the first person may physically respond with an emotional and physical response, including increased heartbeat, clenched fists, and a feeling of fear.

The cerebral cortex helps people regulate emotions such as fear, build relationships, feel empathy for others, and process questions of morality and ethics. Peacebuilding processes aim to help move people out of a purely instinctual or emotional reaction to conflict—based in the brain stem or limbic system—and move to a thoughtful, intentional approach to addressing conflict proactively.[10]

Trauma: Acting in and acting out. Trauma is an event, series of events, or threat of an event that causes lasting physical, emotional, or spiritual injury. Trauma can result from natural causes or perpetual structural violence, or specific acts of crime, abuse, or war. Trauma impacts the biological brain, causing new brain patterns. When societies experience trauma they can also influence cultural beliefs, political systems, and a society's ability to address current problems and conflicts. Peacebuilding in traumatized societies requires helping people to identify harms, assert their needs, and move out of the cycle of violence and onto a path toward reconciliation, acceptance, and contributing toward human security.[11] For this reason, a trauma-sensitive approach to conflict assessment and peacebuilding planning requires basic knowledge of trauma's impacts and common responses to trauma.

As illustrated in the trauma-induced cycle of violence in Figure 7.3 developed by the STAR program (Strategies for Trauma Awareness and Resilience),[12] in the immediate aftermath of trauma, stress hormones flood the body, causing a feeling of shock and pain. Then people move to asking questions such as "Why me?" and often feel shame and humiliation about their victimization as well as survivor guilt. As time passes, people may become depressed, desire revenge, or both, feeling that revenge would alleviate their depression. For some victims, the desire for revenge leads them from a victim cycle to an aggressor cycle, where they use violence on others and put their own needs over others. Figure 7.3 can be a useful map for people to identify their emotional journey and responses to trauma.

Peacebuilding with traumatized people requires understanding and addressing their trauma. Trauma healing and recovery processes are an essential part of peacebuilding. Figure 7.4, also from the STAR program, illustrates the psychological progress that people make when they move out of the victim and aggressor cycles and begin to take part in peacebuilding.[13]

Figure 7.3 Acting In and Acting Out Cycles of Violence

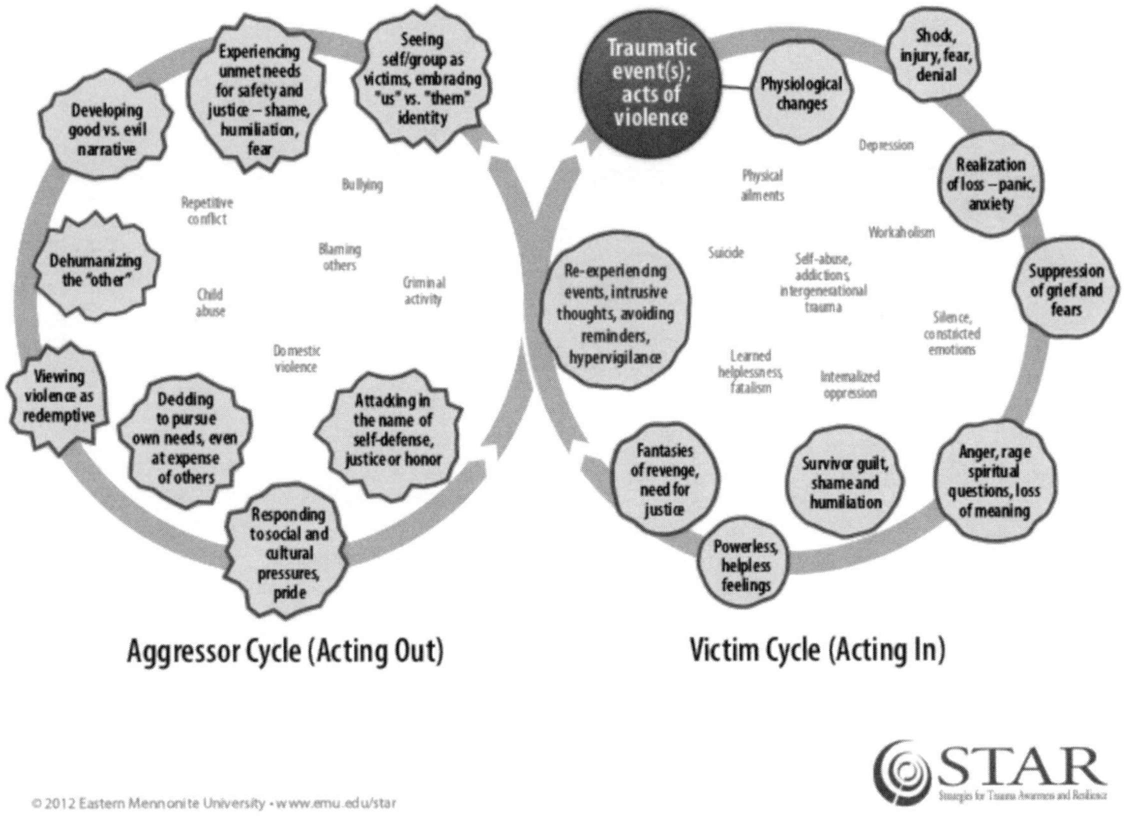

Figure 7.4 STAR Model for Breaking Cycles of Violence

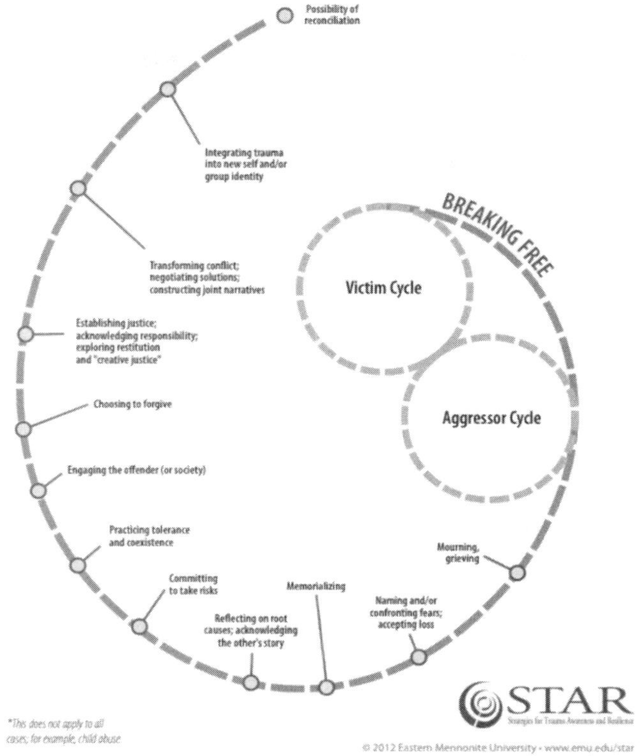

Linking with the lens on Culture and Identity Group Dynamics in Chapter 6, researchers can use Table 7.2 to identify and compare the perceptions, narratives, identities, traumas, and possible brain functioning based on stakeholders' experiences and observable behaviors and statements. While these will remain as guesses and are not verifiable data sources, the insights that come out of the process can help peacebuilding planners have a better sense of the potential cognitive functioning and worldviews motivating key stakeholders.

How Does This Lens Work?

Methodology

Interviews, focus groups, or community consultations or workshops using group discussion. Researchers may also use secondary sources in desk research and polling data.

Table 7.2 Comparative Chart of Stakeholders' Perceptions, Identities, and Traumas

Name of Individual or Group Stakeholders	What life experiences shape these stakeholders' perceptions and narrative of the conflict?	What cultural and identity groups shape how these stakeholders perceive conflict?	What previous traumas may be impacting whether the stakeholders respond instinctually or logically?	How do past traumas affect each stakeholder? Are they acting instinctively from their brain stem, or are they thinking with their cerebral cortex?
Stakeholder A				
Stakeholder B				

Exercise

1. Fill in Table 7.2 to develop for each of the key stakeholders a perception assessment that takes into account the categories in this table.

2. Identify where in Figure 7.3 are the key actors with whom you are most likely to work. Are these key actors behaving in a way that suggests they are acting in or acting out their trauma?

3. Where are key actors on the trauma healing spiral in Figure 7.4? What types of peacebuilding efforts may assist them in moving out of a cycle of violence?

4. In terms of self-assessment, what are potential or actual impacts of trauma affecting you or your organization? Where are you on either or both of the trauma diagrams?

Output Summary

Identify how trauma is impeding the key actors you may work with and consider how a trauma-sensitive approach may enable them to move to more productive and positive relationships with others.

Why 3: Incentives for Peace Lens

What Does This Lens Help Us See?

Incentives for peace increase key stakeholders' willingness and readiness to address conflict through negotiation or dialogue. This lens helps to assess current incentives and identify additional incentives that can be created by insiders or outsiders to the conflict.

How Does This Lens Contribute to Planning Peacebuilding?

Incentives can persuade key stakeholders to pursue peace, helping peacebuilding efforts succeed.

Background

Individuals and groups waging conflict against others make decisions based in part on the perceived costs and benefits of their fight. Recognizing the incentives for groups to continue fighting is an important first step in creating a more valued set of incentives for peace. These groups often conclude that fighting is more beneficial than peace. Individuals who are part of armed groups, for example, may benefit from the predictability of the current order versus an unknown future. Political, religious, and business leaders and others may benefit financially as well. Leaders of groups in conflict may know they have a pathway for promotion through the ranks of their network if they continue to lead aggressively against opposing groups. Maintaining antagonism with other groups and refusing diplomacy may allow leaders to impose order and prevent dissent in their group.

Hurting stalemates. Governments and armed groups often rely on reaching a *hurting stalemate,* in which they force the other side to stop fighting by punishing or hurting them. Armed groups may reach a point of exhaustion from fighting and determine that fighting has more costs than benefits. Determining when a group may decide to give up is not easy. Those groups that fight for identity, religion, or ideology are much more likely to accept any cost to continue fighting than groups fighting for material resources or political power. But often reaching a hurting stalemate requires a great deal of time and destruction of relationships, lives, and infrastructure.[14]

Types of incentives for peace. At least four types of incentives help ready or ripen the stakeholders' readiness for negotiation and create an environment conducive to peace. The ripeness of a peace process centers on whether the groups in conflict believe they have more to gain from peace or continued fighting. Different stakeholders will often desire different forms of incentives.

Security. Armed groups often continue fighting because leaving the network of their group may make them a target for all sides. Making security guarantees for armed individuals and groups is essential and can incentivize them to enter into groups to begin negotiations or support peace.

Political access. Individuals and groups engaged in a civil war seek political access and influence if not control of public decision making. Peace processes are risky for groups with and without political authority. Peace processes require negotiation and sometimes concessions over core interests, risky exchanges of promises, and a transition in which no one knows if they will come out with the same level of political influence. Structural designs lay out how government institutions will relate and who will have access and an ability to participate and represent group interests. Power-sharing or power-dividing deals that give groups influence over political decisions can incentivize groups to enter negotiations or support peace.

Economic access. All sides calculate the economic costs and benefits of continuing fighting or moving toward peace. Linked closely with political considerations, economic motivations can be more creatively addressed with external incentives such as development assistance, payments to armed groups that demobilize, or buying off specific leaders.

Identity/territory. While often overlooked, all sides also assess the impact of a peace agreement on their identity and sense of dignity, self-determination, and group autonomy. Sometimes this is addressed by allowing a group to retain a sense of ethnic or religious identity in a particular territory, such as the Moro Islamic Liberation Army in the Philippines, which has its own territory and separate flag, while belonging to a larger nation. Creative options to recognize identity and create face-saving mechanisms can incentivize groups to enter negotiations or support peace.

Internally or locally generated incentives. When the stakeholders themselves develop their own incentives for working toward peace, these tend to be more successful and creative than outside efforts. For example, the Somali women of Wajir, Kenya, set up a peace prize for the clan chief contributing most to peace. After the first year's prize, other chiefs approached the women to ask for training in mediation and negotiation to improve their chances of winning the prize in subsequent years.

Externally generated incentives. External incentives are most effective when they work in conjunction with internal or intrinsic incentives. External stakeholders can be guarantors for the peace process by assisting with needed economic and technical elements of implementing a peace agreement. However, creating pools of money or financial incentives for key stakeholders to participate in a peace process poses a number of challenges. It can encourage local people to feel like they are participating not because they want to but because they are getting paid to participate. This feeling can lower their willingness to put in their own effort and make their own sacrifices to ensure that peace is sustainable. It can also lead to the idea that the peace process is externally driven and ultimately about making money, taking away local leadership and legitimacy. It can also encourage perceptions of an unlimited pot of funds for peace process activities. In communities where peace dividends financed small-scale projects like building schools or health centers, local people came to see peace as having a financial benefit, which may contribute to devaluing the inherent value of peace. The moral hazard of incentives includes the interpretation of incentives as bribes or buying people off temporarily, but not addressing underlying conditions driving the conflict.

How Does This Lens Work?

Methodology

Interviews, focus groups, or community consultations or workshops using group discussion. Researchers may also use secondary sources in desk research and polling data.

Exercise

1. What types of incentives already exist in this conflict?
2. Do insider or outsider groups create the incentives?
3. What are the dangers of providing incentives in this context?
4. What additional forms of incentives could be created to increase the appeal of peace to key stakeholders?

Output Summary

What types of incentives might work best in this context to incentivize groups to support peace?

Notes

1. John Burton, *Conflict: Human Needs Theory* (New York: St. Martin's, 1990).
2. James Gilligan, *Preventing Violence* (New York: Thames and Hudson, 2001).
3. Lisa Schirch, "Linking Human Rights and Conflict Transformation: A Peacebuilding Perspective," in *Human Rights and Conflict: Exploring the Links Between Rights, Law, and Peacebuilding,* ed. Julie Mertus and Jeffrey Helsing (Washington, DC: US Institute of Peace, 2006), 63–95.
4. See Paul Collier and Anke Hoeffler, "Greed and Grievance in Civil War," World Bank Policy Research Working Paper 2355, Washington, DC, May 2000.
5. Adapted from Howard Zehr, *Changing Lenses: A New Focus for Crime and Justice* (Scottdale, PA: Herald Press, 1990).
6. Roger Fisher and William Ury, *Getting to Yes: Negotiating Agreement Without Giving In* (New York: Penguin Books, 1981).
7. I. William Zartman, *Ripe for Resolution* (New York: Oxford University Press, 1989).

8. See Jayne Docherty, *The Little Book of Strategic Negotiation* (Intercourse, PA: Good Books, 2004).

9. Drawn by Lee Eshleman for Carolyn Yoder, *The Little Book of Trauma Healing* (Intercourse, PA: Good Books, 2005).

10. Yoder, *Little Book of Trauma Healing.*

11. Barry Hart, *Peacebuilding in Traumatized Societies* (Lanham, MD: University Press of America, 2008).

12. These diagrams were developed by the STAR program at Eastern Mennonite University's Center for Justice and Peacebuilding, which began for caregivers of victims and family members of the September 11, 2001, attacks.

13. See the STAR program at Eastern Mennonite University: http://www.emu.edu/cjp/star/.

14. Peter Wallensteen and Margareta Sollenberg, "Armed Conflict, Conflict Termination, and Peace Agreement," *Journal of Peace Research* 34, no. 3 (January 1997), 339–358.

8

WHAT

Systems Mapping of Conflict Drivers and Mitigators

This chapter explores the factors that drive and mitigate conflict. A basic approach will answer the questions in Table 4.1. An intermediate approach will answer the summary questions outlined here from each of the three lenses in this chapter. A more advanced approach will use the suggested methodologies in each lens exercise to answer a longer set of related questions.

Basic conflict assessment questions	What factors are driving or mitigating conflict?
	1. **Conflict tree:** What are the root causes and the effects of the current crisis?
	2. **Systems mapping of conflict drivers and mitigators:** What are the relationships between forces and issues in the context? Do they reinforce or mitigate each other?
	3. **Capacity mapping peacebuilding activities:** What peacebuilding activities are already happening in the context?
Basic self-assessment	What are you capable of doing to address the key drivers and mitigators of conflict?
Theory of change	If x factors are driving and mitigating conflict, what actions will influence these factors?
Basic peacebuilding planning question	What will you do? Given your self-assessment, identify which driving and mitigating factors you will address.

What 1: Conflict Tree Lens

What Does This Lens Help Us See?

This lens distinguishes between the symptoms of conflict and the root causes that are giving rise to a conflict. It can stimulate discussion about the relationships between multiple causes and effects in a conflict. This lens is a very basic, beginners' approach to thinking in terms of systems—useful for groups of people to dialogue with each other about the root causes or core grievances within a context that give rise to symptoms or effects of conflict.

How Does This Lens Contribute to Planning Peacebuilding?

Identifying the root causes of a conflict is important to later identifying how best to intervene to stop the cycle of violence and build peace.[1] This lens can distinguish between efforts that relieve the symptoms of conflict and those that address the underlying causes. The long-term goal of peacebuilding is to address root causes through building society's institutions and structures in a way that meets human needs.

Key Concepts

In many parts of the world, some types of trees or plants, such as the cassava plant or raspberry bush, regenerate even after their tops are cut off. This lens uses these types of plants as a metaphor or symbol to illustrate the power that root causes or latent causes of conflicts have to regenerate symptoms or effects. The tree in Figure 8.1 illustrates the relationship between underlying problems and superficial effects. Efforts to address the presenting issues without addressing the latent root causes will have little effect on the system. Sustainable peacebuilding requires addressing root causes. For example, in Figure 8.1, systemic factors such as social and economic inequality and government corruption are root causes of ethnic clashes and a high crime rate.

How Does This Lens Work?

Methodology

Focus group, workshop, or consultation. This lens is best done in a group to foster dialogue about the differences between root causes and other effects.

Exercise

1. Ask members of a group to identify key issues in the conflict and, if possible, to write each issue on a separate card or to make a list of key issues.

Figure 8.1 Conflict Tree

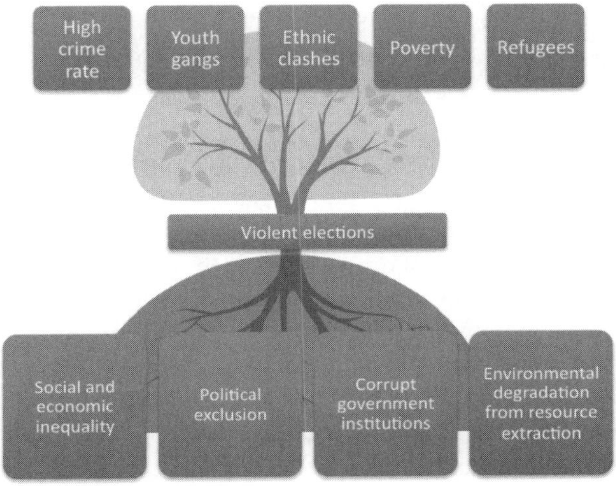

2. Draw a picture of a tree—including its roots, trunk, and branches—on a large sheet of paper, a chalkboard or a flipchart, or on the side of a building or on the ground.

3. Invite people to attach their cards or list issues on parts of the tree . . .
on the trunk, if they think it is the presenting issue or problem.
on the roots, if they think it is a root cause.
on the branches, if they see it as an effect.

4. Many issues can be seen as both causes and effects of the conflict, which is okay; an objective "right answer" may not exist. Sometimes the same word can appear in both places, as root cause and symptom, if there is a cycle of violence.

5. After all the cards have been placed on the tree (see Figure 8.1 for an example), a facilitator asks the group members to find consensus on their analysis of the issues and where they belong.

6. If possible, the group can further divide the root causes into the three or four main roots of the tree, and the related roots that stem out of these main root causes.

Output Summary

Given your self-assessment, what is the best match of your resources to issues listed on the tree? Can your peacebuilding efforts address root causes or resulting effects or both?

What 2: Systems Mapping of Conflict Drivers and Mitigators

What Does This Lens Help Us See?
This lens illustrates the relationships between different factors driving and mitigating conflict.

How Does This Lens Contribute to Planning Peacebuilding?
This mapping of factors driving and mitigating conflict is a more advanced approach to identifying and prioritizing areas for peacebuilding efforts that could change the dynamics of the conflict system. Some factors escalate tension, polarization, and violence. Other factors foster restraint and common ground while helping to depolarize and de-escalate tensions.

Key Concepts
As noted throughout this handbook, conflict acts like a system; its parts are interdependent. There is not a simple cause-and-effect explanation; multiple, interdependent factors influence each other. This lens draws connective lines between issues in conflict to show the ways that issues relate to or reinforce other issues. Like stakeholder mapping, the process itself and the dialogue among people about the relationship between drivers and mitigators of conflict are more important than any actual physical map resulting from the process. Any map will be subjective and will be a shadow of the actual system.

There are two ways of creating a systems map of factors related to conflict. One approach is free form, as in Figure 8.2.[2] The second approach is to prioritize key factors and to create a structured flowchart of how factors build upon each other, as in Figure 8.3.[3]

Systems maps can easily become so complex that they paralyze or confuse more than help. Ultimately, a systems map will be most helpful if it is based on many people's discussions of their own experiences, as well as based on polling data and other research so that the map reflects not the views of one person or a small group of analysts, but of a robust research process that has prioritized and narrowed the number of key factors.

How Does This Lens Work?

Methodology
Interviews, focus groups, or community consultations or workshops using group discussion. Researchers may also use secondary sources in desk research and polling data.

Figure 8.2 Example of Free Form Systems Map of Conflict Factors

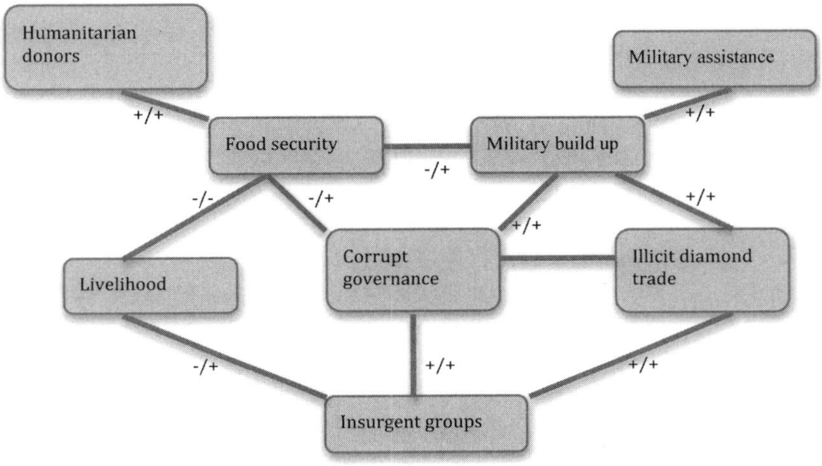

Figure 8.3 Flow-Chart Systems Map of Conflict Factors

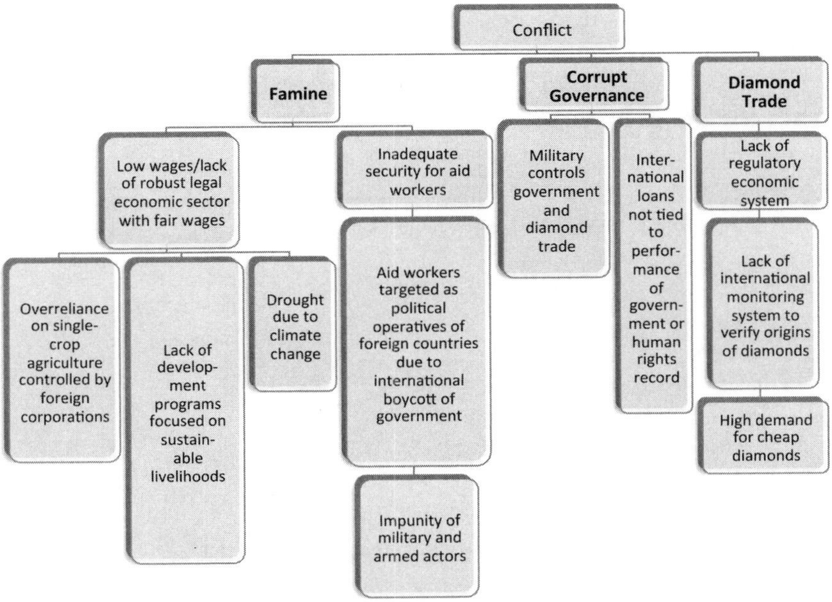

Exercise

1. Use a minimum of three different focus groups. These groups will create their own separate free form map, as in Figure 8.2. Ideally, these focus groups will have access to summarized forms of polling and research data, and will also use their own experience of living and working in the local context. In other words, systems maps are best made by those immersed in the local context who really know how parts of a system relate to each other. But people can also benefit from triangulating their own experiences with polling and research data of how others in their context view the issues. The purpose of having multiple focus groups is to allow comparisons of the different maps through group discussion to further analyze why they see the system in the same or a different way from other groups.

2. Drawing on previous assessment lenses or frameworks, each focus group should identify 10 to 20 key factors or drivers that seem to be important to the ongoing conflict. Separate these into key driving factors and key mitigating factors. Write these factors on small sheets of paper or Post-it Notes, using different colors for drivers and mitigators if possible, that people can move around on a larger sheet of paper. The idea is to make it easy for people to move around the factors and rearrange the map as they discuss the interrelationships.

3. Begin to arrange these factors on a larger sheet of paper or drawing board according to which factors seem to be closer to each other. Ask people to tell narrative stories of the way factors interrelate. What factors support or lead to other factors? What are the impacts of one factor on others? While the groups begin with a longer list, ask them to prioritize, through

Drawing Tips for Free Form Systems Map[4]

- Put six to eight key factors in a central location on the map, to make it easier to show how some smaller factors influence main factors.
- Avoid crossing lines to make the map less cluttered and confusing.
- Draw the lines on the paper with pencil first.
- Avoid repeating a factor unless doing so makes the map less cluttered.
- Use lines and arrows to highlight the most important relationships. Avoid lines, or make them very light, if the relationship between factors makes a map look too complex.

the process of group discussion, to reduce the number on the final map to six to eight key factors.

4. Draw lines of connections with arrows to illustrate which issues impact other issues. Draw loops where issues have a reinforcing impact on each other.

5. *Optional:* Add the words "time delay" along dotted lines when causality or the impact of one factor on another may take longer or be related less directly.

6. *Optional:* Show whether factors have a parallel cause and effect, meaning more of one factor leads to more of another factor. For example, the increased presence of more international corporations logging the forests may correlate to an increase in armed groups. Mark these relationships with a +/+ note next to the line. If factors have an opposite relationship, meaning more of one factor leads to less of another factor, mark this with a +/– sign. For example, an increase in armed groups can correlate with a decrease in economic trade in a region.

7. *Optional:* A free-form systems map such as the one in Figure 8.2 can be processed further into a structured flowchart that prioritizes the key issues, such as the one in Figure 8.3, which organizes factors driving a conflict into three categories of prioritized factors: famine, corrupt governance, and diamond trade. Subfactors that influence each of these key factors are listed underneath. However, a flow chart map can lose important information about relationships between key factors.

8. In a large group, ask people to reflect on the similarities and differences in the different systems maps made by different focus groups. Is there any consensus on the key driving or mitigating factors? Are there similarities or differences in how the groups see the connections or relationships between factors? What experiences of different group members led them to "seeing" different parts of the system?

Output Summary

Given your self-assessment, which factors driving or mitigating conflict relate to you? Identify the six to eight key driving and mitigating factors that you may be most able to influence.

What 3: Capacity Mapping Peacebuilding Activities

What Does This Lens Help Us See?

This lens highlights existing peacebuilding activities taking place in different sectors.

How Does This Lens Contribute to Planning Peacebuilding?

Strategic peacebuilding requires coordination to facilitate a systemic approach, with efforts complementing rather than contradicting each other. Groups contributing to peacebuilding often do not coordinate or even know about each other. Forums for learning about peacebuilding efforts are rare and inadequate. This lens helps insider and outsider peacebuilding organizations learn more about related efforts.

Key Concepts

Table 8.1 identifies a range of different peacebuilding activities that provide examples, not a complete list, of possible peacebuilding efforts. In almost every community around the world, someone or some group is trying to foster peace, whether through using religious rituals, artistic efforts, or symbolic approaches,[5] or intergroup dialogue or psychosocial trauma healing. Others use advocacy and training to foster institutional reform and economic development. Peacebuilding requires improvisation to develop new approaches. Several platforms exist to help identify peacebuilding activities that may help others learn or work in a more coordinated way. These include the following:

- The World Bank's HIVE is a communication platform on fragility, conflict, and violence for the community of practice to share and build knowledge. See www.thehivefcv.org.
- The Global Partnership for the Prevention of Armed Conflict is a network of practitioners in conflict prevention and peacebuilding who share best practices and lessons learned to enable more effective coordinated action. See www.gppac.net.
- The Alliance for Peacebuilding is a US-based network fostering collaboration and shared strategies to support peace. See www.allianceforpeacebuilding.org.
- The International Dialogue on Peacebuilding and Statebuilding is an international forum for political dialogue between countries affected by conflict and fragility, their international partners, and civil society. See www.oecd.org/internationaldialogue.

How Does This Lens Work?

Methodology

Interviews with key people, focus groups, or workshops.

Table 8.1 Five Categories of Peacebuilding and Human Security

Levels of Change	Politically Stable Democracy	Sustainable Economy	Safe and Secure Environment	Justice and Rule of Law	Social and Cultural Well-Being
	Predictable and participatory decision-making and governance	*Access to basic resources and conducive to socially responsible business*	*Personal safety and freedom of movement*	*Perceived equity in social relations and justice systems*	*Respect and dignity between people of different cultures and identities*
	Peacebuilding efforts include these activities in each category:				
Structural	Build formal and informal **governance** institutions Develop independent **media** Foster **civil society organizations** that advocate for public issues	Build **infrastructure** Promote just, sustainable economic policies within the **regulatory and legal environment** Address institutional obstacles to **economic equity**	Conduct **security sector reform** Create institutions to **restrain perpetrators** of violence Use **security forces** to enforce ceasefires, peace zones **Disarm and demobilize** armed groups **Prevent and mitigate natural disasters**	Foster legitimate and just **legal frameworks** Monitor **human rights** Build **independent courts** **Community policing** Create systems for **restorative and transitional justice**	Create **interreligious or interethnic task forces** on preventing violence Support cultural, religious, and media institutions that provide information on **intergroup relations**
Cultural	Use media programs, and religious and cultural venues to discuss **values of citizenship, political equality, and democracy**	Address culture of corruption **Sanction war profiteering** and illicit trade	**Foster respect** for human rights and humanitarian law **Promote understanding** of environmental sustainability	Use media programs, and religious and cultural venues to **promote respect for rule of law and human rights**	Use **media programs, rituals, the arts, and religious and cultural venues** to foster group relations, trauma healing, and peace
Relational	Create **multistakeholder governance processes** Use **mediation and negotiation** to reach political solutions Build state-society relations with **policy advocacy**	Develop processes for **community-based economic development**	Improve relations between security forces and communities **Reintegrate armed groups**	**Mobilize citizens** to advocate for fair and just laws and policies	Use media and the arts for **prejudice reduction** **Intergroup dialogues** Support **women's empowerment and gender sensitivity**
Personal	Train government and institutional leaders in **peacebuilding skills and processes**	Train citizens in starting and supporting **socially responsible businesses**	Train citizens to provide **security sector oversight** and participate in **community watch**		Use rituals, memorials for individual and group **trauma healing**

Exercise

Make a list or draw a chart and identify peacebuilding activities happening in the conflict-affected context. Table 8.1 (also Table 1.3) illustrates many different types of efforts related to peacebuilding. Some of these may not explicitly name the activity as "peacebuilding" but rather reflect a related concept such as governance, democracy, human rights, and so on. The point is not to force a label on them as peacebuilding activities but rather to begin seeing the different diverse activities contributing to peace.

Output Summary

Given your self-assessment, which of these existing efforts most relates to your set of capacities? How might you communicate and coordinate with other existing peacebuilding initiatives?

Notes

1. Simon Fisher, Dekha Ibrahim Abdi, Jawed Ludin, Richard Smith, Steve Williams, and Sue Williams, *Working with Conflict: Skills and Strategies for Action* (London: Zed Books, 2005).
2. Robert Ricigliano, *Making Peace Last* (Boulder, CO: Paradigm Press, 2011).
3. See Deirdre LaPin, African Studies Center, University of Pennsylvania, and her work on "causal influence trees" for conflict in the Niger Delta.
4. Ricigliano, *Making Peace Last,* 127.
5. See Lisa Schirch, *Ritual and Symbol in Peacebuilding* (Bloomfield, MA: Kumarian Press, 2005), and Lisa Schirch and Michael Shank, "Strategic Arts-Based Peacebuilding," *Peace & Change* 33, no. 2 (April 2008): 217–42.

9

HOW

Sources and Uses of Power

This chapter explores the means or sources of power that people use to pursue conflict or peace with others. A basic approach will answer the questions in questions in Table 4.1. An intermediate approach will also answer the summary questions outlined here from each of the three lenses in this chapter. A more advanced approach will use the suggested methodologies in each lens exercise to answer a longer set of related questions.

Basic conflict assessment questions	How is conflict manifested? What are the stakeholders' means and sources of power?

1. Power and means analysis: What are the key stakeholder's means or sources of power? How do other stakeholders depend upon them?

2. Identity and power imbalances: How are power and identity interrelated? How do identity groups use power over other identity groups? How can peacebuilding efforts address the power relationships between stakeholders in different identity groups to foster more egalitarian approaches? For example, is it possible to create multiethnic, male/female, young/old teams for peacebuilding efforts?

3. Gender, conflict, and peacebuilding: What are the gendered dimensions of power in a conflict-affected context? How do the sources of power differ for men and women? Identify strategies for addressing gender-based violence and gender-based roles in peacebuilding. What would gender-sensitive peacebuilding look like in this context?

Basic self-assessment questions	What are your resources, means, or sources of power? How will these shape your efforts? How will these shape your peacebuilding efforts?
Theory of change	If x power sources are driving conflict, what will influence these sources of power?
Basic peacebuilding planning question	How will you shift power sources in support of peace? Given your self-assessment, identify and prioritize your capacity to reduce dividers and to increase local capacities for peace.

How 1: Power and Means Analysis

What Does This Lens Help Us See?

This lens examines key stakeholders' different sources of power or the means with which they drive or mitigate conflict.

How Does This Lens Contribute to Planning Peacebuilding?

Planning for peacebuilding requires identifying existing and potential sources of power, the means with which to fight, and the means for building peace. Peacebuilding is a process of empowerment for all parts of a system, so that each has a voice in the quality of the relationships between them. If groups think they will gain more from fighting than from pursuing their needs through nonviolent avenues, building peace will be difficult. For example, stakeholders with access to money, guns, and recruits to fight may decide to lay down their arms only when offered the possibility of political influence to achieve their goals. "Peacebuilding efforts are most effective when all stakeholders recognize their independence and the extent and limits of each stakeholder's power." Without this awareness, stakeholders may not be willing to negotiate with each other.

Key Concepts

Power is the *ability to do*—to change oneself, others, or the environment. People use power when they participate in decisions that impact their lives. Power exists in relationships between people; power does not exist in a vacuum. There are power dynamics in all relationships. Power is *always shifting:* it is impossible to give a precise measurement of the amount of power that people have at any one time. People can create power by altering the ways they relate to other people.

Sources of power. There are many sources of power. Stakeholders in a conflict can mobilize any of these sources as a means to fight others. People can also use or create these sources of power in peacebuilding efforts.

- Physical or military strength
- Identity (gender, ethnic background, family of origin, position, or authority)
- Personal ability (such as communication skills or professional competency)
- Economic resources
- Access to information
- Education (knowledge and skills)
- Moral or spiritual power
- The personal power of charisma
- Social capital

Social capital refers to the quantity and quality of relationships between people and groups. It is based on the idea that social networks have value providing a way to communicate or collaborate with others. Social capital exists horizontally and vertically within the pyramid in Figure 9.1.

Horizontal social capital exists between groups at the same level. **Vertical social capital** exists between groups at different levels, as illustrated in Figure 9.1. Most peacebuilding focuses on horizontal social capital between divided groups working at the same social level. But vertical social capital is necessary to create system-level impacts.

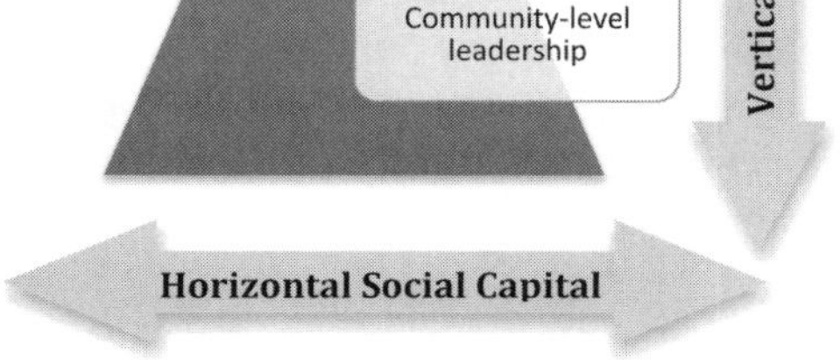

Figure 9.1
Social Capital Pyramid

Bonding social capital refers to the value assigned to social networks *within* a group of people who share a common identity. **Bridging social capital** refers to social networks *between* different identity groups.[1] Bridging social capital is critical to peacebuilding.

Balanced and unbalanced power. People often have different levels of power in conflict-affected systems. People can feel disempowered, as if they have no or little power, when they have a difficult time influencing decisions that affect their lives. People tend to feel especially disempowered when they are not consulted or included in a social process that affects their lives, when others devalue their right or ability to participate in that process, or when one feels that they can have no impact on the world and that death is inevitable.

Misperceptions of who has the "most" power are frequent. People tend to become angry and threaten others when they sense others have more power. Assessing the power each stakeholder has to influence other stakeholders requires a thorough understanding of how stakeholders depend on each other and are interdependent. The power of any stakeholder is related to how dependent others are on them. The power of A over B is equal to the dependence that B has on A and vice versa.

Domination and control versus sharing power. Power over is the *destructive* use of power to impact and influence others' lives without their consent. Domination, control, submission, defiance, threats, and counter-threats are examples of power over strategies. They suggest, "If you do not do what I want, I will do something you do not want."

Power with is the *constructive* use of power to shape the environment with others' consent and participation. **Productive power** is the power to do and create things and the power with others based on exchange relationships that suggest, "If you do something I want, I will do something you want," or **integrative power** to create something with others, such as "I will do something because I care about your well-being."

A government's political power, for example, ultimately depends on the consent and cooperation of its citizens. Governments are not omnipotent. On the contrary, all governments depend on the cooperation of others for their sources of power. They depend on their own population, the institutions of the society they rule, and elites in other countries, and so on. If the population rejects a government's right to rule, the public may use integrative power to create alternative governing structures and cause the collapse of the current government. The more that citizens deny a government authority and come together in a mass movement supporting change, the less power that government can exercise.

How Does This Lens Work?

Methodology

Interviews, focus groups, or community consultations or workshops using group discussion. Researchers may also use secondary sources in desk research and polling data.

Exercise

1. What are the key stakeholders' different sources of power and social capital?

2. How are the stakeholders in the conflict dependent on each other? Are they interdependent, or does one side have more influence on the others?

3. Which stakeholders have "power with" each other or "power over" others? How does power play into the dynamics of the conflict? In what ways do stakeholders use power as a means to wage conflict with each other?

Output Summary

Given your self-assessment, what influence might you have to increase power for disempowered groups, to better enable a negotiation or support for peace? How might you increase or support the power of groups mitigating conflict to play peacebuilding roles? How might you decrease the power sources of groups driving conflict?

How 2: Identity and Power Imbalances Lens

What Does This Lens Help Us See?

This lens examines the way people tend to rank identity groups on a hierarchy, with some identity groups having more power than others. Social ranking reflects power imbalances that can greatly impact the way people behave in a conflict. Many subtle and direct behaviors communicate a power imbalance between people of different identities.

How Does This Lens Contribute to Planning Peacebuilding?

Peacebuilding is a process to transform social hierarchies so all groups are free from fear, free from want, and free to live their lives in dignity without being humiliated or discriminated against because of their identity.

Key Concepts

Research links violent conflict with unequal power distribution among people of different religious, tribal, ethnic, regional, gender, linguistic, racial, and other identities. Public perceptions of inequality between groups may be a leading cause of violent conflict in developing countries.[2]

In many places, children are taught that some people are "superior" and others are "inferior" and to value some people's lives more than the lives of others. These ideas become internalized, leading to what psychologists refer to as "internalized superiority" and "internalized oppression" or inferiority.

Social hierarchies. Where people and structures discriminate between people of different identities, a social hierarchy may emerge. A *social hierarchy* is like a ladder, with some identities viewed as superior to others. Social hierarchies are not natural. Identity groups experience discrimination socially, culturally, and institutionally as jobs, homes, and educational and political opportunities may be denied to some groups because of their identity. People lower on social hierarchies may exert dominance over and prejudice against each other, too. Racism is defined as "prejudice" plus "power," or in other words, a feeling of superiority and disklike for other identity groups with the power to use systems and develop institutional patterns that discriminate against others.

Table 9.1 gives examples of social and institutional patterns that enforce identity and power imbalances.[3] Many people may stereotype and express prejudice over others. But most people do not hold institutional power to enforce these beliefs on others. When groups hold more power than others and

Table 9.1. Examples of Dysfunctional Power Imbalances

Type of Power	Identity	Example of Who May Hold More Power	Example of Who May Hold Less Power
Racism	Race/skin color	White	People of color
Sexism	Gender	Men	Women
Classism	Socioeconomic class	Middle, upper class	Poor, working class
Elitism	Education level Place in hierarchy	Formally educated Managers	Informally educated Clerical, staff
Religious Oppression	Religion	Depending on context	Depending on context
Anti-Semitism	Religion	Christians	Jews
Ageism	Age	Young or old	Elders or younger ones
Heterosexism	Sexual orientation	Heterosexuals	Gay, lesbian, bi, transgender
Ableism	Physical/mental ability	Currently able-bodied	Physically/mentally challenged
Xenophobia	Immigrant status	Citizens	Immigrants/refugees
Linguistic	Language	Dominant language	Minority language

when certain identity groups control institutions, then these social patterns become forms of prejudice with power, or the various "isms."

Dysfunctional power imbalances cause problems both for those with more power and internalized superiority and for those with less power who have internalized inferiority and oppression.

Paulo Freire's *Pedagogy of the Oppressed* created methods for people suffering under oppressive social patterns to "conscientize" themselves by conducting their own social analysis to identify the everyday impacts of identity and power imbalances.[4] For example, based on an analysis of old and new forms of identity and power imbalances, Table 9.2 illustrates modern remnants of racial discrimination and the dynamics among those who continue to suffer under that social pattern.[5] These patterns are found in many conflict-affected regions. People belonging to different identity groups come to reinforce power inequalities on a day-to-day basis. Peacebuilding efforts face challenges to acknowledge and transform the pervasive behavioral and institutional power dynamics between groups.

How Does This Lens Work?

Methodology

Interviews, focus groups, or community consultations or workshops using group discussion. Researchers may also use secondary sources in desk research and polling data.

Table 9.2 Patterns of Racism

Modern Remnants and Continuing Patterns of Racism	Internalized Oppression and Reverse Prejudice
Dysfunctional rescuing: Helping people of color, assuming that they cannot help themselves. Being extra nice and polite to people of color	*System beating:* Getting around the system of racism by learning to play nice and not upset the system, or playing along with the system's low expectations, or using antidiscrimination law as protection and an excuse
Blaming the victim: Criticizing people of color alone for their circumstances and denying the historical impact of racism	*Blaming the system:* Not taking personal responsibility for those things under your control
Avoidance of contact: Living in a diverse country or community but having almost no contact with people of color	*Antiwhite avoidance of contact:* Rejection of all white people; criticizing black people for not being "black enough"
Denial of differences: Ignoring obvious physical differences	*Denial of cultural heritage:* Distrusting other people of color, valuing "all things white"
Denial of the political significance of differences: Minimizing historical differences between groups that continue to impact all people in social, political, economic, and psychological ways	*Lack of understanding of the political significance of differences:* Passivity, turning anger inward or onto other people of color

Exercise

1. How do identity groups within the conflict context rank each other? Is there agreement on the social ranking? Is the social ranking seen as "natural" by all groups?

2. Do groups lower on the social ranking resent their social status? Do these groups work together to increase their social status or work for social equality?

3. Which stakeholders have the means to discriminate against others with the force of social, cultural, and institutional power? Do they use this power over others?

Output Summary

How can peacebuilding efforts address the power relationships between stakeholders in different identity groups to foster more egalitarian approaches? For example, is it possible to create multiethnic, male/female, young/old teams for peacebuilding efforts?

How 3: Gender, Conflict, and Peacebuilding

What Does This Lens Help Us See?

This lens illustrates how the identity and power dynamics between men and women are unlike other identity groups. Gender roles both shape the ways that men and women experience violence and the roles they play in driving and mitigating conflict.[6]

How Does This Lens Contribute to Planning Peacebuilding?

This lens explores how gender sensitivity to gender roles ascribed to men and women pose opportunities and risks for peacebuilding.[7] Women may be able to play important roles in peacebuilding, but gender roles may prohibit them from doing so. Men may be willing to negotiate and forgo violence, but gender roles may push them toward militant solutions.

Key Concepts

Men and women may have different ways of dealing with conflict based on ascribed societal roles. Women may be discouraged from using violence if it is not seen as feminine, while men may be encouraged to be violent to prove their masculinity. Negotiation and dialogue may be seen as feminine, and most cultures value masculine traits more than feminine traits. Peacebuilding roles are more often seen as feminine and less valued than more aggressive masculine efforts to address conflict.

Gender definitions and their relevance to peacebuilding.

Sex. Biological differences between males and females are defined as "sex." Women, for example, can give birth and nurse babies because of their biology. There is little evidence suggesting that women are more peaceful than men because of their biology. There is some evidence that men with high levels of testosterone may be more violent than other men. But biology does not explain why men commit far more acts of violence than women.

Gender and gender roles. Social differences between masculine and feminine characteristics ascribed to men and women are referred to as gender. Families, schools, religious organizations, media programs, and communities encourage boys and girls to take on specific gender roles. Boys who have "feminine" characteristics and girls who have "masculine" characteristics are often punished or sanctioned by their community. Feminine traits include caring for others and interrelational skills that support peace. Masculine traits in many cultures include demonstrating aggression. As a result, gender roles do affect whether men's and women's skills and temperaments support violence or peacebuilding. In practice, many people conflate sex and gender. Other terms described here relate more to sex, but other researchers commonly refer to them as *gender.*

Gender analysis and gender gap. A gender analysis examines how policies and projects affect males and females differently. The gender gap is the difference in levels of participation, qualifications, economic status, or other indicators between males and females. Conflict assessment researchers should pay attention to the possible gender gap between the way women and men experience conflict and support peace.

Gender discrimination. Gender discrimination is any pattern of preferential treatment of males over females. In peacebuilding, there is frequently gender discrimination because men are more often chosen for leadership roles, and women are more often left out of political processes related to violence and peace.

Gender sensitization. Gender sensitization represents an effort to raise awareness about the different needs of males and females and to increase efforts to address these needs. Gender-sensitive peacebuilding requires paying attention to the different experiences and capacities of males and females.

Gender equity and equality. These terms refer to an approach to ensure that men and women are valued equally for the roles they play and benefit equally from policies and projects such as education and compensation for work. Gender equity takes into consideration that women have been historically disadvantaged and may need special programs to overcome this discrimination. In peacebuilding, gender equity means ensuring that women and girls have equal opportunities as men and boys.

Gender mainstreaming. Mainstreaming refers to the inclusion of the goal of gender equality, the use of a gender analysis, and the active inclusion of women and women's groups into all institutional choices and practices.

Women's empowerment—the ability of women to have resources, access, skills, and self-esteem to participate fully in the decisions that affect their lives.

Feminism—The global social movement to address the oppression of women and create gender equality.

Gender dimensions of violence. Gender influences conflict in a variety of ways. Women and men experience different forms of violence.

Men and violence. Most cultures socialize boys and men to be "masculine." Most cultures connect masculinity to concepts of courage, competition, assertiveness, and ambition that are expressed through physical aggression, violence, and repression of other emotions. Young boys are encouraged to repress empathy, to be tough and fearless, not to cry, and to value winning or dominating over others. Many cultures permit and encourage males to act aggressively in order to prove their manhood. Some fathers tell their sons that war will "bring out the man in you." Many boys learn that war is respectable and that heroes are warriors, soldiers, and conquerors.

The language of war is masculine. Military leaders may refer to their enemy in feminine terms, using metaphors like "penetrating the enemy" to describe military strategies. Some voters want to elect leaders whom they believe will be able to make the decision to go to war. Since there are far more men than women in most militaries, women also find it difficult to get into positions of political leadership. Female leaders are questioned whether they "have what it takes" to use violence. Male leaders who favor negotiation or diplomacy rather than war are called "wimps" or "girls," challenging their manhood. In an attempt to act masculine and play the role society has defined for men, many men make "detached decisions" without concern for the human suffering they will bring to others.[8]

Women and violence. Table 9.3 illustrates the types of violence women experience before, during, and after war, even in times of peace. Women experience physical forms of violence such as domestic violence and rape. Psychological forms of violence include harassment, humiliation, and stigmatization. Structural violence against women refers to the way in which many education systems give preferential treatment to boys, or the way in which women are left out of political decision-making processes that impact their lives.

Gender and peacebuilding roles. Socially defined expectations of gender influence the roles women and men can play in peacebuilding. Researchers

Table 9.3 Forms of Violence Against Women

Forms of Violence Against Women			
	During "Normal" Life (No War)	During War or Crisis	Postwar
Physical Forms of Violence AgainstWomen	– Domestic violence – Rape – Female genital mutilation – Female infanticide (killing girl babies) – Trafficking of women as sex slaves	– Increased connection between masculinity and violence leads to increased domestic violence and rape – Forced prostitution and sexual slavery	– Increased domestic violence – Increased rape – Rape victims experience beatings or death by family members who want to return the family's honor
Psychological Forms of Violence Against Women (Emotional abuse, verbal abuse)	– Sexual harassment in the workplace, religious institution, or family – Sexist humor – Shaming women for being raped – Cultural acceptance or glorification of violence against women	– Portrayal of women as victims degrades the worth of women	– War rape victims experience social stigmatization, physical and mental trauma
Structural Forms of Violence	– Giving boys more education, food, and opportunities than girls – Giving girls more work than boys – Paying women less than men for the same work – Feminization of poverty (most poor people are women) – Limitations on female leadership – Excluding women from inheritance and property rights	– As men leave to fight, women are required to provide for all family needs during a time when food and resources are scarce due to war – Women and women's issues are often left out of peace settlements	– Few postwar reconstruction programs are aimed at addressing women's physical and emotional needs resulting from war – 80% of the world's refugees are women – Women are often left out of peace processes where important decisions about the future are made – Truth and reconciliation processes may not make a safe space for the private and sexual nature of the war crimes against women

can use Table 9.4 to conduct a gender analysis of peacebuilding roles. Some peacebuilding roles may be seen as more "appropriate" or "natural" for men or women depending on how different cultures view these roles.[9] Table 9.4 invites researchers to identify the gender gap between men's and women's experiences and opportunities in various peacebuilding roles.

Table 9.4 Examples of Gender-Based Roles in Peacebuilding

	Primarily Male Role	Equal or Shared Role	Primarily Female Role
Raising public awareness about human rights issues			
Providing relief aid to victims of violence			
Serving as peacekeepers by intervening between people or groups that are fighting			
Mediating or facilitating community dialogue on conflicts			
Teaching children about peace and how to handle conflicts without violence			

How gender roles affect women's capacity for peacebuilding. Determining the sources of women's capacity for peacebuilding relies on understanding the ideas of gender discussed earlier. Some women find it useful to draw on skills, assets, and capacities that are available to them in oppressive systems and harness these for productive use in peacebuilding. Women's capacities for peacebuilding are unique from men's in at least four ways.

1. *Socialized and equipped for peace.* Women are not "naturally" peaceful. Women have played a variety of roles throughout history that support war and other forms of violence, from warriors to supportive wives and mothers calling men to the battlefield. Women have the capacity for both violence and peace. Like men, women must be encouraged to use their gifts in building peace. Unlike many boys, many girls are socialized not to express anger toward others, as anger is not seen as "feminine" in many cultures. Many girls are encouraged to develop relationships and relational skills, as these skills are useful for taking care of children and family networks. Believing they are weaker than boys, girls also may develop nonviolent forms of problem solving. This socialization can provide girls and women with skill sets necessary for peacebuilding.

2. *Concerned about ending all forms of violence.* Because many women suffer from structural oppression and domestic violence, they are more likely to conceptualize peace as a way of life rather than an absence of warfare. In peace negotiations and political arenas, women more often include concerns for structural justice, human rights, and an end to domestic violence.[10]

3. *Linked to women's networks.* Women and men have different social networks in many societies. Some women may have unique levels of access to places such as the market or religious networks. Some women may

be uniquely able to mobilize their community to accept a peace settlement or to engage in dialogue through their extensive family and communal relationships.

4. *Mobilized around the ideology of womanhood.* While private and structural violence against women is condoned or ignored, public violence against or repression of women may be harder to justify because of the political need to appear respectful of women's family roles. Women's identities as daughters, wives, and mothers may bring women respect or freedom from repression. As primary caretakers of children, women may be seen as more legitimate conflict activists, since a mother's concern for her children in times of war may be seen as natural. Even in extremely repressive contexts where human rights activists routinely disappear and are tortured and killed, groups of mothers have been able to conduct public demonstrations in times when other groups were not allowed to do so.[11]

How Does This Lens Work?

Methodology

Interviews, focus groups, or community consultations or workshops using group discussion. Researchers may also use secondary sources in desk research and polling data. A variety of websites include reports on women and violence. These include the Women War and Peace site at www.womenwarpeace.org; the United Nations Development Fund for Women (UNIFEM)'s portal on women, peace, and conflict, www.peacewomen.org; and the Initiative for Inclusive Security's Women Waging Peace program site at www.womenwagingpeace.net. Each of these sites links to a range of specialized NGOs providing critical analysis and documentation of gender and conflict issues by country and theme.

Exercise

1. Discuss the connection between masculinity and violence.
   a. Are young boys in your community encouraged to act "tough"?
   b. Are males required to prove themselves using violence? Describe specific examples of boys using violence to earn the respect of being a man.
   c. What role do women play in encouraging men to be violent?
   d. Are there some men who have the reputation of being very masculine but also of being gentle, nonviolent, and working for peace?
   e. In the large group, brainstorm ways that women can affirm men and boys as masculine without needing to prove themselves

through violence. What are ways that women specifically can change the ways that men see themselves and their masculinity?

2. Using Table 9.3, identify the forms of violence women experience in the local context .

3. Using Table 9.4, discuss whether there is a division of peacebuilding roles according to gender. Are men discouraged from negotiating or participating in dialogue? Are women discouraged from being peacekeepers?

Output Summary

Identify strategies for addressing gender-based violence and gender-based roles in peacebuilding. What would gender-sensitive peacebuilding look like in this context?

Notes

1. Alejandro Portes, "Social Capital: Its Origins and Applications in Modern Sociology," *Annual Review of Sociology* 24 (August 1998): 1–24.

2. Frances Stewart, ed., *Horizontal Inequalities and Conflict: Understanding Group Violence in Multiethnic Societies* (New York: Palgrave MacMillan, 2008).

3. Adapted directly from Valerie Batts, "Is Reconciliation Possible? Lessons from Combating Modern Racism," in *Re-Centering Culture and Knowledge in Conflict Resolution* (Syracuse, NY: Syracuse University Press, 2008), 273–301.

4. Paulo Freire, *The Pedagogy of the Oppressed,* 30th ann. ed. (New York: Continuum, 2006).

5. Batts, "Is Reconciliation Possible?"

6. UNIFEM, "Gender and Conflict Analysis," UNIFEM policy briefing paper, New York, October 2006.

7. Sanam Naraghi Anderlini, "Mainstreaming Gender in Conflict Analysis," Social Development Papers 33, World Bank, Washington, DC, February 2006.

8. This section adapted from Lisa Schirch, *Women and Peacebuilding Training Manual* (Harrisonburg, VA: Eastern Mennonite University, 2003).

9. Lisa Schirch, "Frameworks for Understanding Women as Victims and Peacebuilders," in *Victimhood: Women and Post-Conflict Peacebuilding,* ed. Albrecht Schnabel and Anara Tabyshalieva (Tokyo: United Nations University Press, 2012), 48–76.

10. Sanam Naraghi Anderlini, *Women Building Peace: What They Do, Why It Matters* (Boulder, CO: Lynne Rienner Publishers, 2007).

11. Pam McAllistair, *This River of Courage: Generations of Women's Resistance and Action* (Philadelphia: New Society Publishers, 1991).

10

WHEN

Timelines, Triggers, Windows

This chapter explores the historical patterns or cycles of the conflict as well as potential future scenarios. A basic approach will answer the questions in questions in Table 4.1. An intermediate approach will also answer the summary questions outlined here from each of the three lenses in this chapter. A more advanced approach will use the suggested methodologies in each lens exercise to answer a longer set of related questions.

Basic conflict assessment questions

Are historical patterns or cycles of the conflict evident?

1. **Timeline and legacy:** Looking at history, what significant points in history do key stakeholders identify as traumatic or memorable in terms of shaping their identity and leading up to the current crisis? How do these key historic moments link together in a cultural narrative? Identify the key points in history where there are disparate memories in which one side's trauma may be the other side's glory. How can these memories create opportunities for transforming the current crisis and for acknowledgment and apology for past events?

2. **Conflict dynamics and early warning:** Looking at trends over time, what are the indicators that conflict is escalating or deescalating?

3. **Trends, triggers, scenarios, and windows:** Looking forward, what are potential triggers or windows of opportunity and vulnerability that can be forecasted based

	on past patterns? How can peacebuilding efforts prepare to maximize windows of opportunity and minimize threats posed by windows of vulnerability?
Basic self-assessment question	Do you have an ability to respond quickly to windows of vulnerability or opportunity?
Theory of change	If x times are conducive to violence or peace, what will influence these times?
Basic peace-building planning question	What is the best timing for your peacebuilding effort? Given historical patterns, identify possible windows of opportunity or triggers to watch.

When 1: Timeline and Legacy Lens

What Does This Lens Help Us See?

The timeline lens illustrates how different stakeholders understand significant points in history. The goal of using the timeline lens is not to develop a "correct" or "objective" history but to understand people's perceptions. People generally remember what has affected them, had an impact on their lives, or shaped their worldviews. People on opposing sides of the conflict emphasize different events, describe history with different narratives or stories, and attach contrasting emotions to events.

How Does This Lens Contribute to Planning Peacebuilding?

This lens helps key stakeholders better understand each other's perceptions of the historical origins of the conflict so that they can more likely empathize with each other and develop mutually satisfying solutions. The information collected in this process increases understanding of the stakeholder's perceptions of events throughout time, noting the moments in history that created a sense of trauma or glory for a group. This lens also helps groups discover what changes and adaptations stakeholders have made when influenced by adverse circumstances. Identifying these significant moments in history can help opponents understand more about the psychological impact of particular memories. Groups may more readily be able to understand and even apologize to each other once they understand the emotional impact of historic events.

Key Concepts

In a conflict-affected context, groups of people often have completely different experiences and perceptions of history; they see and understand events differently. Research on how different groups perceive history illustrates that different lived experiences shape the worldviews of groups interpreting history. Not all groups remember historic facts the same way. Some groups focus on chosen traumas where their group suffered and chosen glories where their group prevailed.[1]

Chosen trauma refers to groups remembering an event that made them feel helpless, victimized, and humiliated by another group.

Chosen glory refers to the shared memory of an event perceived as a positive element supporting the group's identity and self-esteem, possibly including a triumph over the enemy.

For example, Table 10.1 summarizes some of the disparaties in frequent responses to this exercise carried out with US Americans, Muslims in other countries, and non-Muslims in other countries regarding how they understand the events that led up to the September 11, 2001, attacks. While all

Table 10.1 Comparative Timeline

Dates	US Americans	Muslims in Other Countries	Non-Muslims in Other Countries
September 11, 2001	Unexpected tragedy on 9/11 (trauma)	Terrible tragedy, but not a surprise	Terrible tragedy, but not a surprise
1980s and 1990s		US policies supporting repressive regimes in oil-rich countries (trauma)	US policies supporting repressive governments in other resource-rich countries (trauma)
1970s	Oil crisis causing United States to become more involved in the Middle East (trauma)		
1950s and 1960s			
1940s	US support for creation of Israel (glory)	US support for creation of Israel (trauma)	
1000–1300		Christian crusades against Muslims	

groups see the attacks as a tragedy, they have contrasting understandings about what led up to them. Some groups identified events that happened a thousand years ago as influencing current dynamics.

How Does This Lens Work?

Methodology

Interviews, focus groups, or community consultations or workshops using group discussion. Researchers may also use secondary sources in desk research and polling data.

Exercise

Ideally a timeline is constructed in a large group made up of key stakeholders from different sides of the conflict. This process brings the most insight into symbolic meaning attached to events by different groups. This exercise itself can be a peacebuilding dialogue.

1. Divide the group according to the various "sides," key actors, or identity groups in a conflict.
2. Ask people in each small group to share the major events that have shaped how they see the conflict today. They can start as far back in history as they want to begin telling their story of what has happened. Each group should write a brief three- to five-word summary of each significant historical event, moment of glory, or moment of trauma on a separate sheet of paper.
3. Ask them to write a "G" for "glory" or a "T" for "trauma" in the corner of the paper for each event with a symbolic significance.
4. The facilitator will lay down a line of rope or tape on the floor to mark the line of history along with sheets of paper to mark dates along the timeline. Each side of the conflict will lay down the history in chronological order along the rope line. The historical dates need to be marked so that each group's chronology matches up along the line.
5. When each group is finished laying out their key historic dates, ask everyone to silently walk along the line and read each side's understanding of history. Note how each side remembers different events and has a different interpretation of events as traumatic or as a glory.
6. After everyone finishes silently observing the timeline, reconfigure small groups made up of different identity groups. Ask them to share with each other what they noticed in terms of commonly perceived events versus differences in perceptions. Allow space for people to ask questions of each other about their different perceptions.

Output Summary

Identify the key points in history where there are disparate memories in which one side's trauma may be the other side's glory. How can these memories create opportunities for transforming the current crisis by memorializing, acknowledging, or apologizing for past events?

When 2: Conflict Dynamics and Early Warning

What Does This Lens Help Us See?

This lens helps to identify social and communication patterns that indicate if conflict is escalating or de-escalating. It shows the particular dynamics between people and relates these to common patterns showing that a conflict is escalating. This lens prompts discussion about how people are relating to each other and correlates these with social patterns that often indicate conflict escalation.

How Does This Lens Contribute to Planning Peacebuilding?

Peacebuilding efforts can respond to conflict dynamics, whether conflict is increasing or decreasing. For example, early warning that conflict is increasing can indicate the need for preventive diplomacy. Evidence that conflict is decreasing can indicate the ripeness for negotiation or acts of reconciliation.

Key Concepts

Like the timeline lens, this lens creates an illustrated history of the progression of conflict over time. Many conflicts, even large wars, begin between individual people arguing over a particular issue, such as land, office space, or a goat in the marketplace. As conflict escalates, each person identifies other conflict issues, and the number of problems increases. People often start to see each other as the problem. They may seek a third person's advice on handling the conflict or try to get other people on their side to support them. Each person may choose to punish their opponent in a cycle of vengeance in the pattern of an eye for an eye or "two lives for one life." In the worst cases, whole communities or organizations divide and polarize as each person is forced to take sides in the conflict. Communication decreases and tensions increase as the dynamics evolve.[2]

Conflicts can progress over time like a mountain range, with periods of escalation and de-escalation. In early stages, people often know that conflict is brewing and can be early warners of violence. In order to provide effective early warning about conflict, people need ways of informing others and of organizing themselves in order to respond to conflict before it erupts violently. Figure 10.1 illustrates a common pattern related to conflict escalation.

As conflicts involve more people and issues, the conflict climbs up the mountain or camel's back. The height of the crisis is the top of the arrow. Conflicts eventually transform over time, most often through negotiation or some solution in which both sides achieve some of their goals. Military victory only ends a small percentage of wars.[3] Many peace agreements also fall apart if original grievances remain. Conflicts often escalate and de-escalate many times, resembling a mountain range. Crises and violent conflict can recur many times before there is sustainable peace and stability results.

How Does This Lens Work?

Methodology

Interviews, focus groups, or community consultations or workshops. Researchers may also use secondary sources in desk research.

Exercise

Choose one of the following exercises according to what is most likely to feel comfortable depending on the participant's culture.

1. Ask participants to describe the evolution of the conflict and make a written record.

Figure 10.1 Conflict Dynamics

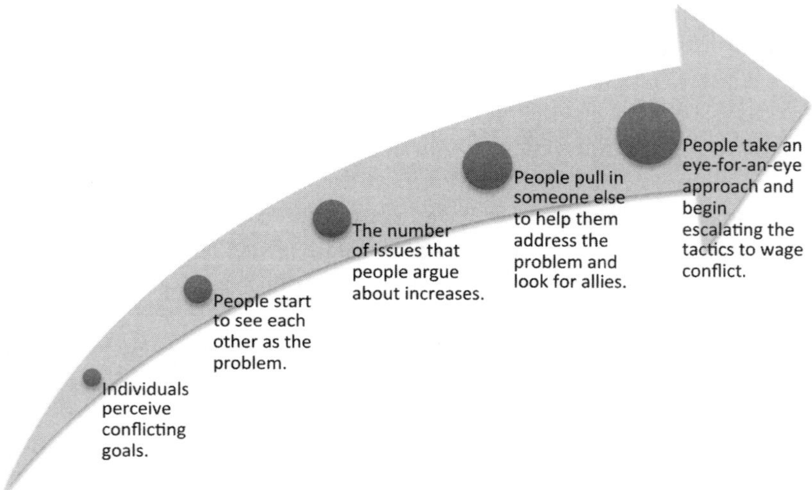

2. Referring to Table 5.1 (see page 91), what are early warning indicators of potential violence or increasing social cohesion and peace? Ask participants to draw the escalation of the conflict in a curve or diagram such as in Figure 10.1. Ask them to identify on the diagram what events and indicators were evident in the escalation or de-escalation of the conflict. The diagram can be a line upward, as in the previous illustration, or it can look more like a mountain range or graph—with ups and downs, and plateaus when conflict is steady.

3. Ask participants to act out the escalation of the conflict in a dramatic way, telling the story through drama methods such as playback theater, in which group members tell a story and either watch or participate in a drama reenacting their story.[4]

Output Summary

Given your self-assessment, are you best situated to work at early or more advanced stages of conflict?

When 3: Trends, Triggers, Scenarios, and Windows

What Does This Lens Help Us See?

This lens draws attention to possible trends, triggers, scenarios, or windows of time that can threaten or create opportunities for vastly increasing the impact of peacebuilding efforts.

How Does This Lens Contribute to Planning Peacebuilding?

Peacebuilding organizations often plan their activities months or years ahead of time with little regard for the political, economic, cultural, or religious calendar year. A surprising event can interrupt a well-planned peace effort. A more informal, unplanned, spontaneous peacebuilding effort can have a much greater impact by virtue of its timing. Forecasting potential risks, tensions, and obstacles arising during a peacebuilding effort is an important step in recognizing that good intentions can lead to counterproductive and harmful impacts. Peacebuilding requires risk-taking. Reducing those risks and finding ways of anticipating possible negative side-effects or second-order impacts is a responsibility of those planning peacebuilding efforts.

Key Concepts

A **trigger** is either a *predictable event* with significance—such as an election, a public census, or an anniversary of a significant event—or a *random event,* such as an assassination, earthquake, corruption scandal, or a final straw such as the 100th person to die from crime in a community. A trigger sets off a chain of reactions leading to larger implications such as violence, political turmoil, civil war, riots, and so on.

Windows of vulnerability are specific times, events, places, or situations that provide an opportunity for groups seeking power to use violence in their efforts to change political or economic structures. For example, passage of a land reform act, an election, return of refugees, a massacre, or a media exposé on a major corruption scandal may all be windows of vulnerability where a system may or may not have the resilience to manage conflict resulting from the event. Sometimes windows of vulnerability allow key stakeholders to magnify underlying core grievances and mobilize public opinion in their favor. If an election or negotiation excludes some stakeholders, or if an election is widely condemned as unfair, the announcement of the results could be a window of vulnerability—a vulnerable moment when violence might easily spark.

Windows of opportunity are specific times, events, places, or situations when there may be more openness to fostering peace; creating new, more inclusive structures through negotiation; and depolarizing relationships between groups by addressing core grievances. Windows of opportunity often bring diverse groups together and foster a sense of unity. For example, a natural disaster or widespread failure of an economic sector such as agriculture or tourism can so devastate a country that all the survivors work together for the common good, regardless of identity.

Windows of uncertainty are specific times, events, places, or situations that may be opportunities for either addressing or magnifying core grievances and structural forms of exclusion.

Forecasting involves identifying trends, potential triggers, and future best- and worst-case scenarios that may impact whether a conflict will escalate or de-escalate. A wide variety of different forecasting datasets pull information together.[5] Matthew Levinger identifies many of these in his book on conflict analysis.[6] Table 5.1 lists a range of indicators of potential escalation of conflict that is useful for identifying future trends. Based on a range of potential events identified through forecasting, researchers can develop possible future scenarios, including the most likely or the most dangerous.

How Does This Lens Work?

Methodology

Interviews, focus groups, or community consultations or workshops using group discussion. Researchers may also use secondary sources in desk research and polling data.

Exercise

1. Looking at the past timeline of the conflict, identify possible political, cultural, religious, or economic events in the coming year that may provide times that would be ripe for a peace effort, or that could possibly lead to violence. Identify particular future triggers or windows, including holidays, sports events, religious rites, or political events like elections that are associated with driving or mitigating conflict. What are future windows of vulnerability or uncertainty?

2. What are predictions or forecasts of future scenarios? If researching with a group, ask the group to role-play possible future scenarios for what might happen.

Output Summary

Identify how peacebuilding efforts can prepare to maximize windows of opportunity and minimize threats posed by windows of vulnerability given a range of possible forecasts and future scenarios.

Notes

1. See Vamik D. Volcan, *The Need for Enemies and Allies: From Clinical Practice to International Relationships* (Northvale, NJ: Jason Aronson Publishers, 1988).

2. Adapted from John Paul Lederach, "Understanding Conflict: Experience, Structure, and Dynamics" in *Conflict Transformation and Restorative Justice Manual: Foundations and Skills for Mediation and Facilitation*, Fifth Edition. Editors: Michelle E. Armster and Lorraine Stutzman Amstuts. Acron, PA: Office on Justice and Peacebuilding, 2008, pp. 47–49.

3. Virginia Page Fortna, *Peace Time: Cease-Fire Agreements and the Durability of Peace* (Princeton, NJ: Princeton University Press, 2004).

4. See the Playback Theatre website, http://www.playbacktheatre.org/.

5. For example, see the University of Texas at Dallas website on political forecasting, http://yule.utdallas.edu/index.html or http://www.forecastingprinciples.com/.

6. Matthew Levinger, *The Practical Guide to Conflict Analysis: Understanding Causes, Unlocking Solutions,* United States Institute of Peace Academy Guides (Washington, DC: US Institute of Peace, 2013).

11

Theories of Change for Peacebuilding

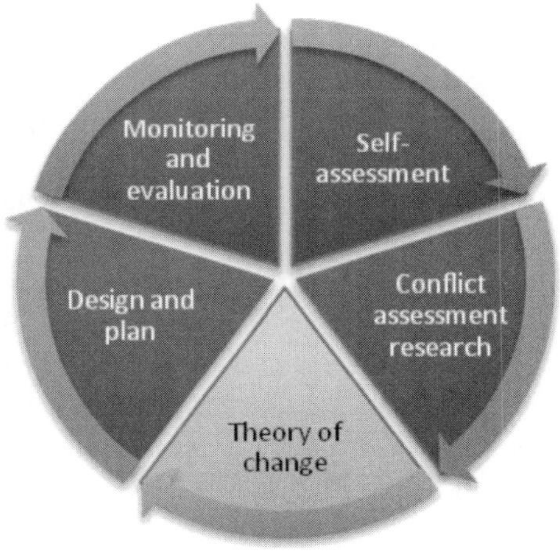

Graphic 11.1

A theory of change or a program rationale is a statement about how a program hopes to foster change to produce intended outcomes and impacts. Theories of change can be either implicit or explicit assumptions about how peacebuilding efforts will affect a conflict-affected context.

Peacebuilding's effectiveness and sustainability relate directly to whether the underlying assumptions informing the design of the peacebuilding effort are accurate. Too often, planners jump from a conflict assessment to planning without first articulating how what they learned in the assessment fits into a hypothesis of what they will do to try to change the system. When urged to articulate the theory of how change will happen within their program, too many groups are unable to state a theory or to show any evidence that the theory might work or explain why a program might address a key conflict driver or mitigator. Without some evidence and logic, peacebuilding efforts rely on unsubstantiated hopes and assumptions.

Untested and unstated assumptions create a gap between intent and impact. Groups intend to contribute toward peace and stability. But at least sometimes, their efforts either have no impact or a counterproductive impact.

For example, in Kosovo many international donors based their programming on the assumption that improving relations between ethnic groups through dialogue and exchanges between students and women's groups would lead to peace. But research found that programs to foster more responsible leadership *within* different ethnic groups produced better outcomes than bicommunal programs.[1]

In Somalia, the international community bases its programming on an assumption that isolating Al Shabaab is the most effective way of undermining their local support. Research suggests that this theory of change through isolation has little empirical grounding and is based on unfounded assumptions.[2] Instead, a strategy of engaging Al Shabaab seems to offer a theory of change that grows out of robust conflict assessment of the local capacities for peace and conflict drivers.[3]

People hold different theories of what causes violence and how change happens, particularly if they are schooled in different fields. Interfield collaboration is difficult when people do not share a common language for understanding conflict.

Change rarely happens in a cause-and-effect pattern with a theory such as "Unemployment causes youth violence." Rather, conflict is more like a system in which various factors and actors interrelate with each other. Ideally, integrated programs grow out of multiple theories of change recognizing the complex and dynamic system of actors, levels, and interacting causes and effects.

Strategic peacebuilding creates a multistakeholder and multisector synergy by beginning with explicit research and assessment processes, as well as an explicit theory of change to lay out a policy or program rationale. It requires an explicit self-assessment of what any actor is and is not able to contribute to peacebuilding. All stakeholders should make transparent and evidence-based decisions about their theories of change that will shape their peacebuilding planning.

Theory of Change Formula

Theories of change have two parts. First is a theory about what factors are driving or mitigating conflict. Second is a theory about what can be done about conflict. A theory of change is about how some driving or mitigating factor of the context (factor) can be changed with some peacebuilding action (action) to achieve an impact that prevents violence or builds peace.

> If these **factors** are driving or mitigating violence, then these **actions** will achieve these **impacts** to reduce violence, foster perceptions of justice, or strengthen peaceful relations between groups.

A theory of change contains each of these three components: factors, actions, and impacts. The following case study provides an example.

Factors (conflict assessment). An Iraqi NGO assessed the local context and found the lack of representative local decision-making bodies, interethnic tensions, and economic deprivation were all important factors driving communities toward violence.

Actions (type of peacebuilding effort). To address these three interrelated drivers of conflict, the organization created an integrated program to set up local community development councils made up of male and female representatives from different ethnic groups to foster local governance, and also incentivized interethnic cooperation through offering microcredit loans to multiethnic business proposals intended to foster economic development.

Impacts (peacebuilding effects). The NGO found that the communities where they worked were less susceptible to insurgent recruitment, experienced less violence, and developed sustainable programs that fostered viable economic systems.

Most theories of change are in fact hypotheses or guesses that need testing to become legitimate theories. Only through monitoring and evaluation can groups gather evidence that the action achieves an impact on the factor.

Some theories focus on *who* needs to change, such as a specific individual or group that is driving a violent conflict or key people who could play a positive peacebuilding role. Peacebuilding would influence these key actors, for example, by drawing them into a political process, removing their sources of power, addressing their grievances, or mediating between conflict groups to address their grievances.

Other theories focus on *what* needs to change in the context, such as a specific policy or institution, or a force like corruption or night raids.[4] For example, if a shortage of water is driving interethnic conflict (factor), then creating an interethnic water management board (action) will help build peace in this region by helping communities communicate peacefully about how to manage water (impact).

Or, if government corruption is driving inequality and division among classes (factor), then building a community's capacities for monitoring and addressing corruption (action) can help build peace in this region by reducing corruption and empowering communities to participate in governance (impact).

These theory of change statements create testable hypotheses for monitoring and evaluating peacebuilding efforts. Identifying a theory of change makes it possible to more usefully assess whether a conflict assessment is accurate, valid, and reliable. Some theories of change fail because a conflict assessment failed to identify key drivers or mitigators of conflict. An organization that wrongly identifies unemployment as a key driver of conflict may design programs that succeed in increasing employment but fail to impact levels of violence. If an organization identifies that women are playing a key role in mitigating conflict, but wrongly theorizes that these women need more training to expand their peacebuilding impact, the theory of change may fail because it has not identified a peacebuilding effort to match the conflict assessment factors.

Results Chains Linking Micro and Macro Peacebuilding Efforts

A theory of change is also sometimes referred to as a "results chain," whereby the peacebuilding action creates a desired result. A "results chain" looks at sequencing programs according to some logical progression.

In Nepal, for example, a peacebuilding project aimed to address structural inequalities (factor) by building the capacity of poor, vulnerable, and socially excluded groups of women and youth (action) so that they could contribute to a local peacebuilding process (impact). The project was successful in building the capacity of these women, who became active in collective advocacy and peacebuilding related to their interests. However, the outcome of the project has not yet led to equality for these women. In other words, the lack of capacity of these groups was only one factor; other factors continue to discriminate against poor women and youth. Capacity building may have been the best starting point. But other peacebuilding efforts were needed to address the factors leading to inequality.[5] It may have been helpful to further analyze what was driving the structural inequalities to develop ideas about how to address these inequalities.

Popular peacebuilding programs such as people-to-people exchanges and interethnic dialogue may play important roles in peacebuilding because they contribute to a results chain that leads to structural changes in the root causes of violence. But these types of programs are also critiqued for not leading to structural change.[6] For example, many dialogues and people-to-people exchanges occur between Israelis and Palestinians. These programs may be an important part of a results chain. But these programs have not been enough to lead to a sustainable peace agreement in the region. A lack of relationships between Israelis and Palestinians is not the only problem holding back efforts to build a peace agreement. Clearly the region needs other types of peacebuilding initiatives as well to address factors driving the conflict.

A dialogue program may be popular simply because there is a snowball effect for people looking for alternatives to violence who know only a little about peacebuilding. Strategic design of a peacebuilding program requires knowing when a dialogue program is the best option or an important step along a sequencing of programs to achieve a results chain and when limited funds should be put into addressing other drivers and mitigators of conflict.

Examples of Theories of Change

There are many hypotheses or theories of change. New articles and books constantly update people's ideas about what drives and mitigates conflict and what can be done to prevent violence and foster peace. This chapter describes a wide range of theories of change related to peacebuilding in the following section. Some of these theories are backed up with extensive qualitative and quantitative data gathered in comparative case studies. For example, we know from several scholars that a comprehensive peace process involving both spoilers and unarmed actors in civil society such as religious leaders makes a peace agreement more likely to succeed.[7] Other theories are less certain. Many people cite democracy as contributing to security, but research on the relationship between democracy and peace illustrates a more complicated relationship.[8]

Given the growth of peacebuilding activities around the world, there is hardly a place where someone has not tried to address some factor driving conflict or mitigating peace. Before planning a new peacebuilding effort, a conflict assessment process should identify whether the assumptions in other groups' theories of change related to a previous peacebuilding effort were accurate.

The theories of change shown in Table 11.1 fall under the five categories of human security: Politically stable democracy, sustainable economy, safe and secure environment, justice and rule of law, and social and cultural

Table 11.1 Sample Theories of Change

Politically Stable Democracy	Sustainable Economy	Safe and Secure Environment	Justice and Rule of Law	Social and Cultural Well-Being
Predictable and participatory decision making and governance with effective governmental and nongovernmental institutions.	*Access to basic resources and conducive to socially responsible trade and business*	*Personal safety and freedom of movement*	*Perceived equity in social relations and justice system*	*Respect and dignity between people of different cultures and identities*

Political Theories

Actors/Fields	Theories of Conflict and Violence	Theories of Change and Approaches to Peacebuilding
Negotiation, Mediation, Peace Process	Armed groups have grievances that drive their desire to fight.	Negotiation, mediation, and comprehensive peace processes can structure a series of official Track 1 diplomatic forums and unofficial or multitrack initiatives to develop mutually satisfying agreements to bring an end to war.
Governance and Institutional Performance	Regions that lack institutions to provide participatory decision-making processes to address human needs and issues are more prone to conflict. States whose institutions perform at low levels cannot endure challenges to their authority during a natural disaster, war, or insurgency.	Improve institutional performance, equity, and participatory processes for the state and other governance institutions to increase the quantity and quality of public services and public legitimacy, and improve state-society relations.
Democracy	People without an opportunity to affect decisions that impact their lives may feel frustrated and disempowered. Violence becomes a tempting option without other channels of political expression.	Foster participatory democracy and active citizenship, and include all relevant stakeholders when making public policy.
Leadership	Ineffective leadership results in political problems escalating toward violence.	Leadership training, including skills in principled negotiation and mediation, enables more effective leaders better able to solve problems through diplomacy.

(continues)

Table 11.1 Cont.

Actors/Fields	Theories of Conflict and Violence	Theories of Change and Approaches to Peacebuilding
Political Elite	Political elites use their power to further their own interests through violence and repression.	International pressure, boycotts, and media campaigns to reduce benefits and increase the costs of elites pursuing their interests through violence.
Advocacy and Activism	Structural violence fosters power imbalances that restrict the ability of some groups to address their issues and meet their needs.	Citizen resistance and social movements employ nonviolent forms of power by raising public awareness and using tactics that highlight a group's political, economic, social, and "people" power through media reports, demonstrations, and other campaigns.
	Economic Theories	
Actors/Fields	**Theories of Conflict and Violence**	**Theories of Change and Approaches to Peacebuilding**
Economic Development	Violence occurs when societies do not have adequate political, economic, and social capacities to address people's basic needs.	Create the political, economic, and social capacity within communities to meet their own needs.
Economic Inequality	Violence can occur when economic disparities are great, as this can lead to a sense of humiliation, frustration, and expectation among those who have less.	Political reforms to address structural constraints that reinforce economic inequalities, targeted economic development, and leveling access to education between groups to foster equality of access.
Resources for War	War requires weapons, money, and other resources.	Arms embargoes, public boycotts, interrupting supply lines, and advocacy for cutting military budgets for repressive governments can increase the costs for using violence and increase the incentives for peace.
Humanitarian Aid	States may not be able to respond to humanitarian crises in the midst of natural disasters or war. Without assistance, people may look to armed groups to help meet their needs.	Alleviate suffering and provide an alternative to people who may otherwise support armed groups.

(continues)

Table 11.1 Cont.

Actors/Fields	Theories of Conflict and Violence	Theories of Change and Approaches to Peacebuilding
	Justice and Rule-of-Law Theories	
Legal and Judicial Systems	Lack of order and social control creates an environment in which violence increases.	Support laws and judicial institutions that enforce laws.
Restorative and Transitional Justice	Crime and violence happen in a social context. Crime and violence create needs for victims and obligations for offenders.	Provide restorative and transitional justice forums for identifying victims' needs, reparations, truth commissions, traditional rituals, and institutional reforms for holding offenders accountable to victims and the community.
International Humanitarian Law	Lack of order and social control creates an environment where war atrocities occur.	Establish and protect international humanitarian law and institutions such as the International Criminal Court.
	Security	
Peacekeeping	The cycle of violence makes it difficult to have the space for negotiation.	Cease-fires, peacekeeping forces, and peace zones reduce the amount of direct violence and create a space where political negotiations can take place.
Security Sector Reform	Traditional military approaches to solving problems often end in increased levels of violence.	Ensure military focus is in protecting "human security" and a positive relationship between citizens and security forces.
Disarmament, Demobilization, Reintegration (DDR)	Armed groups may continue fighting for the economic, security, political, and identity benefits that war brings to them.	DDR creates economic, political, security, and identity incentives to increase the benefits of disarming and demobilzing. Reintegration allows armed groups to reconcile with their communities and address trauma, land claims, and other issues following war.

(continues)

Table 11.1 Cont.

Actors/Fields	Theories of Conflict and Violence	Theories of Change and Approaches to Peacebuilding
Sociocultural and Psychological Theories		
Cultural and Identity-Based Conflicts	People identify themselves according to many cultural groups, such as their religion, ethnicity, sex/gender, or nation. Discrimination by some groups against others is common. People may fight and die to protect their dignity and identity.	Intergroup dialogue, prejudice reduction, training on tolerance and coexistence, people-to-people exchanges, confidence-building measures, and citizen diplomacy foster better understanding and improve intergroup relations.
Psychology/Trauma Healing	Violence creates deep physical, emotional, and spiritual wounds. Many perpetrators of violence were once victims.	Psychosocial trauma healing, involving both individual and group therapy and training, can enable individual and group transformation, so that people stop pursuing revenge and the cycle of violence.
Education, Media	Violence occurs because people are not aware of or do not believe there are other options for addressing conflict.	Educational and training programs in schools, mass media campaigns and edutainment shows, and public symbolic events build capacity and support to communicate, advocate, negotiate, and engage in creative problem-solving and efforts to pursue their interests.
Public Opinion	Cultural and social forces mobilize public attitudes toward violence.	Use the mass media, and empower religious, political, and public figures to denounce violence and thus hope to impact public attitudes toward violence.

well-being. Table 11.1 provides sample theories of change from different fields. This list is not complete but is intended to help identify many of the well-known theories. Some of the theories have been tested and proven. Others are untested assumptions about the way change happens. Ideally, policy and practice is evidence-driven. But in reality, little correlation exists between the most popular, well-funded approaches to peacebuilding, like people-to-people exchanges, and other theories of change. Efforts to achieve peace are often driven by untested assumptions, convenience, or some other motive, such as political expedience or profit. Efforts to achieve successful, sustainable, and strategic peacebuilding require careful articulation of theories of change and evidence supporting these theories.

Developing Theories of Change

Most organizations are not familiar with thinking about theories. Building awareness of the basic assumptions underlying programming requires explicit attention. The following are some practical ideas on how to start developing lists and ideas about theories of change.[9]

Listen carefully to local proverbs, metaphors, and what local people say related to the conflict. Do these sayings hold within them a theory about how things work? For example, in Afghanistan, a Pashto poet said, "War is like a female fly, laying a thousand eggs a day." A related theory is that conflict regenerates itself daily, making new grievances. Change requires stopping the fly from laying eggs, or stopping the violence to prevent creation of new grievances.

Task someone in the organization to interview staff members about their theories of change. Ask them to think about how they would explain their work to their grandmother or someone who does not know about peacebuilding. What is the basic gist of what they think they are doing in their work? Compile these interviews into a list of the theories of change within your organization. Then hold a group discussion about similarities and differences.

Ask staff to add a "theory of change" section to their weekly, monthly, or trip reports. Encourage regular reflection about how new information, conversations with other organizations and local people influence their ideas and assumptions about theories of change.

Take a training or use online worksheets to help capture and develop your theories of change. The Aspen Institute's Theory of Change Community offers a website called Theory of Change Online (http://www.theoryofchange.org/toco-software/).

Compare Theories of Change in a Conflict-Affected Region

How does your assessment of what is driving and mitigating the conflict compare to other groups working in the region? How do your theories of change compare to theirs? Did you identify the same key **factors**? Are you planning similar **actions** to address these factors? Do you hope to have the same **impacts**? How are your theories of change different from other peacebuilding efforts?

Visit the website accompanying this book at www.conflict-assessment-and-peacebuilding-planning.org to learn more or share your own ideas on Theories of Change.

Notes

1. Organisation for Economic Co-operation and Development (OECD), "Guidance on Evaluating Conflict Prevention and Peacebuilding Activities," Working Draft for Application Period, 2008, 35.
2. John Paul Lederach, "Addressing Terrorism: A Theory of Change Approach," in *Somalia: Creating Space for Fresh Approaches to Peacebuilding,* ed. John Paul Lederach et al. (Kalmar, Sweden: Life and Peace Institute, 2012), 7–19.
3. Ibid.
4. OECD, "Guidance on Evaluating Conflict Prevention," 78.
5. Care International UK, *Peacebuilding with Impact: Defining Theories of Change* (London: Care International UK, 2012), 7.
6. Mohammed Abu-Nimer, *Dialogue, Conflict Resolution, and Change: Arab-Jewish Encounters in Israel* (Albany: SUNY Press, 1999).
7. Catherine Barnes, *Owning the Process: Public Participation in Peacemaking: South Africa, Guatemala and Mali* (London: Conciliation Resources, 2002).
8. Howard Wolpe and Steve McDonald, "Democracy and Peace-Building: Re-Thinking the Conventional Wisdom," *Round Table* 97, no. 394 (February 2008): 137–45.
9. John Paul Lederach, Reina Neufeldt, and Hal Culbertson, *Reflective Peacebuilding: A Planning, Monitoring, and Learning Toolkit* (South Bend, IN: University of Notre Dame, 2007), 6.

12

Peacebuilding Planning Guidance

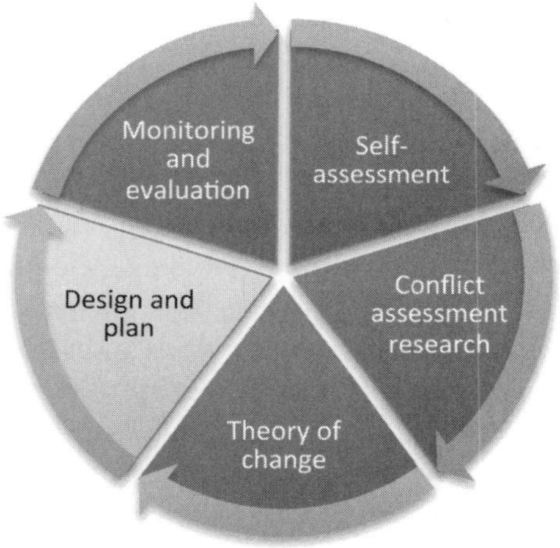

Graphic 12.1

This section of the handbook describes key considerations and conceptual models for designing and planning peacebuilding efforts. The self-assessment, conflict assessment lenses, and theories of change feed directly into these design questions. Planning is a process. Plans may change. But the quality of the process affects the implementation and effectiveness of the peacebuilding effort. The conflict assessment approach in this handbook helps practitioners answer these questions through an assessment process.

Principles of Strategic, Systemic Peacebuilding

Strategic peacebuilding requires long-term actions at all levels, from local to global, by multiple actors coordinating an approach that is led locally and based on explicit decision making informed by a systems approach. A systems approach sees violence as a result of a complex web of people and factors taking place in a complex local, cultural, and historical context. Peacebuilding requires acting in recognition of this complex system.

Peacebuilding aims to add up to national- and regional-level peace and human security at the macro-level peace, system level peace, or "Peace Writ Large."[1] But just as individual development efforts may have an impact at the community level in a country still plagued with poverty, peacebuilding efforts may still prevent or reduce violence locally without succeeding in stopping a war from happening at the national level. Local-level peacebuilding efforts are important, but maximizing the likelihood of peacebuilding efforts leading to national- and regional-level peace requires a strategic approach.

Peacebuilding is strategic when it coordinates the following[2]:

- Planning is deliberate and coordinated, based on conflict assessments.
- Planning includes a "whole of society" approach involving stakeholders from all levels of an institution, community, or society.
- Planning links short-term and long-term focus on systemic change.
- Planning links different kinds and sectors of peacebuilding including economic development, human rights advocacy, and participatory governance programs, all sensitive to reducing divisions and fostering peaceful and just relations between groups. Ideally, planning includes a balance between stopping conflict drivers and starting or supporting conflict mitigators. What beliefs, attitudes, or behaviors at the individual, relational, cultural, and structural levels *need to stop*? What beliefs, attitudes, or behaviors at the individual, relational, cultural, and structural levels *need to start*?[3]

New efforts to identify peacebuilding best practices closely align with key principles in humanitarian and development assistance. The Busan High-Level Forum on Aid Effectiveness, the New Deal for Engagement in Fragile States, the International Dialogue on Peacebuilding and Statebuilding (IDPS), the SPHERE project, the Humanitarian Action Program (HAP), and significant reports such as the World Bank 2011 *World Development Report on Conflict, Security, and Development* all reinforce many of the same principles identified in the accompanying box.

Conflict-Sensitive Peacebuilding Design

Peacebuilding efforts can unintentionally do harm. Too often, outsiders impose peacebuilding efforts on insiders without local consent and

Key Principles of Peacebuilding Design

Based on research—Uses evidence from conflict assessment and self-assessment.

Inclusive—Includes local people on all sides of the conflict.

Local ownership and leadership—Recognizes the self-determination and capacities of local people to identify, lead, and participate in peacebuilding.

Participatory—Involves stakeholders in decision making in the designing of conflict assessment approaches and peacebuilding design, monitoring, and evaluation.

Transparent—Shares information about goals, activities, selection processes, funding, and outcomes of any peacebuilding effort.

Equity—Ensures that the peacebuilding effort contributes to a culture of treating people fairly and does not reinforce social divisions.

Accountable—Responsible for negative impacts on local people and the local context such as elite control, co-optation, or diversion of funds for their own gain.

Do no harm—Invests effort to prevent negative impacts on local people and the local context.

Support human security—Prioritizes the goal that local people view the peacebuilding effort as increasing their human security.

participation. A conflict-sensitive approach to peacebuilding design examines whether there is an inclusive and transparent process for designing the peacebuilding effort, involving local leadership if not input into decision making at every possible step, from design of the effort to who is involved to where and when it takes place. Conflict-sensitive peacebuilding asks, How will this peacebuilding effort exhibit caution in every step so that it does not inadvertently increase tensions or reaffirm existing power structures and divisions between groups?

A conflict-sensitive design of a peacebuilding effort continually addresses the following questions:

1. Where will the peacebuilding effort take place? Will those who live farther away resent the geographical location of the effort? Will there be a local office for the effort? Will the location of this office favor one side of the conflict? How will local people perceive the location of and standard of living at the office in relation to the standard of living of local people?

2. Where will resources for the peacebuilding effort come from? Will funds be used to buy local goods and services? How will decisions be made about which local vendors are used? Will they come from all sides of the conflict?

3. Who will benefit from the peacebuilding effort? Will those left out of the effort resent those who benefit or those who helped them? Is there a way of structuring the effort so that neighboring communities can also benefit at some point?

4. **Who will staff the peacebuilding effort?** Do they represent people from all sides of the conflict? Will those not represented resent those who are? Will all staff be evacuated if violence should take place? If not, how will security decisions be made and prepared for ahead of time?

5. **Why will local people participate?** Is there a financial incentive for participating? Will they volunteer? Could use of a financial incentive have a negative impact on community volunteerism?

6. **What will the peacebuilding effort do?** How might the effort be negatively impacted by the conflict-affected context? How might the context be negatively affected by the peacebuilding effort?

7. **How will resources be brought into the local context to support the peacebuilding effort?** What positive and negative impacts will these financial, material, or human resources have on the local context?

8. **When will the peacebuilding effort take place**? Will some people be left out because of the time of day or year when it will happen?

Moving from Micro to Macro Change

Strategic peacebuilding addresses the question of scale. Ideally, efforts build on each other to progress toward macro changes. Designing peacebuilding so that it impacts macro-level change requires considering how to link micro peacebuilding efforts to macro changes to the system. A variety of strategies involve scaling up peacebuilding from micro to macro approaches.

Reaching More People with Geographic and Demographic Replication

One way to increase the impact of peacebuilding is to replicate a program across geographic (territory) or demographic (population) planes. Replication or adaptation at a large scale can help move a small peacebuilding effort to one that impacts macro-level change in a system.

For example, including peace education curriculum in one school district is a positive outcome. But peace education programs are unlikely to have a macro effect on a country unless they are replicated in every district, at every grade level, in every year of school to reinforce learning among youth about the skills and processes needed to address conflict constructively, without violence. But replication can have problems if there is great diversity in the local context.

In Afghanistan, for example, districts and provinces are very different in terms of their cultures, their decision-making processes, their geography, their level of security, and so on. A program to reduce violence by generating local employment that works in one place in Afghanistan may fail in another place.

Program replication is often thought of as cost-effective in that it saves money on assessment or program design. But in a diverse country, a program that works in one area may not work at all in another region. Replication thus may not be saving money in the end, nor may it be the most effective way to scale up peacebuilding.

Reaching More People Using the Media

The mass media is also an important strategy for scaling up peacebuilding efforts to reach more people.[4] Mediation and negotiation processes usually involve only one or two dozen key people at most. Peacebuilding training programs can reach dozens or hundreds of people, and peace education programs in schools can reach thousands of youth. A radio program on negotiation can reach thousands of people and at least help them understand the process going on behind closed doors in highly sensitive diplomacy. And an edutainment TV show that teaches about peaceful conflict management can reach hundreds of thousands of people.

For example, in Macedonia, few people participated in peacebuilding dialogues between ethnic groups. However, most people in Macedonia have watched *Nashe Maalo*, a television program that intentionally fostered interethnic understanding and tolerance. *Nashe Maalo* was able to reach far more people than any other peacebuilding effort.[5]

Linking Vertical and Horizontal Peacebuilding Social Capital

Strategic peacebuilding efforts coordinate different peacebuilding actors and build social capital to improve the quality and quantity of relationships between them. Peacebuilding efforts often start at the kitchen table with a small number of stakeholders. But ultimately, peacebuilding works best when those attempting to foster peace communicate with each other to harmonize their work. Too often, peacebuilding efforts are like discordant notes creating chaos. Mechanisms and an infrastructure of communication channels can maximize and synchronize conflict assessment processes, as well as the design, monitoring, and evaluation of how individual efforts add up to systemic change.

The conflict assessment lens on peacebuilding actors asked who can foster "vertical capacity" between the grassroots, middle, or top levels of society in addition to horizontal social capital across these levels. Are there people at the mid-level who could help build a bridge between the top- and community-level leaders by creating forums and meetings between them?

Strategic peacebuilding connects efforts to influence more people and key people. The Reflecting on Peace Practice research project found that approaches concentrating on including more people, but not linking to key leaders or groups, do not add up to effective peacebuilding. *Key people approaches* involve certain important leaders, or groups of people, who are seen as able to bring about change in a situation. *More people approaches* aim to engage large numbers of people in processes to address an issue. Broad involvement of the public is seen as necessary to change. Conversely, the research found that strategies focusing on key people without thinking through how this connects with critical masses of people were also ineffective.[6] In other words, peacebuilding strategies to foster vertical social capital are important (see Figure 12.1).

In countries like South Africa that have experienced massive social change, thousands of small-scale efforts aimed at individual change happened simultaneously with coordinated large-scale international media efforts linking those supporting change from inside and outside the country. These strategies aimed to achieve a critical mass of people seeking change in the country as well as reaching key people at the national and international levels. The fall of apartheid and the rise of democracy in South Africa were not the result of one or two peacebuilding efforts. It took hundreds and

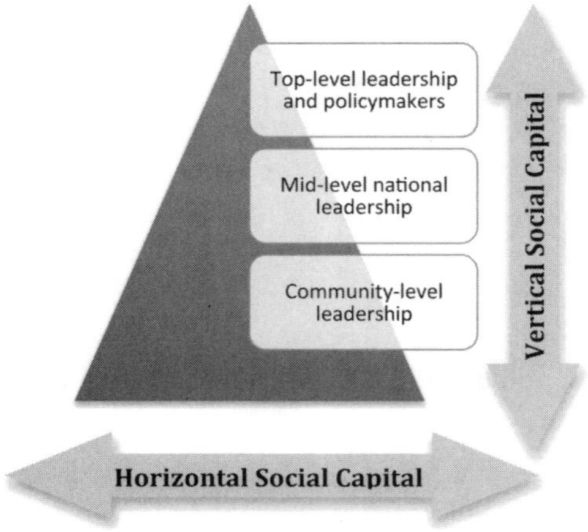

Figure 12.1
Social Capital Pyramid

thousands of people working for change to transform the country. While that process started with the historic peace accord and first free democratic elections, that process of transformation continues today as the country continues to wrestle with the economic disparities continuing to impact human security.[7]

Connecting Personal with Structural Change Strategies

Macro-level change usually does not happen unless an explicit goal and strategy exist for linking local-level peacebuilding to higher-level efforts to affect structures. The Reflecting on Peace Practice research project found that peacebuilding efforts that just focused on individual- or personal-level change did not seem to create systems-level change.[8] *Individual-level* approaches seek to change the attitudes, values, perceptions, or circumstances of individuals as an important first step in bringing about any type of real and lasting wider social change. Intergroup dialogue is an example of this approach. *Structural-level* approaches more directly aim to change sociopolitical or institutional structures. These programs support the creation or reform of institutions that address the grievances that drive conflict and institutionalize nonviolent modes of handling conflict within society. Peacebuilding efforts that intentionally try to link individual with structural efforts are more likely to bring about change.

Policy advocacy connects people at the community level who have experienced peacebuilding processes at the community level with key people who make decisions that affect root causes and policies at the structural level. The Aspen Institute's program on strategic design of policy advocacy through evaluation models gives online tools and best practices for impacting domestic and foreign policies.[9]

For example, in Israel and Palestine, intergroup dialogues have personally transformed many people. But this individual transformation does not impact structural-level policies. Delegations of Israeli and Palestinian citizens who meet with international policymakers on how they could support peace make a key link between individual-level peacebuilding and structural-level peacebuilding.

Integrating Multisector Programming

Integrated peacebuilding efforts aim to address as many drivers and mitigators as possible in multisector programming. Peacebuilding designs weave together goals to improve intergroup relations in other sectors such as food security, health, rule of law, education, or security-sector reform.

For example, a traditional development program such as health education can include a component that brings together women from different ethnic groups to learn basic health and conflict transformation skills. Humanitarian assistance such as setting up a refugee camp can be done in a way that is both conflict-sensitive and fosters peace. A conflict-sensitive approach would conduct a conflict assessment to understand divisions among refugees so as not to unintentionally increase conflict within the camp. It would also look at ways of fostering an intergroup governance structure within the camp that could begin discussing tensions. Or would it set up a combined peace education and literacy program for refugees, thus achieving a mixture of goals related to education, literacy, governance, and peacebuilding capacity.

Two other forms of integration relate to multisector programming.

Institutional integration. Peacebuilding organizations may need to build their own institutional capacity to design multisector efforts that address multiple drivers and mitigators of conflict. Or they may need to develop partnerships with other organizations to design integrated programs.

Message integration. An integrated approach to multisector peacebuilding can include and coordinate peaceful messages in different sectors. A health or rule-of-law program could be part of the same messaging campaign.

Sequencing Programs for a Hierarchy of Results

Like the "results chain" described in Chapter 11, planners can design peacebuilding so that a series of efforts or programs reinforce and build on each other over time to achieve a hierarchy of results that leads from peacebuilding efforts at the micro-level to macro-level system change.

As a first example, a peacebuilding program may start with a literacy project that teaches peacebuilding concepts. Next, students learn conflict transformation skills such as negotiation and problem solving in a basic accounting and business education program. Then the program offers microcredit loans to students who create business plans with someone from across the ethnic or religious lines of conflict in their community. The program then fosters a local business association among small businesses and offers training in global economic dynamics related to the conflict. Next the program helps business leaders do policy advocacy related to their economic interests in peace in their region.

As a second example, building peace and security in a country that faces a corrupt government, ethnic and religious conflicts, a local insurgency, violence against women, and foreign corporations and elite control over oil resources requires a complex set of peacebuilding activities. Stage one might include a network of local and international universities and NGOs working together to offer workshops in conflict assessment and peacebuilding, to build broad understanding and buy-in for understanding a peacebuilding approach. Middle- and higher-level religious stakeholders could convene a national dialogue. And international donors and stakeholders could hold an international conference to explore options for incentivizing a reduction in government corruption and corporate accountability. Stage two could involve a variety of projects at all levels of society to hold dialogues to discuss where they want their country to be in five to ten years. Developing a national consensus on the future direction of a country can then help various stakeholders begin to work together to take concrete steps toward their joint vision.

Adam Curle's sequencing model in Figure 12.2 illustrates that steps toward macro-level change move in two directions,[10] increasing the awareness of the interdependence between parts of a system and balancing the power between parts of a system. This model offers insight into the different types of peacebuilding efforts that may be relevant at different stages of conflict and at different levels of society.

Figure 12.2 Curle Model of Power and Awareness

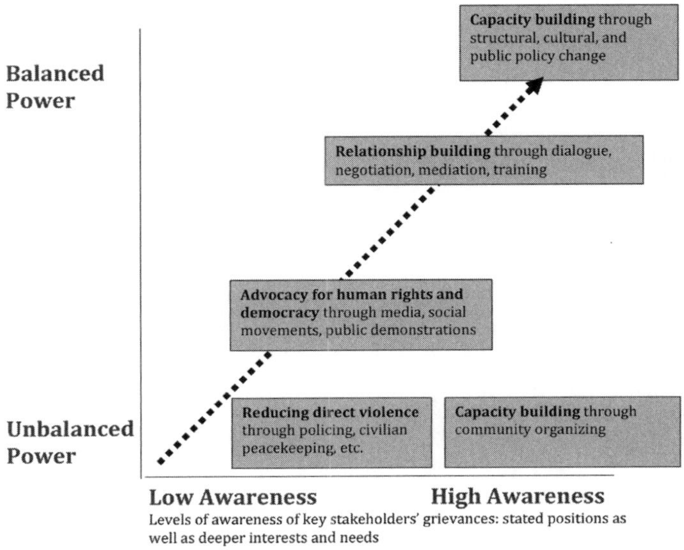

Awareness. When awareness of a conflict is low, peacebuilding efforts best seek to expose underlying injustices or tensions and increase understanding of the core issues driving conflict through advocacy and media education programs. Once a critical mass of people gain awareness of conflict's driving factors and the core interests and needs of other stakeholders, other peacebuilding options become more possible.

Power. When power is unbalanced, negotiation and dialogue often fail. More powerful stakeholders have little to gain from negotiation if they perceive that they can maintain the status quo that benefits them without negotiating. Successful negotiation requires a perception that all stakeholders have an interest in change. If the best alternative to a negotiated agreement (BATNA) is more appealing than working out other options with adversaries, then negotiation is likely to fail or be only for show.

The process of peacebuilding in a situation where power is unbalanced and awareness of key issues is low begins with capacity-building efforts such as community organizing and education. In situations of severe violence that inhibits community organizing, peacebuilding can include community-based policing and community watch programs. Advocacy strategies that can increase a group's power and increase awareness of interdependence between groups, perceived injustices, violations of human rights, or lack of democracy are another key step.

Successful advocacy strategies begin to ripen the conditions for relationship-based strategies such as dialogue, mediation, negotiation, and other efforts to transform relationships. As power becomes more balanced and awareness of the key issues increases, policy proposals and structural change become possible (see Figure 12.2).

Leveraging System Dynamics

The principles of a systems approach detailed earlier in this handbook can help design peacebuilding that most effectively identifies key leverage points or centers of gravity in a system. Leveraging change in one part of a system in a small way can in some cases lead to massive change in other parts of the system. Systems have many different leverage points. They are identified in this book as key conflict drivers or mitigators. The most significant system levers are the basic paradigm or values, or the goals and purposes of the system.[11]

As a first example, industrial cultures tend to treat the environment as a resource for humans to use in pursuit of economic growth. Indigenous cultures tend to see the environment endowed with spiritual dimensions and interdependent with the survival of human beings. These two paradigms lead to different approaches to land, food, economic, social, and political systems. Changing the paradigm of thinking of land as an endless resource versus an interdependent part of humanity would create significant system change.

As a second example, in security-sector reform, changing operational-level procedures to avoid civilian casualties could take much effort, but produce little change if the fundamental goal of the system remains primarily to hunt down and kill the enemy. But a change to the mission of the security forces to protecting civilians and not hunting and killing would lead to massive system change in terms of all levels of recruitment, training, and operations.

Breaking or weakening a link in a system can also create system change. Protecting civilians may enable security forces to better peel away community support from insurgent groups in the region and enable civil society to support broader democratic movements.

Systems are also like rivers, always moving and shifting. It is easier to redirect a river than to try to build a dam or get the river to reverse directions. A peacebuilding effort that moves parts of a system in a direction that is in everyone's interests is more likely to work than one that seems to go against the interests of some groups.

Peacebuilding efforts can move *with* the system in at least three ways[12]:

1. Peacebuilding efforts have a *cumulative effect* on a system when they affect as many of the factors driving or mitigating conflict as possible (in other words, an integrated program that achieves multiple outcomes). For example, a peacebuilding effort that provides microcredit loans to multiethnic business proposals incentivizes a change not only in economic development but also in interethnic relations.

2. Peacebuilding efforts have a *ripple effect* when they make a change in key factors that influence more factors driving or mitigating conflict. For example, addressing the lack of security for journalists reporting on corruption can have a ripple effect of not only ensuring more independent media coverage of corruption, but also more international and community awareness and pressure on corrupt actors in government from above and below.

3. Peacebuilding efforts have an *amplifier effect* when they work closely with the interests of those people related to key drivers and mitigators of conflict. Peacebuilding efforts that align with key factors in the system that are already changing are more likely to affect macro-level changes in that system.

For example, if military expenditures are a key factor driving violent conflict, a peacebuilding program attentive to the larger system would look for elements in the system that have an interest in curbing or changing military expenditures. This could mean working with parts of the military and defense contractors to evaluate their longer-term interests in supporting a more sustainable security and business plan centered on peacebuilding and human security as opposed to their shorter-term interests in profiting from arms sales. Other businesses depend on peaceful conditions and would seem to have an interest in stopping arms sales. Bolstering these capacities could then change the system itself, by reducing profiteering driving military expenditures and making peacebuilding a profitable activity.

Increasing Connectors, Decreasing Dividers

Connectors and dividers are key leverage points in a system. Building on the conflict assessment of the dividers and connectors from CDA Collaborative Learning Projects in Chapter 5, the design of peacebuilding can begin by brainstorming what can be done to increase or support the connectors and decrease the force of the dividers. In the center column of Table 12.1, identify how the design of a peacebuilding effort decreases the factors contributing to division or increases the factors contributing to peace and connection.

The most conflict-sensitive peacebuilding efforts support connectors and decrease dividers. Those that at least seek to do no harm are aware of the potential for peacebuilding activities of any kind (development, human rights advocacy, peacekeeping, and security-sector reform, for example) to increase divisions and expose people to violence. The least conflict-sensitive peacebuilding efforts inadvertently do cause harm, despite good intentions.[13]

At best, peacebuilding includes all stakeholders in designing the effort; increases mutual dependency and communication between communities; models and promotes tolerance, acceptance of differences, and empathy for others; and increases the capacity of people and communities to abstain from being involved in or exposed to violence. Peacebuilding should always reduce harmful competition, suspicion and biases between communities, promote tolerance toward others, and reduce the vulnerability of people and communities to violence.

At a minimum, peacebuilding avoids obstructing the needs of other stakeholders; avoids increasing competition, suspicion, and biases between communities; avoids negative behaviors that would model intolerance toward others; and avoids placing people and communities at more risk from violence.

Planners need to use extreme caution that their peacebuilding efforts do not inadvertently obstruct the needs of some stakeholders in neighboring communities; increase competition, suspicion, and biases between communities; model behavior that decreases tolerance, acceptance of difference

Table 12.1 Using Connectors and Dividers to Design or Redesign Peacebuilding

Dividers or Sources of Tension	Peacebuilding Effort	Connectors or Local Capacities for Peace
Examples: School textbooks that promote racism Media coverage that shows one group of people responsible for most crime Unfair housing regulations that show preference for people of one ethnic background Different religious beliefs and holidays Different languages Different schools or sections of a city for different cultural groups	Peacebuilding programs and projects should • Decrease the dividers or sources of tension • Increase the connectors or support the local capacities for peace	Examples: Electrical systems Common holidays that everyone celebrates Grocery stores or markets that everyone uses Shared belief in helping neighbors Shared experience of a hurricane or flood Shared pride in national flag Shared love of music Shared respect for elders as mediators of conflict

or empathy for others; or accidentally or negligently place people and communities at more risk from violence.

Integrated Model of Peacebuilding

This peacebuilding planning model, adapted from John Paul Lederach,[14] incorporates a number of the conflict assessment lenses and methods for scaling up peacebuilding from micro to macro impacts. Adapting the micro-macro nested model from the assessment lens, this planning model asks what different types of programs could address the conflict at different levels of society (see Figure 12.3).

Whether at the community, district, national, or regional level, peacebuilding takes time. It is not something accomplished within a six-month time frame. Stable peace can emerge, but it usually takes years and decades of concerted effort. Media coverage that leads to short-term focus following the headlines from crisis to crisis, leaving behind a trail of "donor orphans" without sustained funding to support peacebuilding, makes long-term strategic peacebuilding difficult.

Looking into the future, the model asks what types of programs could address conflict at different levels in the next 3 to 6 months, 5 to 10 years, 10 to 20 years, and also much more long term, looking at 20 or even 50 years into the future. The model offers insight into the different types of

Figure 12.3 Integrated Model of Peacebuilding

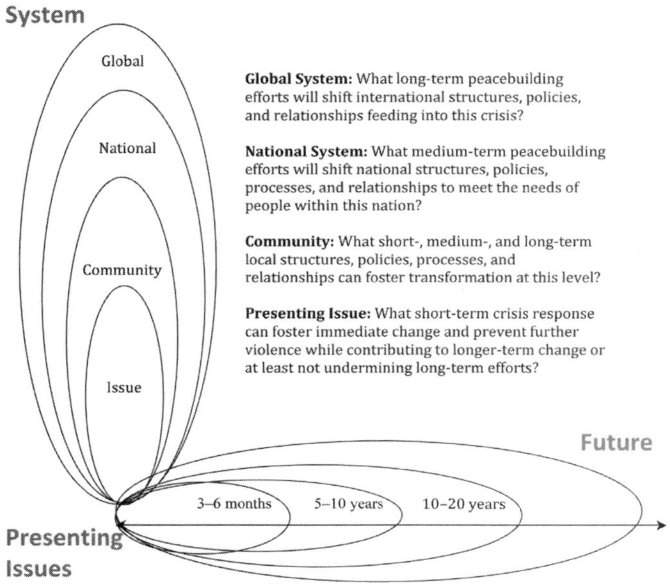

peacebuilding efforts that may be relevant at different stages of conflict and at different levels of society.

System
Global
National
Community
Issue
Global System: What long-term peacebuilding efforts will shift international structures, policies, and relationships feeding into this crisis?
National System: What medium-term peacebuilding efforts will shift national structures, policies, processes, and relationships to meet the needs of people within this nation?
Community: What short-, medium-, and long-term local structures, policies, processes, and relationships can foster transformation at this level?
Presenting Issue: What short-term crisis response can foster immediate change and prevent further violence while contributing to longer-term change or at least not undermining long-term efforts?
Future
3–6 months
5–10 years
10–20 years
Presenting Issues

Strategic peacebuilding designs short-term efforts that will feed into medium- and long-term efforts. And it designs long-term efforts that will also have immediate short-term impacts.

SMART Peacebuilding Goals

Setting goals on how to influence a conflict-affected system requires knowing a great deal about the way a system works. Most organizations set goals with very limited knowledge of the level of complexity in a system. So a goal is best thought of as a hypothesis. Organizations best influence a system if they allow themselves to keep learning about the system, which takes humility. Peacebuilding planners cannot and do not know how some goal will interact in a complex system. The most we can do is plan carefully and then watch and listen to the system to see what happens. And in most cases, planners will have to revisit and adapt goals as learning about the system takes place.

The Reflecting on Peace Practice research project found that many groups make two main mistakes when they develop goal statements. First, they confuse activities with goals. They will state a goal as "Holding a training for ethnic leaders," which is an activity, not a goal. Second, they make the mistake of being vague and overly general, such as a goal to "strengthen democratic processes."[15]

A goal statement should be SMART, meaning that it is Specific, Measurable, Attainable, Relevant, and Time-bound.[16] A SMART goal helps planners be more explicit about the decisions they are making on how to influence the system. Goals should aim to affect macro-level changes. Designing policies, programs, and projects with impact requires careful consideration of key principles, which are outlined here.

Specific

A specific goal identifies the purpose and who will be involved. These are examples of specific peacebuilding goal statements:

> To develop the capacity of youth to play positive peacebuilding roles through a national-level peace education curriculum that will be incorporated in all 25 school districts in the next five years.

> To facilitate the social and economic reintegration of 500 former soldiers back into their home communities over a 12-month period in five provinces.

Measurable

A measurable goal identifies how much change will happen so as to know whether the peacebuilding effort is making progress. In the previous example, the first goal states two measures: 25 school districts and five years. The second goal states three measures: 500 soldiers and 12 months in five provinces. A goal is measurable when it has definable benchmarks and indicators. But the degree of youth capacity and the amount and types of social and economic integration also require definition in order to be measurable.

Attainable

An attainable goal is realistic and achievable. The first example may not be attainable if only one small NGO is working on the project. But if that NGO is working with the National Ministry of Education, the goal could be attainable. A self-assessment of an organization's financial, staff, and other resources and networks helps develop realistic goals.

Relevant

A relevant goal is one that relates to the conflict assessment and theory of change. In the first example, it would be important to have first identified whether youth were in some way a primary factor driving violence or whether they were a potential mitigator of social divisions. In the second goal, it would also be important to know whether unemployed and socially transient former soldiers were viewed widely as drivers of conflicts or significant potential threats.

Time-bound

A time-bound goal provides a time frame for the peacebuilding effort. It can be short term (6 months) or long term (10 years). Governance transformations almost always take 10 to 20 years. Both of the example goal statements provide a clear time frame.

Peacebuilding Log Frames

A log frame helps to lay out a logical framework so as to improve the design and effectiveness of a peacebuilding effort. Log frames are not perfect tools. They can force people to think too simplistically about a complex context. Just as with a systems map, a logframe boils down the complexity of a system into a manageable amount of information. Log frames may make reality too simple, suggesting a direct cause-effect relationship between some peacebuilding effort and an intended outcome. On the other hand, without tools like log frames, designing and planning peacebuilding for a complex conflict-affected system is even more perplexing and paralyzing.

A self-assessment, conflict assessment, and theory of change all lay out the foundation for a design log frame (see Table 12.2). This normally also includes elements of monitoring and evaluation shown in Table 12.3.

Table 12.2 Peacebuilding Design Log Frame

Self-Assessment, Organizational Capacity, Inputs	Goal	Activities	Theory of Change	Key Audience	Time Frame
What resources (economic, skills, and social capital) do you have to achieve this goal?	What are you trying to change?	What efforts will you use to foster change?	What is your rationale for this strategy?	Who will be involved?	When will these activities take place?

Table 12.3 Peacebuilding Monitoring and Evaluation Log Frame

Outputs	Indicators or Benchmarks	Intended and Actual Outcomes	Goals, Intended and Actual Impacts
What activities actually took place, how many people were involved, etc.?	How will you measure change?	What are the *desired* effects of the effort? What were the *actual* effects? What did you learn about the system?	What will the change look like if you are successful? What were the actual impacts? What did you learn about the system?

Visit the website accompanying this book at www.conflict-assessment-and-peace building-planning.org to learn more or share your own ideas on Peacebuilding Design and Planning.

Notes

1. "Peace Writ Large" is a term that CDA and others use to indicate system-wide sustainable peace at the societal or regional level.

2. Lisa Schirch, *The Little Book of Strategic Peacebuilding* (Intercourse, PA: Good Books, 2004).

3. Anderson, Mary B., and Lara Olson. *Confronting War: Critical Lessons for Peace Practitioners* (Cambridge, MA: Collaborative for Development Action, 2003) 4.

4. See Lisa Schirch, *Amplifying Peace: Mass Media and Peacebuilding* (forthcoming).

5. Vladimir Bratic and Lisa Schirch, "Why and When to Use the Media for Conflict Prevention and Peacebuilding," Global Partnership for the Prevention of Armed Conflict, the Hague, December 2007.

6. Anderson, Mary B., and Lara Olson. *Confronting War: Critical Lessons for Peace Practitioners* (Cambridge, MA: Collaborative for Development Action, 2003) 48.

7. Susan Collin Marks, *Watching the Wind: Conflict Resolution During South Africa's Transition to Democracy* (Washington, DC: US Institute of Peace, 2000).

8. Anderson and Olson, 55.

9. See http://fp.continuousprogress.org.

10. Adapted from Adam Curle, *Making Peace* (London: Tavistock Press, 1971).

11. Donella H. Meadows, *Thinking in Systems: A Primer* (White River Junction, VT: Chelsea Green Publishing, 2008), 145–65.

12. Robert Ricigliano, *Making Peace Last* (Boulder, CO: Paradigm Press, 2011), 163–65.

13. CDA Collaborative Learning Projects. *The Do No Harm Handbook: The Framework for Analyzing the Impact of Assistance on Conflict* (Boston: Collaborative for Development Action, 2004).

14. Adapted from John Paul Lederach, *Building Peace: Sustainable Reconciliation in Divided Societies* (Washington, DC: US Institute of Peace, 1997).

15. Anderson, Mary B., Diana Chigas, Lara Olson, and Peter Woodrow. *Reflecting on Peace Practice Handbook* (Cambridge, MA: Collaborative for Development Action. 2004) 14.

16. Peter Drucker, *The Practice of Management* (New York: Harper and Row, 1954).

13

Monitoring and Evaluation

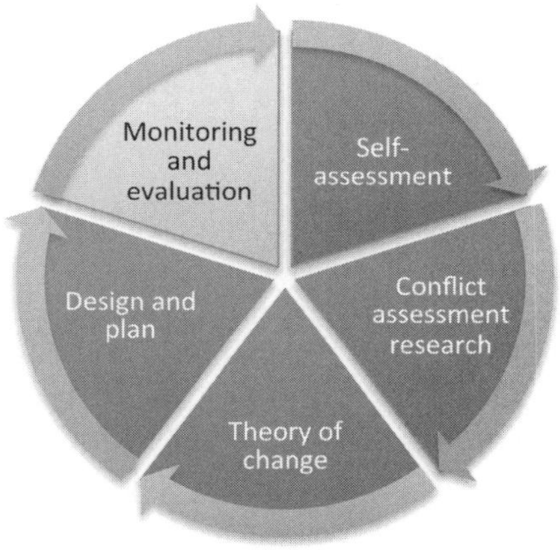

Graphic 13.1

This section of the handbook comes last in the diagram. But in reality, good monitoring and evaluation require thinking and planning during all the other stages.

Assessing whether a peacebuilding effort carried out intended activities and achieved intended outputs, outcomes, and impacts is challenging. Measuring levels of direct or structural violence and the quality of relationships between groups or the strength of efforts for peace are intangible compared to counting number of schools built or number of literate citizens in the population. In the words of Albert Einstein, "Not everything that can be counted counts, and not everything that counts can be counted."[1]

Ultimately, speculating what would have happened if a peacebuilding effort had not taken place is impossible. Researchers can make "contingent predictions" about what might have happened, but these are not certain.[2] Peacebuilding monitoring and evaluation relies on looking at patterns to determine the trends in this context before and after peacebuilding efforts. How do these also compare with the trends in similar contexts?

The field of peacebuilding is working extensively to improve monitoring and evaluation and to identify key indicators for measuring improvements.[3] The New Deal for Fragile States is identifying indicators of systemwide impacts of peacebuilding efforts. Catholic Relief Services runs a program to develop globally accepted peacebuilding indicators.[4] The Learning Portal for Design, Monitoring & Evaluation (DM&E) for Peacebuilding (http://dmeforpeace.org/) is a community of practice for DM&E peacebuilding professionals. It provides a transparent and collaborative space for sharing evaluation reports and data, and methodologies and tools. By making this material easily accessible it hopes to improve the practice of DM&E for peacebuilding and increase the effectiveness of peacebuilding programs.

Conflict-Sensitive Monitoring and Evaluation

Just as with the design of the conflict assessment research process at the beginning of a peacebuilding effort, monitoring and evaluation research follows all of the same advice cautioning perceptual biases, distorted data, and careful design of who conducts the monitoring and evaluation research and who is consulted in the research process.

First and foremost, following the earlier section on "Conflict-Sensitive Design of Peacebuilding," researchers should ask whether the intent of the design matched the impact in the real world. How are local people involved in monitoring and evaluating the context, the program, and the program's relationship with the context? Participatory processes like focus groups and consultative meetings that include people involved as well as excluded from the peacebuilding effort can generate a list of the evaluation indicators.[5] Local people can develop meaningful indicators since they know firsthand if and how their human security is improving.

The Differences Between Monitoring and Evaluation

Monitoring and evaluation research processes are similar, but they are not the same. Monitoring goes on continually to track progress throughout a peacebuilding effort. Monitoring focuses more on internal learning and redesigning a program so that it can work. Monitoring research processes are often done by a small, internal group of people who keep an eye on a small number of indicators.

Evaluation happens at the end or at a natural break in the peacebuilding effort. Usually, donors want an evaluation of the peacebuilding effort they funded. Evaluations tend to be focused on showing a donor what they want to hear. Evaluation usually involves an outside research group that looks at the peacebuilding effort and its impacts. Outside evaluators ideally have a more objective approach less biased by the internal desire to have had one's work contribute to peacebuilding. They may also use a wider range of qualitative and quantitative methods and look at a broader scope of the context before and after the peacebuilding effort.

Just as with assessment, there are basic and advanced approaches to monitoring and evaluation. Figure 13.1 illustrates each of the key steps of the monitoring and evaluation processes.

Figure 13.1 Steps in Monitoring and Evaluation

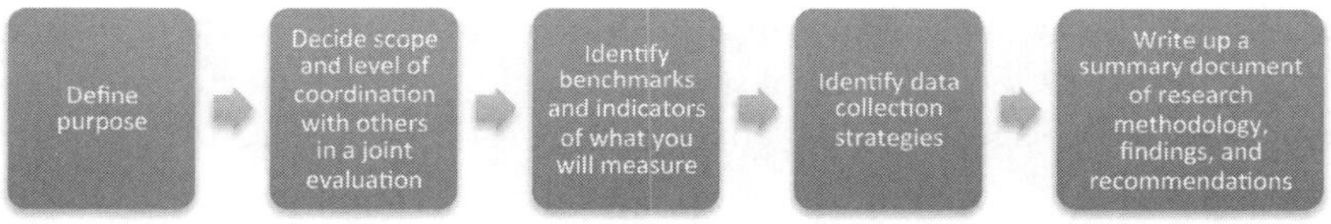

Purpose of Monitoring and Evaluation

Monitoring and evaluation (M&E) can serve multiple purposes, including the following.[6]

Risk assessment. M&E can serve as a way of assessing the ongoing risks that changes in the local context will negatively impact the peacebuilding effort or that the peacebuilding effort will negatively impact the context.

Report to donors. M&E can serve as a way of reporting to funders on the investment of their funds.

Report to local community. M&E can serve as a way of involving and reporting to local communities about the impact of the peacebuilding effort on their lives.

Learning. M&E can help organizations learn about what worked and did not work so they can adapt their future strategies on these lessons. Failures offer great opportunities to learn. Failures can teach us about what we missed during a conflict assessment, what did not factor into a self-assessment, what key assumptions of theories of change were wrong, or what mistakes were made in planning and implementing the program.[7]

Learning should be at the center of the monitoring and evaluation. Monitoring and evaluation should lead to the active improvement of the peacebuilding effort while it is being implemented. Good monitoring and evaluation offer real-time feedback to immediately improve and continue to adapt and innovate dimensions of the effort to increase its effectiveness in changing the conflict system.[8] This means constantly looping back to the conflict assessment and theories of change to ask: *Do the conflict assessment conclusions and key theories of change assumptions hold? Are the assumptions made during the design phase still relevant to the current context and conflict dynamics?*

Scope and Dimensions of Monitoring

Ideally, monitoring takes on four dimensions, detailed in Table 13.1. These dimensions include a systemwide monitoring and evaluation of the *outputs* of a specific project, a group of projects and programs by multiple organizations, the *outcome* focusing on a particular subregion or sector within a society (such as training journalists in conflict-sensitive reporting) and incremental progress toward a benchmark, and *impacts* on the conflict-affected context or system.

Monitor and Evaluate Quality of Program Implementation

Most monitoring focuses only on identifying whether an organization carries out the goals, activities, and budget of a peacebuilding effort as planned. Organizations can most easily measure how they implemented the peacebuilding effort and whether they followed the original design. How do the lessons from monitoring feed back into the redesign of the peacebuilding effort?

Table 13.1 Dimensions of Monitoring and Evaluation

Indicators	Outputs	Intended and Actual Outcomes and Benchmarks	Intended and Actual Impacts
How will you measure change?	What activities actually took place, how many people were involved, etc.?	What are the desired direct effects of the effort? What were the actual effects? Do the outcomes of the peacebuilding effort meet preestablished benchmarks, indicating progress toward desired impacts? What did you learn about the system?	What will the change look like if you are successful? What were the actual impacts? What did you learn about the system?

An *implementation failure* occurs when a group is not able to implement a program as designed because of a lack of staff capacity, an issue of access to location, inadequate budget, an unexpected crisis interrupting the program, or some other problem.[9]

A more advanced approach to monitoring the implementation of a peacebuilding effort looks outside of the organization to those involved in the effort. How do local people, both those involved and excluded from the peacebuilding effort, describe the effort? What is the story or narrative they used to describe what happened and its impact on their lives?

What were the negative and positive unintended impacts?

How did groups not involved in the effort perceive it? How do they see its impact on the larger context? Do they think the effort increased or decreased tensions between groups involved in the effort?

Did the program set up expectations for future programs that build on this one? What is the level of sustainability of the program? Do local people feel ownership?

How will some or all of the learning from the monitoring and evaluation be shared with local people and other organizations? Are there internal and external formats for reporting?

Were resources invested in coordination with other peacebuilding efforts? Did coordination lead to a more coherent and strategic approach that maximized synergy and complementarity between efforts?

Monitoring Context

Monitoring a peacebuilding effort includes regularly revisiting and updating the conflict assessment on a monthly basis. This starts with a risk assessment. What possible changes in the local context would disrupt the peacebuilding effort? What is changing in the political, economic, social, cultural, religious, media, and security sectors? Are levels of violence and crime increasing or decreasing? Are there new policies or initiatives beginning? Do news media reports or recent polling report changes in behavior, attitudes, or beliefs? Are new actors involved? What other peacebuilding efforts have begun?

Measuring local perceptions of human security and comparing these with baseline data can give a sense of whether indicators are improving or worsening. Measuring change at this level is best done in coordination with other peacebuilding efforts in the context to examine cumulative impacts.

Monitoring Theories of Change[10]

Is the peacebuilding effort changing the factors driving or mitigating conflict in the way intended? How accurate were the original theories of what needed to change in the system? What new insights shift understandings of how the system works? What new theories of change are emerging?

A *theory failure* or flawed theory of change means that basic assumptions about what was driving or mitigating conflict and what peacebuilding effort would address those factors were wrong. This could be due to inaccurate or misinterpreted data in a conflict assessment.

Monitoring Peacebuilding Impacts on the Context

What impact is the peacebuilding effort having on the context? Are there indicators that a peacebuilding effort is directly impacting change in some part of the conflict system? Is this change impacting other factors? Is there a "results chain" moving micro-level changes to macro-level changes?

Strategic monitoring and evaluation include not just short-term outcomes of specific programs but long-term interrelated impacts of multiple actors, multiple programs, and multisectors.[11] Most monitoring and evaluation focus only on the specific peacebuilding effort itself and whether the short-term objectives were met with the promised activities. Project-level outcomes rarely lead directly to massive system-level changes. But the cumulative effect of strategic and coordinated peacebuilding should have an impact on the conflict-affected system.

Baselines, Benchmarks, and Indicators

Baseline information can be drawn from the conflict assessment, particularly information in the "Where: Context Assessment" section. Baseline information about the context allows a comparison of what changes happened in the context in the time before, during, or after a peacebuilding effort.

Benchmarks are objectives set to determine whether a peacebuilding effort is making progress toward its goal. *Indicators* are used to measure progress toward a benchmark. Indicators are measures used to see if the peacebuilding effort or action is impacting the driving or mitigating factors according to your theory of change.

Like peacebuilding goals, indicators should be SMART (specific, measurable, attainable, relevant, and time-bound) as described in Chapter 12.

Etic indicators are quantitative measures that can be seen from the outside, such as the number of trainings that take place.

Emic indicators are qualitative measures developed by local people related to the quality of the programming and their perceptions of its impacts, such as improved perceptions of security or freedom of movement. As with each part of this handbook, insiders should be involved in identifying and measuring indicators of whether a program is having its intended impact.

Qualitative indicators have a descriptive unit of measurement. For example, twenty community leaders may describe their projections for the future as "hopeful" (a qualitative measure) rather than "depressing."

Quantitative indicators have a numerical unit of measurement. For example, there may be 500 more people (a quantitative measure) involved in a community dialogue program.

Identity-based indicators look at the different impacts of a peacebuilding effort on different identity groups. For example, the peacebuilding effort may impact women differently than men.

Pragmatic indicators can be more easily counted because someone is already collecting the information. For example, does the peacebuilding effort impact the number of forested acres in the district? Geospatial mapping already counts forested districts, so this information would be easy to obtain.

Indicator Examples

Fewer cases of domestic violence reported to local shelter
Increase in multiethnic business plans funded with microcredit loans
Increase in cases heard by local courts using mediation and restorative justice
Increase in intercommunal communication (phone calls, e-mails)
Increase in number of parliamentarians visiting communities and holding forums

The Reflecting on Peace Practice research project identified five indicators of effective peacebuilding.[12] These include the following:

- The effort results in the creation or reform of political institutions to handle grievances in situations where such grievances do, genuinely, drive the conflict.
- The effort contributes to a momentum for peace by causing participants and communities to develop their own peace initiatives in relation to critical elements of context analysis.
- The effort prompts people increasingly to resist violence and provocations to violence.
- The effort results in an increase in people's security and in their perception of security.
- The effort results in meaningful improvement in intergroup relations.

Other research identify broader principles as indicators, for example[13]:

- What was the **impact and coverage** of the peacebuilding effort?
- How **relevant and appropriate** was the peacebuilding effort?
- How **timely** was the peacebuilding effort?
- How **sustainable** was the peacebuilding effort?
- Was the peacebuilding effort **coherent**, and did it work in a way that **coordinated** and was **complementary** to other peacebuilding efforts?

Table 13.2 provides a range of sample peacebuilding indicators for the five categories of peacebuilding and human security described throughout this handbook.

Key questions for each of these indicators include the following:

1. Is it feasible to collect data on these indicators? If police reports do not capture levels of violence against women, or government records on income disparity between ethnic groups do not exist, it may not be possible or easy to collect data relevant to the indicator.[14]

2. Is it possible to establish a connection between the peacebuilding effort and the indicator, or could other changes in the system have created the change? In other words, might the change have happened regardless of the peacebuilding effort?

3. Are those leading the peacebuilding effort open to learning and adapting their strategies during monitoring and evaluation? Or are they resistant to evaluation or fundamentally convinced that their efforts work already?

4. Why do people say they participate in the peacebuilding effort? Are they coerced or paid to participate, or is it voluntary?[15]

5. How do these indictors interact with each other in the conflict system? Is there a harmony effect of each indicator being like a note in a musical chord that creates a larger effect? Or are the notes discordant, creating tension and chaos?

Data Collection Strategies

As detailed in Chapter 2, data collection strategies for monitoring and evaluation can include interviews, focus groups, community consultations, polling, mobile phone and Internet surveys, or the use of local research teams such as youth who are given cameras to ask and document people's responses to a peacebuilding effort. In addition to those data collection

Table 13.2 Sample Peacebuilding Indicators

Levels of Change	Politically Stable Democracy	Sustainable Economy	Safe and Secure Environment	Justice and Rule of Law	Social and Cultural Well-Being
	Sample Peacebuilding Indicators				
Structural	Three new radio stations constructed, owned and operated by multiethnic teams. Civil society assembly created to develop joint proposals for revising the constitution.	Poverty reduction strategy begins with creation of national taskforce composed of government and civil society organizations.	Two insurgent groups participate in a mediation with local elders to identify conditions for disarmament and demobilization.	International criminal court works with national justice system to design a transitional justice process.	National-level interreligious taskforce is created.
Cultural	New radio shows producing news content on the peace process.	University conducts a poll of national attitudes on corruption.	Religious leaders release statement calling for an end to war.	Six public school districts teach students about transitional justice options in their country.	Labor unions create statement for their members on national reconciliation.
Relational	Political leaders hold negotiation to design the peace process.	Five community forums take place for community members to talk with government about corruption.	Four community-level forums bring security forces and community members together for dialogue.	Two major ethnic groups hold a dialogue to discuss their perspectives on amnesty for crimes committed during the war.	Women's groups meet to discuss their recommendations and strategies for the national peace process.
Personal	Key government agency approaches a peacebuilding organization to conduct training for them.	Citizens receive training from an NGO in community-based corruption monitoring.	Trauma recovery units offer PTSD services to 50 members of security forces.		Four national-level workshops held for community leaders on psychosocial awareness and trauma healing.

methods already detailed, a variety of other strategies are particularly useful for monitoring and evaluation, including the following:

Anonymous mechanisms. Provide anonymous mechanisms for collecting information and complaints from local people where people may risk their safety or experience some sort of political, social, or economic harm from sharing their perspectives on a peacebuilding effort.

Vulnerable and marginalized groups. Develop mechanisms to hear perspectives from vulnerable and marginalized groups.

Conflict diaries. Provide a notebook or conflict diary to help community members identify day-to-day challenges that could increase conflict and ideas for project redesign to address local tensions.[16]

Transparency boards or announcements. Put up a board to state the peacebuilding goals, activities, and funding as a way of informing community members. Radio announcements, e-mails, or SMS text messages may also be used to heighten local knowledge and ownership of a project; a phone number or e-mail for people to share ideas or to make complaints ensures that communication channels with the community are open.

Vigilance committees. Create a structured mechanism to monitor and evaluate the impact of a peacebuilding effort on those not directly involved. A vigilance committee made up of community members not involved in the peacebuilding effort receives training in supervising and oversight. The group then provides day-to-day monitoring and offers feedback on whether the peacebuilding effort is carried out as intended in the planning documents and records the positive and negative impacts of the peacebuilding effort on the community.

Community meetings. Those leading a peacebuilding effort can meet with local government officials, other civil society organizations, the Vigilance Committee, and the public to share bills and vouchers for peacebuilding effort expenses, to hear any grievances or complaints, and to discuss the outcomes and impact of the peacebuilding effort.[17]

Table 2.2 illustrated a chart for research gaps. This chart is also helpful for monitoring and evaluation. Researchers should seek to identify missing information, make plans to identify who may have critical information, and design a plan for filling the research gaps.

Summary Document

A monitoring and evaluation document can summarize information on the purpose, scope, indicators, data collection strategies, and conclusions on the implementation of the peacebuilding effort (outputs), the effect of the peacebuilding effort on the specific objective of the effort (outcomes), and the macro-level impacts on the conflict-affected system (impacts).

The document will also revisit the theories of change to assess whether the assumptions hold or need to change, and the self-assessment to examine changes to the group or partnerships leading the peacebuilding effort. From the very beginning, if outsiders are leading a peacebuilding effort, they should consult with insiders to design their own exit strategy or to establish clear timelines for reevaluating the relationship between insiders and outsiders, depending on the evolution of the conflict system and the peacebuilding effort. If it becomes clear that peacebuilding efforts are creating more harm to local people, then outsiders should consider whether their presence should end immediately. Inside groups should also examine whether their identity and mission remain relevant and appropriate to the context.

Visit the website accompanying this book at www.conflict-assessment-and-peace building-planning.org to learn more or share your own ideas on Peacebuilding Monitoring and Evaluation.

Notes

1. Cheyanne Church and Julie Shouldice, *The Evaluation of Conflict Resolution Interventions: Framing the State of Play* (Londonderry, Northern Ireland: INCORE, 2002).
2. Albrecht Schnabel, "One Size Fits All? Focused Comparison and Policy-Relevant Research on Violently Divided Societies," in *Researching Violently Divided Societies: Ethical and Methodological Issues,* ed. Marie Smyth and Gillian Robinson (Tokyo: United Nations University Press, 2001), 193–206.
3. Andrew Blum, "Improving Peacebuilding Evaluation," US Institute of Peace, Washington, DC, June 2011.
4. Tom Bamat, Aaron Chassy, Clara Hagens, Guy Sharrock, "GAIN Peacebuilding Indicators," Catholic Relief Services, Baltimore, MD, 2010.
5. Organisation for Economic Co-operation and Development (OECD), "Guidance on Evaluating Conflict Prevention and Peacebuilding Activities," Working Draft for Application Period, 2008, 66.
6. Ibid., 26–27.
7. John Paul Lederach, Reina Neufeldt, and Hal Culbertson, *Reflective Peacebuilding: A Planning, Monitoring, and Learning Toolkit* (South Bend, IN: University of Notre Dame, 2007), 5.

8. Michael Quinn Patton, *Developmental Evaluation: Applying Complexity Concepts to Enhance Innovation and Use* (New York: Guilford Press, 2011), 1.

9. OECD, "Guidance on Evaluating Conflict Prevention," 41.

10. These four categories of peacebuilding monitoring and evaluation are identified in Care International UK, *Peacebuilding with Impact: Defining Theories of Change* (London: Care International UK, 2012), 9. Some of them are also detailed in the Conflict Sensitivity Consortium, "How to Guide to Conflict Sensitivity," Conflict Sensitivity Consortium, London, February 2012.

11. Koenraad Van Brabant, "Peacebuilding How? Assessing the Design of Peacebuilding Interventions," Interpeace, Geneva, 2010, 2.

12. Anderson, Mary B., and Lara Olson. *Confronting War: Critical Lessons for Peace Practitioners* (Cambridge, MA: Collaborative for Development Action, 2003).

13. Mark Hoffman, *Peace and Conflict Impact Assessment Methodology* (Berlin: Berghof Research Center for Constructive Conflict Management, 2001).

14. Ken Menkhaus, "Impact Assessment in Post-Conflict Peacebuilding: Challenges and Future Directions," Interpeace, Geneva, July 2004, 6.

15. Lederach et al., *Reflective Peacebuilding,* 40.

16. Conflict Sensitivity Consortium, "How to Guide to Conflict Sensitivity," 19.

17. Adapted from ibid., 27.

Appendix A

Writing a Conflict Assessment and Peacebuilding Planning "Learning Document"

Peacebuilding that is coordinated, system-based, strategic, and participatory requires a sense of shared understanding. A shared learning document in the form of a written report, video, or output from another medium can facilitate this broader sense of ownership and understanding. The process of creating the learning document can help groups that coordinated a conflict assessment and peacebuilding process reflect on the whole process from self-assessment, conflict assessment, and theories of change, to designing, implementing, monitoring, and evaluating a peacebuilding effort. The process itself can help further build understanding and strengthen relationships.

Background, initial self-assessment. Provide an overview of the interests and goals of the group or groups that commissioned, facilitated, or organized a conflict assessment and peacebuilding planning process.

Research methods. Provide a description of the research methodology, including who carried out the research, who was involved, and how and when they collected data.

Conflict assessment. Describe the output summary from each of the lenses in the Where, Who, Why, What, How, and When framework.

Theories of change. Describe the key theories of change that link the short list of drivers and mitigators of conflict with ideas about how peacebuilding could address these.

Self-assessment. Discuss decisions about Where, Who, Why, What, How, and When the peacebuilding effort relates to the peacebuilding group's identity, relationships, and capacity.

Design and planning. Describe the goals, activities, outputs, outcomes, and impacts of the peacebuilding effort, detailing how the effort coordinated with other groups to address key conflict drivers and mitigators.

Monitoring and evaluation. Describe results of the research process, ideally coordinated closely with other insider and outsider peacebuilding organizations.

Appendix B

Recommendations for Coordination and Donors

Peacebuilding at the macro level requires capacity and expertise in a wide range of areas. No one group can do it alone. A benefit of shared conflict assessment and peacebuilding planning is the creation of a strategic plan that includes synergistic work with other organizations. Coordination can take many forms. It can mean sharing information, integrating conflict assessment processes, sharing planning and programming information, forming partnerships and integrating planning, sharing information about evaluation, and jointly conducting research or advocacy.[1]

The United Nations; regional organizations; international NGOs; government diplomatic, development, and defense agencies; local governments; and local civil society organizations (CSOs) often conduct separate, overlapping conflict assessments. A multiplicity of conflict assessment processes can waste precious time and resources. Local CSOs are increasingly being asked to participate in uncoordinated conflict assessments by different countries and donors. Local leaders spend a great deal of time providing insights to their international partners. This lack of international coordination consumes local leaders' energy and wastes international resources. Coordinating conflict assessment processes can increase the quality of conflict assessment while decreasing the duplicative number of processes costing both money and time and resulting in assessment fatigue. A coordinated more strategic approach fosters coordination of donors' short-term, high-impact investments and local actors' interest in long-term, sustainable change.

In Nepal, local and international NGOs set up communities of practice to share their conflict assessments, theories of change, and program designs as well as monitoring and evaluation data. Groups shared design flaws in their projects, gained confidence and trust to honestly assess their own failures, and adapted a cooperative learning model that improved their conflict assessment and program design.[2]

Ideally, shared assessment leads to more coordinated missions. But coordination and harmonization can also have negative effects. If outsiders hold too much control over the funding and direction of peacebuilding, coordination may undermine local, insider ownership of peacebuilding. Too much control-based coordination can also reduce the ability of a small group of insiders or outsiders to quickly respond or to be flexible and adaptive to changing circumstances.[3] Too much coordination and integration can also compromise needed impartiality that allows some groups to work across the lines of conflict.

But these dangers are not reasons to avoid coordinating in a broad sense of sharing information. Coordination can take many forms. Sharing information in a forum that promotes communication between different peacebuilding actors is a low-level time investment that can have large payoffs in terms of program quality.

Recommendations for Donors

Donors are in the best position to incentivize coordinated conflict assessment and peacebuilding planning processes.

Invest in assessment. The quality of a peacebuilding program relates directly to the quality of the assessment. Donors can improve their investments in peacebuilding by requiring participation in or facilitation of a conflict assessment process with other local and international actors.

Donors can ensure quality programming by budgeting for the following elements:

- Budget for conflict assessment at the start, either in a standalone assessment or funding participation in a coordinated assessment forum with other donors and organizations.[4]
- Budget for staff capacity-building in conflict-sensitive program design.
- Budget for monitoring and evaluation that includes local participants, both those who benefited directly from the peacebuilding effort and those who did not to provide their feedback on the effort.
- Require identification of theories of change in the underlying assumptions column of their logical frameworks (log frames) so that donors are aware of the logic of what a program aims to achieve.

Incentivize coordination. Ideally, the United Nations, the World Bank, or an independent conflict assessment center could create a platform in every conflict-affected country to enable ongoing, multistakeholder, multisector conflict assessment, as described in earlier chapters. Few individual donors or peacebuilding planners have enough convening power, facilitation skills, trusted relationships, or resources, however, to conduct a multistakeholder conflict assessment on their own. As such, most donors continue to skimp on conflict assessment, resulting in inaccurate and inadequate analysis. Donors can work together to reduce duplication and maximize complementary research that produces accurate and balanced results with triangulated data. Often donors are not sharing or learning from conflict assessment processes conducted by local or international NGOs. A repository of conflict assessment research is not available for all areas of the world. Resource websites like the Human Security Gateway are gathering reports and conflict assessments for some regions of the world. A coordinated conflict assessment center would create more reliable and comprehensive data sets and knowledge banks to complement a multistakeholder dialogue of insiders and outsiders working in a conflict-affected region to support peace.

Explicit statement of interests. Some donors will have explicit political and economic interests in a region where they want to support peacebuilding. Local people will assume that these interests shape their conflict assessment and support for peacebuilding. The more donors can be explicit about their interests and how these support and do not contradict the human-security interests of local people, the more likely peacebuilding donors will be seen as legitimate.

In addition, donors should be clear that they are making a commitment to invest in developing local solutions if they are asking local people to commit time and effort to a conflict assessment. Local people often complain that they took part in a donor's conflict assessment process, but then never learned about what the donor decided to do with its programming. At minimum, donors should be accountable for reporting back to local communities that participated in a conflict assessment to provide basic information about the outcome of their research.

Notes

1. Mark Rogers, Aaron Chassy, and Tom Bamat, "Integrating Peacebuilding into Humanitarian and Development Programming: Practical Guidance on Designing Effective, Holistic Peacebuilding Projects," Catholic Relief Services, Baltimore, MD, 2010, 27.

2. Care International UK, *Peacebuilding with Impact: Defining Theories of Change* (London: Care International UK, 2012), 8.

3. Koneraad Van Brabant, "Peacebuilding How? Criteria to Assess and Evaluate Peacebuilding," Interpeace, Geneva, 2010, 4.

4. Donors reluctant to spend limited funds on assessment can find ways of building on assessments done by other groups working in the local context, although this strategy can backfire if these assessments processes had design flaws resulting in inaccurate assessments.

Bibliography

Abu-Nimer, Mohammed. *Dialogue, Conflict Resolution, and Change: Arab-Jewish Encounters in Israel.* Albany: SUNY Press, 1999.

Anderlini, Sanam Naraghi. "Mainstreaming Gender in Conflict Analysis." Washington, DC: World Bank. Social Development Papers 33. February 2006.

———. *Women Building Peace: What They Do, Why It Matters.* Boulder, CO: Lynne Rienner Publishers, 2007.

Anderson, Mary B. *Do No Harm: How Aid Supports Peace—or War.* Boulder, CO: Lynne Rienner Publishers, 1999.

———, Diana Chigas, Lara Olson, and Peter Woodrow. *Reflecting on Peace Practice Handbook.* Cambridge, MA: Collaborative for Development Action, 2004.

———, and Lara Olson. *Confronting War: Critical Lessons for Peace Practitioners.* Cambridge, MA: Collaborative for Development Action, 2003.

Augsberger, David W. *Conflict Mediation Across Cultures: Pathways and Patterns.* Louisville, KY: Westminster/John Knox Press, 1992.

Avruch, Kevin. *Culture and Conflict Resolution.* Washington, DC: US Institute for Peace, 1998.

Baker, Pauline. *Conflict Assessment System Tool (CAST).* Washington, DC: The Fund for Peace, 2006.

Bamat, Tom, Aaron Chassy, Clara Hagens, and Guy Sharrock. "GAIN Peacebuilding Indicators." Baltimore, MD: Catholic Relief Services, 2010.

Barnes, Catherine. *Owning the Process: Public Participation in Peacemaking: South Africa, Guatemala and Mali.* London: Conciliation Resources, 2002.

Batts, Valerie. "Is Reconciliation Possible? Lessons from Combating Modern Racism." In *Re-Centering Culture and Knowledge in Conflict Resolution,* 273–301. Syracuse, NY: Syracuse University Press, 2008.

Blum, Andrew. "Improving Peacebuilding Evaluation." Washington, DC: US Institute of Peace, June 2011.

Boulding, Kenneth. *The World as a Total System.* Newbury Park, CA: Sage, 1985.

———. *Three Faces of Power.* Newbury Park, CA: Sage, 1989.

Bradbury, Mark. "Do They Think We're Stupid? Local Perceptions of US 'Hearts and Minds' Activities in Kenya." http://www.odihpn.org.

Bratic, Vladimir, and Lisa Schirch. "Why and When to Use the Media for Conflict Prevention and Peacebuilding." The Hague: Global Partnership for the Prevention of Armed Conflict, December 2007.

Bryant, Coralie, and Christina Kappaz. *Reducing Poverty, Building Peace.* Bloomfield, MA: Kumarian Press, 2005.

Burton, John. *Conflict: Human Needs Theory.* New York: St. Martin's, 1990.

———. *Resolving Deep-Rooted Conflict: A Handbook.* Lanham, MD: University Press of America. 1987.

Bush, Kenneth. *A Measure of Peace: Peace and Conflict Impact Assessment (PCIA) of Development Projects in Conflict Zones.* Ottawa: The Peacebuilding and Reconstruction Program Initiative and The Evaluation Unit, 1998. http://www.conflictsensitivity.org.

Capra, Fritjof. *The Web of Life: A New Scientific Understanding of Living Systems.* New York: Anchor Books, 1996.

Care International UK. *Peacebuilding with Impact: Defining Theories of Change.* London: Care International UK, 2012.

Carnegie Commission on Preventing Deadly Conflict. *Preventing Deadly Conflict: Final Report.* New York: Carnegie Corporation of New York, 1997.

CDA Collaborative Learning Projects. *The Do No Harm Handbook: The Framework for Analyzing the Impact of Assistance on Conflict.* Boston: Collaborative for Development Action, 2004.

Chassy, Aaron. "Civil Society and Development Effectiveness in Africa." In *Problems, Promises and Paradoxes of Aid: Africa's Experience,* edited by Muna Ndulo and Nicolas van de Walle. Athens: Ohio University Press and University of Cape Town Press, forthcoming.

Cheldelin, Sandra, Daniel Druckman, and Larissa Fast, eds. *Conflict.* New York: Continuum, 2003.

Church, Cheyanne, and Mark Rogers. *Designing for Results: Integrating Monitoring and Evaluation in Conflict Transformation Programs.* Washington, DC: Search for Common Ground, 2006.

———, and Julie Shouldice. *The Evaluation of Conflict Resolution Interventions: Framing the State of Play.* Londonderry, Northern Ireland: INCORE, 2002.

Collier, Paul, and Anke Hoeffler. "Greed and Grievance in Civil War." World Bank Policy Research Working Paper 2355. Washington, DC: World Bank, May 2000.

Collin Marks, Susan. *Watching the Wind: Conflict Resolution During South Africa's Transition to Democracy.* Washington, DC: US Institute of Peace, 2000.

Conflict Sensitivity Consortium. "How to Guide to Conflict Sensitivity." London: Conflict Sensitivity Consortium. February 2012.

Cooperation for Peace and Unity. *Human Security Indicators.* Kabul, 2010.

Cooperrider, David L., Diana Whitney, and Jacqueline M. Stavros. *Appreciative Inquiry Handbook.* Bedford Heights, OH: Lakeshore Publishers, 2003.

Cortright, David, George A. Lopez, Alistair Millar, and Linda M. Gerber-Stellingwerf. "Friend or Foe: Civil Society and the Struggle Against Violent Extremism." A Report to Cordaid from the Fourth Freedom Forum and Kroc Institute for International Peace Studies at the University of Notre Dame. October 27, 2008.

Curle, Adam. *Making Peace.* London: Tavistock Press, 1971.

Dart Center for Journalism and Trauma. "Self Study Unit 2: Covering Terrorism." http://www.dartcenter.org.

Diamond, Louise, and John McDonald. *Multi-Track Diplomacy: A Systems Approach to Peace.* Grinnell: Iowa Peace Institute, 1991.

Docherty, Jayne. *The Little Book of Strategic Negotiation.* Intercourse, PA: Good Books, 2004.

Doyle, Michael, and Nicholas Sambanis. *Making War and Building Peace.* Princeton, NJ: Princeton University Press, 2006.

Drucker, Peter. *The Practice of Management.* New York: Harper and Row, 1954.

Dugan, Maire. "A Nested Theory of Conflict." *Women in Leadership* 1, no. 1 (Summer 1996): 9–20.

Dziedzic, Michael, Barbara Sotirin, and John Agoglia, eds. *Measuring Progress in Conflict Environments (MPICE): A Metrics Framework.* Washington, DC: US Institute of Peace, 2010.

Fisher, Roger, and William Ury. *Getting to Yes: Negotiating Agreement Without Giving In.* New York: Penguin Books, 1981.

Fisher, Ron. *The Social Psychology of Inter-group and International Conflict Resolution.* New York: Springer-Verlag, 1990.

Fisher, Simon, Dekha Ibrahim Abdi, Jawed Ludin, Richard Smith, Steve Williams, and Sue Williams. *Working with Conflict: Skills and Strategies for Action.* London: Zed Books, 2005.

Fishstein, Paul, and Andrew Wilder. "Winning Hearts and Minds? Examining the Relationship Between Aid and Security in Afghanistan." Medford, MA: Feinstein International Center at Tufts University, January 2012.

Fortna, Virginia Page. *Peace Time: Cease-Fire Agreements and the Durability of Peace.* Princeton, NJ: Princeton University Press, 2004.

Foure, Guy Oliver, and I. William Zartman, eds. *Negotiating with Terrorists.* New York: Routledge Press, 2010.

Freire, Paulo. *The Pedagogy of the Oppressed.* 30th anniversary ed. New York: Continuum, 2006.

Galtung, Johan. "Violence, Peace, and Peace Research." *Journal of Peace Research* 6, no. 3 (1969): 167–91.

Gilligan, James. *Preventing Violence.* New York: Thames and Hudson, 2001.

Goodhand, Jonathan, Tony Vaux, and Robert Walker. *Conducting Conflict Assessments: Guidance Notes.* London: Department for International Development, 2002.

Gurr, Ted R. *Why Men Rebel.* Princeton, NJ: Princeton University Press, 1970.

———, and Barbara Harff. *Ethnic Conflict in World Politics.* Boulder, CO: Westview Press, 1994.

Hart, Barry. *Peacebuilding in Traumatized Societies.* Lanham, MD: University Press of America, 2008.

Heath, Dan, and Chip Heath. "Analysis of Paralysis." FastCompany.com, November 1, 2007.

Hicks, Donna. *Dignity: The Essential Role It Plays in Resolving Conflict.* New Haven, CT: Yale University Press, 2011.

Hiscock, Duncan, and Teresa Dumasy. "From Conflict Analysis to Peacebuilding Impact: Lessons Learned from People's Peacemaking Perspectives." London: Conciliation Resources and SaferWorld, March 2012.

Hoffman, Mark. *Peace and Conflict Impact Assessment Methodology.* Berlin: Berghof Research Center for Constructive Conflict Management, 2001.

Human Security Report. Vancouver, BC: Human Security Research Group, 2009–2010.

International Alert. *Codes of Conduct for Conflict Transformation Work.* London: International Alert, 1998.

Janis, Irving L. *Groupthink: Psychological Studies of Policy Decisions and Fiascoes.* Boston: Houghton Mifflin, 1983.

Kanyinga, Karuti. "The Legacy of the White Highlands: Land Rights, Ethnicity, and the Post-2007 Election Violence in Kenya." *Journal of Contemporary African Studies* 27, no. 3 (July 2009): 325–44.

Kelly, Max, with Allison Giffen. "Military Planning to Protect Civilians." Washington, DC: Henry L. Stimson Center, 2011.

Kriesberg, Louis. *Constructive Conflicts: From Escalation to Resolution.* Second ed. Lanham, MD: Rowman and Littlefield, 2003.

Krishna, Anirudh, and Elizabeth Shrader. *Social Capital Assessment Tool.* Washington, DC: World Bank, 1999.

Lederach, John Paul. "Addressing Terrorism: A Theory of Change Approach." In *Somalia: Creating Space for Fresh Approaches to Peacebuilding,* edited by John Paul Lederach et al., 7–19. Kalmar, Sweden: Life and Peace Institute. 2012.

———. *Building Peace: Sustainable Reconciliation in Divided Societies.* Washington, DC: US Institute of Peace, 1997.

———. *The Little Book of Conflict Transformation.* Intercourse, PA: Good Books, 2003.

———. *The Moral Imagination: The Art and Soul of Building Peace.* New York: Oxford University Press, 2005.

———. *Preparing for Peace: Conflict Transformation Across Cultures.* Syracuse, NY: Syracuse University Press, 1995.

———. "Resilience and Healthy Communities: An Exploration of Image and Metaphor." In *Community Resilience: A Cross-Cultural Study Revitalizing*

Community Within and Across Boundaries. Washington, DC: Fetzer Institute and Woodrow Wilson International Center for Scholars, 2009.

———, and Scott Appleby. "Strategic Peacebuilding: An Overview." In *Strategies of Peace,* edited by Daniel Philpott and Gerard F. Powers, 19–44. New York: Oxford University Press, 2010.

———, and Janice Moomaw Jenner, eds. *Into the Eye of the Storm: A Handbook of International Peacebuilding.* San Francisco: Jossey-Bass, 2002.

———, Reina Neufeldt, and Hal Culbertson. *Reflective Peacebuilding: A Planning, Monitoring, and Learning Toolkit.* South Bend, IN: University of Notre Dame, 2007.

Leonhardt, Manuela. *Conflict Analysis for Project Planning and Implementation,* Bonn: GTZ, 2002.

Levinger, Matthew. *The Practical Guide to Conflict Analysis: Understanding Causes, Unlocking Solutions.* US Institute of Peace Academy Guides. Washington, DC: US Institute of Peace, 2013.

Liebler, Claudia, and Cynthia Sampson. "Appreciative Inquiry in Peacebuilding: Imagining the Possible." In *Positive Approaches to Peacebuilding,* 55–79. Washington, DC: Pact Publications, 2003.

Marshall, Monty G., and Benjamin R. Cole. *Global Report 2001: Conflict Governance, and State Fragility.* Vienna, VA: Center for Systematic Peace, 2011.

McAllistair, Pam. *This River of Courage: Generations of Women's Resistance and Action.* Philadelphia: New Society Publishers, 1991.

McNair, Rachel. *Perpetration-Induced Traumatic Stress: The Psychological Consequences of Killing.* Lincoln, NE: Praeger, 2002.

———. *The Psychology of Peace: An Introduction.* Westport, CT: Praeger Publishers, 2003.

Meadows, Donella H. *Thinking in Systems: A Primer.* White River Junction, VT: Chelsea Green Publishing, 2008.

Menkhaus, Ken. "Impact Assessment in Post-Conflict Peacebuilding: Challenges and Future Directions." Geneva: Interpeace, July 2004.

Mitchell, C.R. *The Structure of International Conflict.* London: Macmillan, 1981.

———, and Michael Banks. *Handbook of Conflict Resolution: The Analytical Problem-Solving Approach.* London: Pinter, 1996.

Montville, Joseph. *Conflict and Peacemaking in Multiethnic Societies.* Lexington, MA: Lexington Books, 1990.

Muggah, Robert, Timothy D. Sisk, Eugenia Piza-Lopez, Jago Salmon, Patrick Keuleers. *Governance for Peace: Securing the Social Contract.* New York: United Nations Development Program, 2012.

Nilsson, Desiree. "Partial Peace: Rebel Groups Inside and Outside of Civil War Settlements." *Journal of Peace Research* 45, no. 4 (2008): 479–95.

Nixon, Hamish. "The Dual Face of Subnational Governance in Afghanistan in DCAF Afghanistan Working Group, Afghanistan's Security Sector Governance

Challenges." DCAF Regional Programmes Series 10. Geneva: Geneva Centre for the Democratic Control of Armed Forces, 2011.

Northrup, Terrell A. "Dynamic of Identity." In *Intractable Conflicts and Their Transformation,* edited by Louis Kriesberg, Terrell A. Northrup, and Stuart J. Thorson, 55–82. Syracuse, NY: Syracuse University Press, 1989.

Organisation for Economic Co-operation and Development (OECD). "Guidance on Evaluating Conflict Prevention and Peacebuilding Activities." Working Draft for Application Period, 2008.

———. *Supporting Statebuilding in Situations of Fragility and Conflict.* Paris: Organisation for Economic Co-operation and Development, January 2011.

Paffenholz, Thania. *Civil Society and Peacebuilding.* Boulder, CO: Lynne Rienner Publishers, 2009.

Patton, Michael Quinn. *Developmental Evaluation: Applying Complexity Concepts to Enhance Innovation and Use.* New York: Guilford Press, 2011.

Poole, Alice. "Political Economy Assessments at Sector and Project Levels." How-To Note. Washington, DC: World Bank, May 2011.

Portes, Alejandro. "Social Capital: Its Origins and Applications in Modern Sociology." *Annual Review of Sociology* 24 (August 1998): 1–24.

Pruitt, Dean G., and Sung Hee Kim. *Social Conflict: Escalation, Stalemate, and Settlement.* Third ed. New York: McGraw Hill Higher Education, 2004.

Redekop, Vern. *From Violence to Blessing.* Ottawa: Novalis, 2002.

Reychler, Luc, and Thania Paffenholz. *Peacebuilding: A Field Guide.* Boulder, CO: Lynne Rienner Publishers, 2001.

Ricigliano, Robert. *Making Peace Last.* Boulder, CO: Paradigm Press, 2011.

Rogers, Mark, Aaron Chassy, and Tom Bamat. "Integrating Peacebuilding into Humanitarian and Development Programming: Practical Guidance on Designing Effective, Holistic Peacebuilding Projects." Baltimore, MD: Catholic Relief Services, 2010.

Ross, Marc H. *The Culture of Conflict.* New Haven, CT: Yale University Press, 1993.

Rothman, Jay. *Resolving Identity-Based Conflicts.* San Francisco: Jossey-Bass, 1997.

Schirch, Lisa. *Amplifying Peace: Mass Media and Peacebuilding.* Forthcoming.

———. "Frameworks for Understanding Women as Victims and Peacebuilders." In *Defying Victimhood: Women and Post-Conflict Peacebuilding,* edited by Albrecht Schnabel and Anara Tabyshalieva, 48–76. Tokyo: United Nations University Press, 2012.

———. "Linking Human Rights and Conflict Transformation: A Peacebuilding Perspective." In *Human Rights and Conflict: Exploring the Links Between Rights, Law, and Peacebuilding,* edited by Julie Mertus and Jeffrey Helsing, 63–95. Washington, DC: US Institute of Peace, 2006.

———. *The Little Book of Strategic Peacebuilding.* Intercourse, PA: Good Books, 2004.

———. *Ritual and Symbol in Peacebuilding.* Bloomfield, MA: Kumarian Press, 2005.

———. *Strategic Peacebuilding.* Intercourse, PA: Good Books, 2004.

———. *Women and Peacebuilding Training Manual.* Harrisonburg, VA: Eastern Mennonite University, 2003.

———, and Michael Shank. "Strategic Arts-Based Peacebuilding." *Peace & Change* 33, no. 2 (April 2008): 217–42.

Schnabel, Albrecht. "One Size Fits All? Focused Comparison and Policy-Relevant Research on Violently-Divided Societies." In *Researching Violently Divided Societies: Ethical and Methodological Issues,* edited by Marie Smyth and Gillian Robinson, 193–206. Tokyo: United Nations University Press, 2001.

Schrock-Shenk, Carolyn, ed. *Mediation and Facilitation Training Manual.* Akron, PA: Mennonite Conciliation Service, 2000.

Schwartz, Barry. *The Paradox of Choice: Why Less Is More.* New York: Harper Perennial, 2005.

Serwer, Daniel, and Patricia Thomson. "A Framework for Success: International Intervention in Societies Emerging from Conflict." In *Leashing the Dogs of War,* edited by Chester Crocker, Fen Osler Hampson, and Pamela Aall, 368–87. Washington, DC: US Institute of Peace, 2007.

SIDA. *Manual for Conflict Analysis.* Division for Peace and Security through Development Cooperation, Methods Document, Stockholm: Swedish International Development Cooperation Agency, 2006.

Smith, Dan. "Towards a Strategic Framework for Peacebuilding: The Synthesis Report of the Joint Utstein Study on Peacebuilding." Oslo: PRIO, 2003.

Specht, Irma. "Conflict Analysis: Practical Tool to Analyse Conflict in Order to Prioritise and Strategise Conflict Transformation Programmes." Utrecht, the Netherlands: ICCO, Kirk in Action, and Transitional International, 2008.

Stedman, Stephen. "Spoiler Problems in Peace Processes." *International Security* 22, no. 2 (Fall 1997): 5–53.

Stewart, Frances, ed. *Horizontal Inequalities and Conflict: Understanding Group Violence in Multiethnic Societies.* New York: Palgrave MacMillan, 2008.

Sutcliffe, K., and K. Weber. "The High Cost of Accuracy." *Harvard Business Review* 81 (2003): 74–82.

Thompson, Edwina. "Principled Pragmatism: NGO Engagement with Armed Actors." Monrovia, CA: World Vision International, 2008.

UNIFEM. "Gender and Conflict Analysis." UNIFEM policy briefing paper. New York: UNIFEM, October 2006.

United Nations. Report of the Secretary-General on Peacebuilding in the Immediate Aftermath of Conflict. New York: United Nations, June 11, 2009.

United Nations Human Security Unit. United Nations Human Security Unit PowerPoint, October 2011.

University of Foreign Military and Cultural Studies. "Red Team Handbook." Volume 5, no. 15. U.S. Army, April 2011.

USAID Afghanistan. Community Development Program (CDP) Fact Sheet. June 2011. http://afghanistan.usaid.gov.

USAID Conflict Management and Mitigation Office. *Conflict Assessment Framework (CAF) 2.0.* Washington, DC: United States Agency for International Development, June 2012.

US Department of State, Office of the Coordinator for Reconstruction and Stabilization. *InterAgency Conflict Assessment Framework (ICAF).* Washington, DC: United States Department of State, 2008.

Van Brabant, Koenraad. "Peacebuilding How? Assessing the Design of Peacebuilding Interventions." Geneva: Interpeace, 2010.

———. "Peacebuilding How? Criteria to Assess and Evaluate Peacebuilding." Geneva: Interpeace, 2010.

———. "Peacebuilding How? 'Insiders'-'Outsiders' and Peacebuilding Partnerships." Geneva: Interpeace, 2010.

———."The Uses of Video in a Participatory-Action-Research Process for Peacebuilding." Geneva: Interpeace, 2005.

Varshney, Ashutosh. *Ethnic Conflict and Civil Life: Hindus and Muslims in India.* New Haven, CT: Yale University Press, 2002.

Verstegen, Suzanne, Luc van de Goor, and Jeroen de Zeeuw. "The Stability Assessment Framework: Designing Integrated Responses for Security, Governance and Development." The Hague: Clingendael Occasional Paper, prepared for the Netherlands Ministry of Foreign Affairs, 2005.

Volcan, Vamik D. *Bloodlines: From Ethnic Pride to Ethnic Terrorism.* Boulder, CO: Westview Press, 1999.

———. *The Need for Enemies and Allies: From Clinical Practice to International Relationships.* Northvale, NJ: Jason Aronson Publishers, 1988.

Wallensteen, Peter, and Margareta Sollenberg. "Armed Conflict, Conflict Termination, and Peace Agreement." *Journal of Peace Research* 34, no. 3 (January 1997): 339–358.

Wolpe, Howard, and Steve McDonald. "Democracy and Peace-Building: Re-Thinking the Conventional Wisdom." *Round Table* 97, no. 394 (February 2008): 137–45.

Woocher, Lawrence. "Conflict Assessment and Intelligence Analysis Commonality, Convergence, and Complementarity." Washington, DC: US Institute of Peace, June 2011.

World Bank. *2011 World Development Report on Conflict, Security, and Development.* Washington, DC: World Bank, April 2011.

World Vision. "Making Sense of Turbulent Contexts." Washington, DC: World Vision International, 2006.

Yoder, Carolyn. *The Little Book of Trauma Healing.* Intercourse, PA: Good Books, 2005.

Zartman, I. William. *Ripe for Resolution.* New York: Oxford University Press, 1989.

———, and Jeffrey Z. Rubin. *Power and Negotiation.* Ann Arbor: University of Michigan Press, 2000.

Zehr, Howard. *Changing Lenses: A New Focus for Crime and Justice.* Scottdale, PA: Herald Press, 1990.

———."Us and Them: A Photographer Looks at Police Pictures: The Photograph as Evidence." *Contemporary Justice Review* 1 (1998): 377–85.

Zolli, Andrew and Ann Marie Healy. *Resilience: Why Things Bounce Back.* New York: Free Press, 2012.

Index

About the Book

Offering a systematic approach that links practical conflict-assessment exercises to the design, planning, monitoring, and evaluation of peacebuilding efforts, *Conflict Assessment and Peacebuilding Planning* has been carefully—and realistically—designed to enhance the effectiveness of peacebuilding practice.

Lisa Schirch presents a convenient, logical framework and a wealth of tools for improving planning and implementation. She also helps us to fruitfully question widely held assumptions. Her concise handbook, informed by on-the-ground realities, is an essential resource for building true human security.

Lisa Schirch is research professor of peacebuilding at Eastern Mennonite University and founding director of 3P Human Security at the Alliance for Peacebuilding. Her publications include *The Little Book of Strategic Peacebuilding*, *Civilian Peacekeeping: Reducing Violence and Making Space for Democracy*, and *Ritual and Symbol in Peacebuilding*.